The Code of Putinism

The Code of Putinism

BRIAN D. TAYLOR

OXFORD
UNIVERSITY PRESS

OXFORD
UNIVERSITY PRESS

Oxford University Press is a department of the University of Oxford. It furthers
the University's objective of excellence in research, scholarship, and education
by publishing worldwide. Oxford is a registered trade mark of Oxford University
Press in the UK and certain other countries.

Published in the United States of America by Oxford University Press
198 Madison Avenue, New York, NY 10016, United States of America.

© Oxford University Press 2018

CIP data is on file at the Library of Congress
ISBN 978–0–19–086732–4 (pbk.)
ISBN 978–0–19–086731–7 (hbk.)

5 7 9 8 6 4

Paperback printed by Webcom, Inc., Canada
Hardback printed by Bridgeport National Bindery, Inc., United States of America

To Renée

CONTENTS

LIST OF FIGURES AND TABLES

PREFACE AND ACKNOWLEDGMENTS

In December 2017, Vladimir Putin announced his intention to run for a fourth term as Russian president. By the time this book is published, it is virtually certain that Putin will have been re-elected to a fourth term in a process more like a coronation than an actual contest. With Putin having won another six-year term, Putinism will carry on. The goal of this book is to capture the essence of Putinism. More precisely, this book aims to explain Putinism as a system, and especially Putinism as the collective mentality of Putin and his team—what I call The Code of Putinism.

Many people and organizations helped in making this book possible, none of whom are responsible for the contents, and especially the deficiencies. Principal funding for the research came from the Smith Richardson Foundation; I especially thank Nadia Schadlow for her support for this project. I thank the Department of Political Science and the Maxwell School of Syracuse University for financial and institutional support; I especially thank Jacquelyn Meyer for her assistance. PONARS Eurasia helped in multiple ways. Some of the ideas in this book were first explored at PONARS conferences; I thank PONARS members who participated for their comments. Most centrally, PONARS helped organize a manuscript workshop on the first draft of the book, in November 2015. I owe a huge debt of gratitude to the participants in the workshop: Daniel Goldberg, Henry Hale, Steve Hanson, Fiona Hill, Marlene Laruelle, Robert Orttung, Robert Otto, Nikolay Petrov, Peter Rollberg, Gulnaz Sharafutdinova, and Cory Welt. Bob Otto read the penultimate draft and provided valuable comments; he also helpfully provided many relevant articles from the Russian press.

Lauren McCarthy of the University of Massachusetts very generously agreed to use the first draft as a text for her Russian politics class. The comments sent by Lauren and her students were of enormous help in shaping the manuscript. Additional comments on chapter 5 were provided by participants in the FiDiPro "Critical Issues in the Research of Contemporary Russian Politics" Conference, Aleksanteri Institute, University of Helsinki, June 2017. I thank all of the participants, and especially Irina Busygina, Vladimir Gel'man, Marina Khmelnitskaya, and Ella Paneyakh. Renée de Nevers read several chapters and provided very helpful comments as I staggered across the finish line.

Special credit to the two primary research assistants on this project, Matthew Povlock and Mikhail Strokan. I couldn't have done it without them. Li Shao also provided last-minute assistance. Ivan Grigoriev saved me from a couple of careless errors about judicial politics. I also thank David Hoffman and Roger Haydon for helpful advice.

I am very grateful to Dave McBride of Oxford University Press for his interest in this book, and his efficiency in the publication process. Thanks also to his editorial assistants Claire Sibley and Emily Mackenzie for all of their support. Two external reviewers provided extraordinarily helpful and detailed comments, for which I am grateful. I thank Nancy Peterson for her excellent work in preparing the index, Sylvia Cannizzaro for copy editing, and Edward Robinson for managing the production process.

I owe a special debt of gratitude to everyone in Russia who consented to be interviewed for this book; their insights greatly influenced the arguments in this book. I also thank my friends and colleagues in Russia who made my research trips enjoyable.

A couple of notes on the mechanics. Generally I have placed endnote callouts at the end of the paragraph, to avoid littering the text with too many distracting notes, so many endnotes contain multiple citations. I use the transliteration system of the US Board on Geographic Names, which I believe is easier for non-Russian speakers to read than the Library of Congress system, although I have used the familiar English form for well-known names. Soft signs are omitted from the main text, but preserved in the notes. All translations from Russian are mine unless otherwise noted.

My final thank you is to my family, especially my parents and my sons Anatol and Lucian de Nevers. I dedicate this book to my wife, Renée de Nevers, with love and gratitude.

The Code of Putinism

Introduction

"There is Putin—There is Russia. There is no Putin—There is no Russia." This dramatic pronouncement was made by a top Kremlin official named Vyacheslav Volodin in 2014. The statement seems absurd, since Russia has existed for hundreds of years, and presumably will continue to do so long after Putin has left power. One might have thought that outspoken Russian patriots would be offended that Russia was considered so fragile that its existence depended entirely on one man. But one of the most outspoken, a former member of parliament named Sergey Markov, wholeheartedly agreed. Markov reasoned that Russia has "very weak institutions and a very strong leader. In that sense Putin is higher than institutions, he is stronger than institutions." Without Putin, he continued, "weak institutions might not be able to maintain the unity of the country and social stability, and the country could move further toward collapse."[1]

This paradox, in which Putin seems to grow ever stronger, his famous muscles bulging powerfully, while Russian institutions remain weak and ineffective, is at the heart of understanding Putinism. The goal of this book is to capture the essence of Putinism, and to explain why a strong Putin does not mean a strong Russia, and may in fact be a problem rather than a solution. I hope to describe in a relatively straightforward fashion what the Harvard sovietologist Merle Fainsod, in his classic book *How Russia Is Ruled*, called the "anatomy and physiology" of the system of rule in Russia under one specific leader.

Does Vladimir Putin deserve his own "ism?" Definitely. His longevity as ruler (eighteen years and counting), and his impact on Russian political development, justify this tribute. If he stays in office until 2024, which he can do quite legally under the Russian Constitution, he will have served over twenty-four years as the primary leader of Russia, longer than any leader since Stalin and considerably longer than such world-historic figures as Lenin, Mikhail Gorbachev, and Boris Yeltsin. And the option of making Putin "president for life" could be engineered at some point in the future, a not-uncommon pattern in post-Soviet Eurasia.

Putin also deserves his own "ism" because there is a coherent set of political practices and especially an operating "code" that has remained fairly consistent over time. Thus, Putinism is more like "Thatcherism" or "Reaganism" than like "Marxism"—it is not a fully developed, all-encompassing ideology, but a system of rule and a guiding mentality, a personality and a historical moment.

The central claim of this book is that we can understand Putin and Putinism if we understand the "code" or mentality of Putin and his close associates. To continue the biological analogy, the code of Putinism is the nervous system. It is the coordinating center, the brain, and the depository not just of reason but also of emotions, habits, and ideas. The nervous system controls the rest of the body. The code of Putinism has guided the political decisions that have shaped the political and economic system, domestic and foreign policy.

The code of Putinism is not simply the worldview of leading Russian elites but also a set of habits and emotions that guide policy and decision-making. The dominant beliefs of the current regime are basically conservative and stress the need for a strong state to protect Russia against internal and external enemies. This core idea is reinforced by habits of control, order, and loyalty acquired in the Soviet state, especially its security organs, and emotions related to loss of status, resentment, the desire for respect, and vulnerability. The notion of a "code," therefore, is meant to highlight that Putin—like all people—is motivated not simply by rational self-interest but also by ideas, habits, and emotions. This combination of emotion, habit, and ideas is what I call a code, or mentality.[2] It is the code of Putinism, and not the code of Putin, because it reflects the mentality of not just Putin but also many of his closest and most influential associates, people who have worked with Putin for decades. There is a Team Putin, with a distinct and coherent mentality.

There are three major implications of the core argument about the existence and importance of the code of Putinism, and these implications distinguish my argument from some important alternatives to understanding Russian politics. First, Putin matters. Second, what matters about Putin and his team is the "code." Third, the code of Putinism has made Russia an underperforming country at the domestic level and an overambitious one at the international level.

There are important and influential alternatives to each of these three arguments. Although everyone would agree, one would think, that "Putin matters," many would argue that what he believes and feels is relatively unimportant, because he is tightly constrained by what we might call "preexisting conditions"—Russian culture, dependence on oil and gas, the legacies of communism, and so on.[3] I contend that, although these conditions obviously matter, Putin was able to make consequential decisions that greatly shaped Russia's trajectory.

Second, he made these important choices under the influence of the code, the ideas and habits and emotions that are shared by Putin and much of his circle. Although Putin and his allies are obviously somewhat constrained by circumstances and have their own interests to pursue, including power and wealth, their behavior cannot be understood solely or even primarily as motivated by narrow calculations of personal gain. Rather, rational interests combine with elements of the code. For example, Putin is often portrayed as a cold-blooded schemer. One of his closest friends, however, once described him as "a very emotional person, but he was completely incapable of expressing emotion. . . . He had strong emotions, but he couldn't present them properly." This friend was the cellist Sergey Roldugin, who was later revealed to have secret foreign bank accounts showing that he was a billionaire, riches seemingly acquired through insider deals involving companies controlled either by the Russian state or other friends of Putin. What should we conclude from this? The obvious story is that Putin is enriching his old friends, and perhaps himself—some have speculated that Roldugin's wealth is actually Putin's. But if we have a broader view of what motivates people, we also see that Putin has remained steadfastly loyal to an old friend whom he could have left behind in his ascent to power, and that one of his closest friends knows Putin to be a "very emotional person." Roldugin stated that over time Putin learned to express his emotions well, and I have to agree—Putin's emotions come out clearly in many speeches and interviews. Throughout the book, we will see how a mix of habits, ideas, emotions, and, yes, interests influence the actions of Putin and his circle. Within a highly centralized and personalistic political system, the mentality of the ruler and his close allies has a large impact. Understanding Putinism requires understanding this broader code—rational self-interest is not enough.[4]

Third, some experts don't think Russia is underperforming at the domestic level or overambitious at the international level. Rather, Russia looks like what they labeled a "normal country," having all of the pluses and

minuses of a country at its level of economic development. This argument is
an important corrective to the too-easy tendency to compare Russia to countries like France or the United States, wealthy countries with long democratic
traditions. But this approach goes too far, because Russia does in fact under-
perform, with a much less effective state than it should have, given its level
of development. Putin's Russia is misruled: the way Putin pursues his ideal
of a strong state actually leads to a weak state. The code of Putinism helps
explain the paradox of this disappointing performance, with Putin adopting
an approach to ruling that sells Russia short. Similarly, in the international
realm, the mentality of Putin and his team has led to foreign policy choices
that, while understandable, are holding back Russia's standing in the world
and hurting its own internal development.[5]

The central task of this book, then, is to explain the code of Putinism
and show its importance for Russian politics, economics, and foreign
policy. In terms of politics, the code has shaped how the system operates
and what we might think of as the outputs of this system. The Putinist political system combines a set of formal rules and institutions that I call
"hyperpresidentialism" and an informal system of clan networks. The 1993
Russian Constitution is frequently described as "superpresidential" because
of the considerable powers it gave to the head of state. Putin took this existing "superpresidential" system and made it "hyperpresidential." He and his
team took a series of steps to weaken the countervailing structures in the
formal political system, such as the judiciary, the parliament, and the regions,
thereby concentrating more and more power in the presidency.

Thinking more broadly, hyperpresidentialism is a highly centralized
version of what political scientists call electoral authoritarianism. Electoral
authoritarianism is a political system that on paper is a democracy but in
reality is authoritarian, because the elections that do take place, although
ostensibly competitive, are not free and fair enough for the ruling party to
lose. When the formal democratic system is predominantly for show it can't
serve as a mechanism of competition and elite rotation, so these crucial political processes take place in behind-the-scenes battles between informal clan
networks composed of small groups of political and economic elites.

Taking these two features of the political system together, hyperpresidentialism and informal clan networks, points to a fundamental tension
and potential weakness at the heart of Putinism. The building of an authoritarian political system behind an electoral façade was supposed to en-
able Putin to control the state while maintaining ostensibly democratic

credentials. But because the formal institutions are to a significant degree fictitious, political and economic elites have to rely more than ever on informal networks to pursue their objectives and get things done. Understanding this tension at the heart of Putinism helps explain many seeming paradoxes, such as Putin's domination of the political system while he fails to achieve many of his specific policy goals. In other words, a political system like Putinism, combining informal clan competition with hyperpresidentialism, cannot help but be an ineffective system of governance. Real policy achievements—and Putin certainly has those—are more despite the system rather than because of it.[6]

The code of Putinism has also shaped the economic system. "Putinomics" is also a hybrid system, combining the formal institutions of market capitalism with a set of informal clan networks. At the top of the Putinist economic system are Putin and his circle, who make the most important decisions and benefit from and sustain the system. State domination of the oil and gas sector is central to Putinomics, as are Putin's personal links to the key players in this industry. Throughout the economy, the arbitrary power of state officials is often central to who wins and who loses, given the weakness of the rule of law and formal property rights.

Finally, the code of Putinism has shaped Russian foreign policy. Putin is determined to claim, or reclaim, Russia's rightful role as a great power. According to the code, only a Russia that is strong at home can be strong abroad, and vice versa. Weakness, brought about by the traumatic collapse of the Soviet Union, represented an existential threat to the country that had to be reversed. Resentment at Russia's lost status, and suspicion that the West in general and the United States in particular were determined to keep Russia weak, created a Putinist foreign policy increasingly frustrated that Russia was not given its due and was even under serious threat, leading ultimately to the annexation of Crimea, war in Ukraine and Syria, interference in the 2016 US presidential election, and major tensions with the United States and Europe.

When did Putinism begin? Logically one might expect it to have started in 2000, when Vladimir Putin became Russian president. But Putinism in its true form really only appeared around 2003–2004. It was only then, when his first term as president ended and his second term began, that Putin cast aside several top officials inherited from Boris Yeltsin, including his chief of staff and prime minister. He replaced them with a prime minister with KGB roots and a chief of staff who had been a loyal aide in St. Petersburg, a certain Dmitriy Medvedev. This time period also was when Russia's richest man,

Mikhail Khodorkovsky, was arrested and thrown in jail and his oil company Yukos was taken over by the state-controlled oil company Rosneft, headed by one of Putin's closest allies. After 2004 the effort to create what was called a "vertical of power" achieved its fully centralized form as governor elections were canceled, with governors now basically appointed by the Kremlin (although governor elections returned after 2012, a series of "filters" were put in place to ensure that only candidates acceptable to the Kremlin could actually win the elections). And this period was when, after the 2003 Iraq War, the 2004 Beslan terrorist attack in southern Russia, and the 2004 Orange Revolution in Ukraine, Putin became fully convinced that the United States was out to get Russia in general and him personally, willing to make common cause with terrorists and revolutionaries in pursuit of the goal of keeping Russia weak.

Putinism has changed somewhat over time, but its core tenets have remained quite consistent. Further, it is not monolithic, so there is room for some pluralism and disagreement within the code. For example, despite its fundamental conservatism, economic liberalism—meaning a larger role for the market and a smaller role for the state—at times has balanced this conservative tendency, especially in Putin's first term (2000–2004). But the code pointed in a definite direction, and as Putin grew more comfortable and confident as ruler, he began to trust his gut more and more, taking him in a more conservative direction in his second term (2004–2008). Although the system remained largely Putinist during the presidency of Medvedev (2008–2012), when Putin served as prime minister due to constitutional limits on more than two consecutive terms as president, it was definitely a more moderate version, with more room for advocates of political and economic liberalization. When Putin returned to the presidency in 2012, he tightened up the system and the code of Putinism became more anti-Western and conservative, and the authoritarianism became more severe. This direction reached full expression in 2014 after the annexation of Crimea and the war in Ukraine.

Thus, the most important changes have been in a particular direction, with the code pointing the way. If we compare the Putinism of today with that of the year 2000, over time it has moved in a more closed and restrictive direction. The code increasingly stressed Russia's position as a "besieged fortress" under threat from internal and external enemies working together to weaken the Russian state. The political system became more authoritarian, with Putin almost always choosing, at each fork in the road, to head toward greater control concentrated in the Kremlin and less room for independent actors outside the state, including in the media and civil society. Finally, over time Putin managed to elevate himself ever further above the informal clan networks, which continued to fight among themselves, but were less and less of a restraint on the boss at the top.

Does Putinism travel? After all, many "isms" are important not just because they are associated with one leader and one country but also because they are emulated by other leaders in other states. Analysts have pointed to the "Putinization" of politics in the former communist world, especially in places like Hungary and Macedonia. "Putinization" in this context usually refers to a combination of electoral authoritarianism, cronyism, opposition to European liberal values of openness and tolerance, and sometimes a cult of personality of the leader. Turkish Prime Minister Recep Tayyip Erdogan has been called the "Turkish Putin" and seems to employ similar rhetoric about his opponents and institutional maneuvers to prolong his rule.[7] What makes it difficult for Putinism to travel fully, however, is the Putinist code that draws much of its energy and focus from feelings of resentment and disrespect associated with Russia's fall from superpower status. For this reason, Putinism is primarily a Russian phenomenon.

Putinism is not simply a return to a traditional form of Russian rule, after a brief liberalization under Gorbachev and Yeltsin. Although there is a long history of authoritarianism in Russia, and an equally long tradition of what we now call corruption, Russia is not doomed by history, geography, or culture to remain as it was in the past. Democratic government and contemporary standards of law-based rule and rational administration are, in the great sweep of human history, relatively new phenomena everywhere, but they have spread considerably around the planet in the last century. Moreover, Russia today is a very different country, with a very different society and a different international situation, than the Russia of Ivan the Terrible, Peter the Great, or Joseph Stalin. Russian society is now highly educated, predominately urban, relatively wealthy in comparative terms, and more connected to the outside world than ever before. In these circumstances, authoritarianism was a choice, not some cultural curse.

This book argues that these choices were the product of a particular mentality widely shared among much of the Putinist elite, most importantly Putin himself. At the same time, Putinism does have firm roots in Russian society, and many elements of the code resonate strongly among average Russians. Something like Putinism without Putin was certainly possible at the turn of the millennium, given the collective trauma of the Soviet collapse and the difficult effort to build a new state and a new economy in the 1990s; the social demand for a strong state and a strong Russia was real. Ultimately, however, the specific form of Russia's political and economic system under Putin owes a great deal to the man himself, and the mentality of those around him.

Finally, it is important to emphasize what this book is *not*: it is not a biography of Vladimir Putin, it is not a history of the period from 2000 to the present, and it does not aspire to be a comprehensive account of current Russian politics. It also is not a work of academic political science, trying to test general theories about the comparative nature of political systems. Although the framing of issues is sometimes informed by more general social science concepts, jargon is either avoided or explained in a language that is meant to bear some resemblance to standard English. The emphasis is on elite politics and policymaking, so the dynamic and fascinating Russian society is largely confined to the background. The goal is to provide a clear and accessible discussion of the key features of Putinism.

Putinism Decoded

What makes Putinism an "ism?" For students of Russia in particular, "isms" are generally associated either with major ideological systems of thought or with comprehensive systems of rule, especially when they carry a person's name—Marxism, Leninism, Stalinism. Marxism and Marxism-Leninism were overarching ideological visions of the world that served as inspiration and guide to action for millions. In contrast, Leninism and Stalinism as labels could be applied either to an ideology or to a system of rule. Thus, political systems in communist countries were often characterized as Leninist or Stalinist, which implied some kind of model or template.

Vladimir Putin seems like an unlikely founder of an ism. He studied law, not philosophy, in college (incidentally, so did Lenin). He served his entire career as a state official—first in the KGB (Committee for State Security), then in the St. Petersburg's mayoral office, then for the Russian federal government—before becoming president. Party politics and programmatic debates seem to hold little interest for him. Russian parliamentarian Vyacheslav Nikonov, a strong Putin supporter, says, "Putin hates the word ideology." An American academic characterized Putin as a "problem solver" and "the ultimate pragmatist," accurately capturing a common view of Putin, both within and outside Russia.[1]

It would indeed be an exaggeration to say that Putinism is an ideology in the pure sense of that word, what the Oxford English Dictionary calls "a systematic scheme of ideas." A former member of the Duma (the national parliament) from St. Petersburg, someone who knew Putin back when he started his political career in the early 1990s as an assistant to Mayor Anatoliy Sobchak, told me that there is "no such thing" as Putinism, because it has no serious ideological basis. Rather, it is a "simulacra of ideology"—meaning that it looks kind of like an ideology, but without real substance.[2]

If it would be a mistake to see Putinism as a fully developed and coherent ideological scheme, it would be an even bigger mistake to reduce Putin's actions to pure pragmatism and a cold-blooded pursuit of his own self-interest. Indeed, we cannot truly understand Putin's Russia by attributing all of his actions to the rational pursuit of power and advantage. Yet this is the dominant mode of analysis of much contemporary political science writing, including about Russia. As one political scientist puts it, "the ultimate goal of politicians is the maximization of power. . . . they aspire to stay in power by any means for as long as possible and to acquire as much power as possible." The only other goal that might motivate rulers, according to this perspective, is the accumulation of wealth—a different type of self-interest. Thus, for the preeminent American scholar Karen Dawisha, Putin is not just an autocrat but a kleptocrat, ripping off Russia for the benefit of himself and his cronies.[3]

This form of reasoning, which academics call "rational choice theory," tells us something about Putin and Putinism, but far from everything. As the great German sociologist Max Weber observed long ago, rational self-interest is not the only motive for human action. In addition to what Weber called "instrumental rationality," other important motives for human behavior include values or ideas ("value rationality"), emotion ("affect"), and habit ("tradition").[4] This is a much more convincing account of human decision-making than one based purely on individual self-interest. All of us can think of times when our actions have been guided by emotions, or habit, or a set of values or principles. Indeed, much of what we do on a daily basis we do because that's what we've done before, and many of our most consequential choices in life are guided by emotions (whom do I love?) or ideas (what do I believe?). As one political scientist recently observed, the "contemporary scholarly stereotype of the autocrat as a super-rational being narrowly focused on political survival" needs to give way to a broader account of motives, including factors such as personal experiences, ideas, memories, and emotions.[5]

I refer to this combination of motives that fall outside the realm of instrumental rationality—habit, emotions, and ideas—as a "code." A code is both more and less than an ideology; more, because it involves not just ideas but also other stimuli for action, and less, because it is not a coherent and encompassing system of thought.[6] The distinction here between code and ideology is similar to that made by the prominent scholar Juan Linz between ideology and "mentality." For Linz, fully formed ideologies were organized and well-developed "systems of thought" that are characteristic of totalitarian regimes, whereas mentalities "are ways of thinking and feeling, more emotional than rational" that are characteristic of authoritarian regimes. The central point is that people's motives for action should not be reduced to one thing; they are the product of different types of influences.[7]

It is worth reiterating that it is not Putin's code, but the code of Putinism—which means these beliefs, emotions, and habits are shared to a large extent by other members of Putin's team. Although he is obviously the most important person in the system and the central decision-maker, he has surrounded himself with many people who share similar backgrounds and beliefs. Further, as I discuss toward the end of the chapter, one reason for Putin's popularity with Russians for the past eighteen years is that many aspects of the code have a wider resonance in society, particularly in the aftermath of the collective trauma of the Soviet collapse and the painful transition to a new economic system.

This code has several key features. Members of the Putinist elite believe in both the importance of a strong state and the necessity of Russia retaining its status as a great power in a dangerous and competitive international system. They value order, unity, and state power over individual freedoms or societal interests. This is particularly true because Russia is, in their view, a besieged fortress, with the West in general and the United States in particular working to undermine it, often in league with disloyal Russian citizens. A basic distrust of spontaneity and uncontrolled behavior fuels a desire to bring others under control; further, since people are generally weak, if you don't control them, then someone else will. Loyalty to one's team is essential, especially because institutions are weak and vulnerable to destabilization. The Putinist elite are sensitive to perceived slights to themselves and to Russia, and thus feelings of resentment about lost status and a desire for respect are prominent.

These are sweeping claims; obviously there is a lot more nuance within this code, and contradictions and exceptions. The rest of the chapter will unpack this code and substantiate these claims, especially with the help of speeches by Putin and other key elites and interviews with Russian experts and observers. Further, this code took some time to fully develop and reveal itself, and has evolved over time. Some elements were clearly present from the beginning, such as statism, an impulse toward control, and resentment about Russia's perceived lower status in the world. Other components were more contested and in flux, such as anti-Westernism.

Another reason that the code only became clear over time is because at the beginning of his rule Putin was both less confident and felt more constrained. But, as is true in other realms of Putinism, a key break occurred in 2003–2004. This is the moment when Putin freed himself from the remaining constraints of his predecessor Boris Yeltsin, jettisoning the prime minister and Kremlin chief of staff he had inherited and throwing the richest tycoon from the 1990s in jail. Television, the parliament, and the regions were all brought even further under control in this time period. Further, the Iraq war of 2003, the Beslan terrorist attack of September 2004, and the Orange Revolution in Ukraine in December 2004 cemented certain ideas about the internal and external dangers facing Russia, threats that might be aimed ultimately at Putin and the Kremlin.[8]

Putinist Ideas

What does Vladimir Putin believe? This is a thorny problem, since only in riddles are there people who either always tell the truth or always lie. The middle-ground position is that we can have greater confidence that he means what he says when he says it a lot, in settings both scripted and unscripted, and his actions are generally consistent with these statements. Further, to the extent views are shared by other leading members of Putin's circle, our confidence that these are truly held views increases somewhat. In this case we have more than fifteen years of statements and actions to draw on, so some central ideas do stand out.

Perhaps the most fundamental component of Putin's thinking is that he is a *statist* (in Russian, a *gosudarstvennik*). In his first major programmatic statement as Russia's ruler, on the eve of the millennium in December 1999, he made this point quite emphatically. Russia, he averred, was different from the United States or England, with their liberal traditions; in Russia, the state "has always played an exceptionally important role ... [and] is the source and guarantor of order, the initiator and driving force of any change." Building a strong state, Putin stated, was "the key to the rebirth and rise of Russia." At the same time, he reassured his readers that this strong state would be a "democratic, law-based, capable, federal state." The following year he declared, "Russia from the very beginning was created as a super-centralized state. It is fixed in her genetic code, her traditions, the mentality of the people."[9]

This commitment to statism and state-building has been a consistent theme of Putinism. In 2006 Putin listed "strengthening Russian stateness" as his first major achievement, and in 2007 the first two things he mentioned were "restoration of the territorial integrity" of the country and "the strengthening of the state." Putin biographers Fiona Hill and Clifford Gaddy stress, "the first key to Vladimir Putin's personality is his view of himself as a man of the state, his identity as a statist."[10]

The centrality of statism to Putinism is clear. The important question, though, is what *kind* of state does the Putinist code envision? After all, although a boatload of social science research has demonstrated the importance of a strong and effective state for maintaining social order and delivering services to citizens, there is a lot of variation in terms of how states do this, and the degree to which states uphold and advance the interests of their population.[11] Here there are ample grounds for skepticism about Putin's stated commitment to a state that is democratic, law-based, and federal, especially since Putin also insisted from the beginning that the Russian state must be "super-centralized." The next chapter details how Putin undermined democracy and federalism and weakened the rule of law, and chapter 5 shows how Putin has largely failed to build a strong and effective state, but the immediate question here is the Putinist vision for the state.

According to the Putinist code, the state has primacy over society and the individual. As one former KGB officer put it in 2001, the "main state ideology" for Russians is the view that the state is "sacred and indivisible . . . its greatness and interests are higher than any individual citizen." This primacy is reflected in the traditional Russian notion of a "service state"—not one that provides services *to* its citizens, but one that expects citizens to serve *it*. This service state mentality has deep roots in Russian history, and scholars have established how powerful tsars like Ivan the Terrible (1533–1584) and Peter the Great (1682–1725) put in place a system in which the nobility had little independent power and were subordinate to the tsar and the state. As one Russian scholar put it, commenting on the centrality of statism to Putinism, "the state is omniscient and the people are powerless."[12]

This notion of the primacy of the state was particularly strong in the KGB, where Putin and many of his closest allies began their careers. KGB agents saw themselves as being at the pinnacle of state service, an elite class, the "sword and shield" of the state. Nikolay Patrushev, one of Putin's closest and oldest KGB allies who has served Putin both as director of the KGB's main successor agency, the Federal Security Service (FSB), and as secretary of the Security Council, once asserted that FSB personnel are united by a "sense of service" and are the "new nobility" of post-Soviet Russia. Another Putin KGB ally, Viktor Cherkesov, maintained that secret service personnel ("chekists," the term used for secret police officials in the early Soviet state) had a special responsibility to preserve the Russian state. "History has arranged it," Cherkesov wrote, "that the burden of upholding Russian statehood has to a considerable extent fallen on our shoulders." Indeed, Cherkesov asserted that the chekists were a "hook" that society was clinging to in order to avoid plunging into an abyss. Putin and the chekists, he continued, were preventing Russia from falling to its death, and if they failed Russia itself was at risk, "awaiting the fate of many African nations—practically complete an-nihilation, plunging into chaos and multiracial genocide."[13] The importance that Putin and his allies attach to strong state control as necessary to prevent chaos and collapse is so strongly ingrained it is as much a habit as it is an idea, a point to which I return later.

Putin is not only a statist, but a particular type—a *great power statist* (in Russian, a *derzhavnik*). States in the modern world are sometimes called Janus-faced, like the Roman god, because they look both inward at their own societies and outward at other states in the international system. For Putinism, both faces of the state, whether facing inward or outward, must be strong and powerful. Putin has repeatedly talked about the dangers to Russia of being weak internationally. In the aftermath of the horrific 2004 Beslan terrorist attack, in which over three hundred people died, half of them chil-dren, after being taken hostage inside a school by Islamic terrorists from the North Caucasus region of Russia, Putin observed, "We appeared weak. And the weak are beaten." The statement that "the weak are beaten" consciously or unconsciously referenced a famous 1931 speech by Stalin, in which he jus-tified his industrialization campaign by arguing that the Soviet Union must not fall behind the leading industrial powers, because "those who fall behind get beaten."[14]

Putin saw it as his historic mission to restore Russia's status as one of the world's great powers. He stated in 2003, "All of our historical experience shows that a country like Russia can live and develop in its existing borders only if it is a great power. In all periods when the country was weak—politically or economically—Russia always and inevitably faced the threat of collapse." By the end of his second term as president he was taking credit for having accomplished this goal, stating in 2008 that "Russia has returned to the world arena as a strong state."[15]

Putinist ideas contend that Russia needs to reestablish itself as a great power so it can join forces with other great powers such as China to challenge and supplant the unjust international order established by the United States after the Cold War. Putin complains frequently about this issue. For example, at a security conference in Munich in 2007 he objected to a unipolar world with "one center of power, one center of force, one center of decision-making. A world of one boss, of one sovereign." In 2014 Putin went further, accusing the US of trying to dominate the world, of using "total control over global media" to portray white as black and black as white, of having not allies but "satellites," of only recognizing the legitimacy of those states who demonstrated loyalty and using "open blackmail" to keep states in line, of spreading chaos by supporting "open neo-Nazis and Islamic radicals," of behaving like "Big Brother," and of "constant interference in all issues in the world." He compared those who don't accept US dominance to rape victims who are told, using a sexist expression, that they "should just relax and enjoy it."[16]

According to core Putinist ideas, Russia should be a great power not only so it won't be pushed around globally but also so it can resist infringements on its sovereignty. The threats to sovereignty are not so much military ones, although the Russian military and political elite worry about those threats as well, but political. In particular, Russia needs to be strong to be able to resist pressure to change its domestic political system, and to stand up to those lecturing Russia about the deficiencies of its domestic political system.

One manifestation of this idea was the conception of "sovereign democracy" propagated in 2006 by Putin's deputy chief of staff Vladislav Surkov, sometimes referred to as the chief Kremlin ideologist. The adjective "sovereign" was more important than the noun "democracy," with Surkov arguing that Russia must pursue its own conception of democracy without outside interference. It would be "stupid," Surkov stated, to think that the "unprecedented pressure on Russia" was due to deficiencies in its democracy. Rather, the true motive of external critics was "control over Russia's natural resources by means of weakening its state institutions, defense capability, and independence."[17]

The need to be a strong state internally and externally, and to forcefully resist Western pressure aimed at weakening Russia, is connected to another core Putinist idea, that of *anti-Westernism* in general and *anti-Americanism* in particular. This claim is more controversial than the previous ones, and perhaps it is more accurate to say that Putin is deeply suspicious of the United States than completely "anti." Indeed, many observers contend that Putin and his closest associates are fundamentally European and pro-Western at heart. Putin himself on many occasions has stressed that Russians are Europeans; for example, in 2003 he told the BBC, "in terms of geographic location, history, culture, the mentality of its people, Russia is a European country."[18] Putin speaks fluent German and some English, and many of his core allies have spent time living in the West and have children who have studied in the West or even live there, from New York to London to Helsinki. Clearly the Putinist elite is more comfortable personally in the West than other points of the globe, and they are not storing their riches in, or sending their children to, Beijing or Mumbai or Johannesburg. This European orientation is evident at the mass level as well; as one Novosibirsk journalist put it, when a new sub-urban housing development goes up, the project isn't called "Hong Kong" but "Marseilles."[19] For Russian elites and masses alike, even those living in the Asian part of Russia, the West is still the dominant point of reference, what is taken as "normal."

On the other hand, the outpouring of anti-Western rhetoric in recent years has been unmistakable. A 2014 draft Ministry of Culture policy document baldly declared that "Russia is not Europe," although this phrase was dropped from the final document. One way to reconcile the recent anti-Western and anti-American language with the more positive pro-Western statements of Putin's early years is to see this as a fundamental shift in Putinism. For ex-ample, David Remnick, the editor of *The New Yorker* and a long-time Russia watcher, referred in 2014 to "Putin's new anti-Americanism."[20]

Another way to square the circle of a combination of anti-Westernism and anti-Americanism with a simultaneous identification with Europe on a cultural and even financial level is to remember that "Putinism" is not a co-herent ideology but an amalgamation of ideas, habits, and emotions.[21] We need not search for complete consistency and coherence in this code, and it has evolved over time. Still, a certain anti-Westernism has been evident from the beginning of Putinism in its complete form, which took effect in 2003–2004. This became clear in the aftermath of the Beslan attack mentioned above. Not only did Putin maintain that it was Russia's weakness that led to the terrorist assault, but he implied that the United States was behind the attack. Specifically, Putin stated:

> They want to cut from us a tasty piece of pie, others are helping them. They help because they believe that Russia—as one of the world's great nuclear powers—still represents some kind of threat. And this threat must be eliminated. Terrorism, of course, is only an instrument for achieving these goals.[22]

Putin did not specify who these "others" were who were helping international terrorists. But given his references to "the world's great nuclear powers," his 2006 blast at "Comrade Wolf" who "knows who to bite and doesn't listen to anybody," his 2007 Munich speech cited previously, followed by a May 2007 Victory Day comparison of those who advance "claims of exceptionality and diktat in the world" to Nazi Germany, it seems pretty obvious he was referring to the United States. This was confirmed in 2015 when he alleged directly that the United States helped Chechen terrorists in the 2000s.[23]

Russian international relations expert Sergey Medvedev was one of the first to identify the Beslan speech as a crucial moment in "the construction of the new Russian identity." According to Medvedev, who bears the unique distinction among Russian professors of being called a "moron" by Putin because of his advocacy of multilateral stewardship of Arctic resources, Putin used the Beslan speech to rally support for national unity behind his "authoritarian modernization" project. He did so in part by playing on widespread ideas about a Western conspiracy to weaken Russia and undermine its status as a great power. When I caught up with him in Moscow in June 2015, Medvedev observed that although the Beslan address at the time caught many people by surprise, especially the way in which Putin blamed the West for the tragedy, in hindsight it "looks natural." The Beslan speech, Medvedev suggested, represented "the first appearance of the real Putin."[24]

Putinist anti-Americanism takes a rather specific form. Although there are those among the Russian elite who seem to dislike American culture and society in general, for Putinism the problem with America is much more specific—that the United States is out to get them.[25] According to this view, for more than a decade the West has been trying to shift the balance of power in Eurasia against Russia, with the ultimate goal of overthrowing Putin himself. Russian leaders believe that the United States has developed the technology of "colored revolutions" as a form of political warfare against Russia. A series of uprisings, ostensibly brought about either by electoral fraud or by corrupt and unpopular leaders, are really all provoked by Washington's not-so-hidden hand. Most importantly for Russia, the Ukrainian 2004 "Orange Revolution" and 2014 "Maidan Revolution" were both part of this American approach, but other upheavals in the region are also explained according to this framework. Uprisings in the Middle East during the Arab Spring, particularly the ones in Libya and Syria, are likewise seen as Western efforts to bring new regimes to power through the use of revolutionary upheaval.[26]

Putin and his circle believe that the West has every intention of infecting Russia with what is called the "Orange plague," after the 2004 "Orange Revolution" in Ukraine. Domestic opponents of Putin are believed to be part of this same conspiracy to weaken Russia; in November 2007, he told supporters that "those who oppose us . . . need a weak, sick state," accusing them of being "jackals" scavenging for foreign support. This fear was seemingly confirmed for Putin when large public protests broke out in Moscow after falsified parliamentary elections in December 2011. When US Secretary of State Hillary Clinton criticized the conduct of the elections, Putin stated that opposition leaders "heard the signal and with the support of the US State Department began active work." In June 2013 Putin complained again about Western double standards and interference, saying, "your [the US] diplomatic mission works together [with] and directly supports them [the Russian opposition]."[27]

Why are the United States and its European allies pursuing this colored revolution strategy? According to Putin and his team, it's partially for the reason above—that "Comrade Wolf" wants a world of "one boss, one sovereign," and thus states that don't toe the line must be brought under control. But ultimately the American goal goes beyond simply encircling Russia with pro-American regimes or punishing other great powers like Russia that refuse to submit to US domination. The real and final objective is to weaken Russia, force it to break up, and grab its natural resources. Patrushev, the secretary of the Security Council, has made this argument on several occasions. For example, in February 2015 he stated that the United States doesn't particularly care about Ukraine; rather, its goal is to use the situation in Ukraine to weaken Russia: "The Americans are trying to drag Russia into an inter-state military conflict, using the Ukrainian events to bring about a change in power [in Russia] and in the final analysis dismember our country." Patrushev likes to quote former Secretary of State Madeleine Albright as saying Russia is too big and "unjustly" controls too many natural resources and therefore must be broken up. It perhaps doesn't matter that Albright never said this, and the source of the claim is a statement by a retired KGB general about an alleged secret program to read the minds of American leaders—what matters is that Patrushev and other Russian political elites believe it to be a true indication of American policy.[28]

Another ideational attribute of Putinism is what might be called *conservatism* but is probably more properly seen as *antiliberalism*. Conservatism and liberalism are used here not as they are in the United States, as some kind of left–right political spectrum in which most Democrats are liberals and most

Republicans are conservatives, but the way the terms are used in Europe (including in Russia) and in political philosophy. Thus, liberals tend to stress the importance of individual rights and freedoms, and have a generally positive view of human nature and the possibility of rational progress. Conservatives, in contrast, tend to stress the group over the individual, be more skeptical about human nature, and prioritize order and tradition over change and reform. Contemporary political and economic liberalism emphasizes curbing the state's power to infringe on individual rights, whether that be on private property rights in the economic realm or rights of free expression and belief in politics.

Putin's embrace of conservative ideology became most explicit in his third term as president, which began in 2012. In his 2013 annual address to parliament he defended traditional values and spirituality, declaring this a "conservative position" that prevents society from falling into "chaotic darkness, a return to a primitive state." But his very first major statement of his political views in December 1999 also stressed that Russia was historically very different from liberal America and England, contending that "collective forms of life have always dominated over individualism" in Russia and that the Russian people look toward the state and society as a whole for support, rather than believing in their own efforts. This collectivist and statist orientation is decidedly conservative.[29]

Putin's conservatism also helps explain his sometimes contradictory attitudes about Europe. One Russian political commentator observed that the European civilization with which Putin identifies is the world of the nineteenth-century German chancellor Otto von Bismarck, Britain's World War II prime minister Winston Churchill, and the former French general and president Charles de Gaulle. This Europe of hierarchy and traditional institutions is one that Putin "learned about in history books." Putin's conservative values suggest "he wanted to become part of a West that no longer exists." He doesn't like the West he sees today, with same-sex marriage, multicultural societies with large migrant populations, and powerful nongovernmental organizations (NGOs), creating a West that, according to this expert, Putin thinks is "creepy."[30]

Although conservative and antiliberal elements were prevalent in the Putinist code from the beginning, there is no doubt that these tendencies became more pronounced after 2012. The reason for this ideational shift are easy to find. From 2008 to 2012 Putin's hand-picked stand-in as president, Medvedev, had embraced a more liberal and pro-Western rhetoric and image.

In late 2011 and early 2012 the largest demonstrations since the 1991 Soviet collapse broke out in Moscow, in response to clear evidence of electoral fraud in the December 2011 parliamentary elections as well as Putin's decision to return to the presidency for a third term rather than allow Medvedev to run for a second term. Putin and his conservative allies responded to these protests with a political campaign to tighten the screws and a conceptual embrace of conservatism. Liberal protestors were painted as out of step with traditional Russian values, an alien element inspired and even funded by the West. New legislation criminalized "abusing the religious feelings of believers" and spreading "homosexual propaganda," and three members of the punk feminist protest group "Pussy Riot" were subjected to a modern-day show trial and sentenced to two years in prison for their admittedly provocative "punk prayer" staged in Moscow's Church of Christ the Savior. One Russian scholar labeled this ideational project "paleoconservatism," with its embrace of traditionalism, spirituality, patriotism, and anti-Westernism.[31]

The embrace of conservatism inspired a range of government and progovernment officials, commentators, and scholars to develop a more coherent ideological justification for this shift. References to Russian religious and conservative thinkers of the past such as Nikolay Berdyayev and Ivan Il'in began to appear occasionally in Putin's speeches (Putin had cited Il'in in the 2000s as well), and the deputy head of the Presidential Administration gave their books as New Year's presents to state officials. But it would be a mistake to treat this emphasis on conservative thought as a full-blown ideology, rather than a "mentality" or part of a more general "code." Putin and other officials drew on a rather diverse array of thinkers with different philosophical and ideological positions—this was not some new equivalent of Marxism-Leninism, a relatively coherent and state-mandated set of beliefs. As one Russian academic put it, Putin's conservatism was a "hybrid . . . that draws on several schools of thought." The head of a centrist and generally pro-Kremlin Moscow think tank saw the efforts by some officials to develop and promote conservative thought as a "search for political language, not a political strategy," with bureaucrats responding to signals from above and trying to guess what the boss wants.[32]

To summarize, these are the key ideas of the Putinist code:

+ statism, including great power statism
+ anti-Westernism, and in particular anti-Americanism
+ conservatism/antiliberalism

Missing from this list is the idea of *nationalism*. To some this may come as a surprise, because it is commonplace to describe Putin as a nationalist. The historian Walter Laqueur, in his book on Putinism, contends that "the most important component in the new ideology is nationalism accompanied by anti-Westernism." But what does it mean to say nationalism is a core part of Putinism? Nationalism is a political ideology that holds that each nation should control its own political unit (in the modern world, usually a state) because, as one scholar puts it, "the nation is the chief repository of legitimate political authority." Much here hinges on what we mean by "nation," which this author defines as "a community of people who share kinship based on race, culture, language, ethnicity, religion, and/or citizenship."[33]

The problem for Putin, and indeed any Russian ruler of the last several centuries, is defining the boundaries of the Russian nation. Although ethnic Russians have always been the largest nation by far, in both Imperial Russia before 1917 and the Soviet Union between 1917 and 1991, roughly half of the population was non-Russian, the rest of the population made up of other nationalities, such as Ukrainians, Tatars, Georgians, Uzbeks, and so on. Post-Soviet Russia, in contrast, is about 80 percent Russian, but that still leaves tens of millions of Tatars, Ukrainians (living inside Russia, not Ukraine), Chechens, et cetera. Defining the boundaries of the Russian nation by ethnicity would thus leave out millions of citizens of the current Russian state— including groups who have advanced independence or autonomy claims in the recent past, such as the Chechens—and suggest territorial designs on neighboring countries where 25 million ethnic Russians live. For this reason Putin, like Russian and Soviet leaders before him, has emphasized, "Russia emerged and developed over the centuries as a multinational state." Because of this long-standing difference between the boundaries of the state and the boundaries of the nation, Russia's rulers have tended to privilege the imperatives of the state or empire over those of the nation.[34]

Given this tension, it makes more sense to see Putin and his team (some of whom are not ethnically Russian, by the way) as embracing ideas of Russia as a strong state and a great power than nationalism per se.[35] Nationalist ideas do have some influence, and nationalist phrases can appear in the speeches of Putin and other top officials, but nationalism should not be thought of as a core part of the code, even in the aftermath of the Crimea annexation, when notions of a wider "Russian world" became most prominent; the implications of nationalist ideas for Russian policymaking are too contradictory to serve as a reliable guide. It is notable that Laqueur's discussion of "the new Russian national idea" rarely, if ever, quotes Putin, instead relying on the writings of long-dead philosophers or contemporary publicists of uncertain influence. Putin himself, rather than lauding nationalism, has compared it to a "virus" and a "bacteria," maintaining that it represents a threat to Russia's historic "multiconfessional and multinational state." A leading Russian editor, who has met with Putin often, stressed in 2014—when the idea that Putin was an ethnic Russian nationalist became particularly widespread in the West—that Putin "always stressed the danger of nationalism for preserving Russia. He has always felt that any manifestation of nationalism will lead to the collapse of Russia, and he has talked about that constantly."[36]

Of the ideas that do serve as the core of Putinist ideas—statism, anti-Westernism, and conservatism—experts differ as to which ideas deserve priority. Some argue that the one key idea now is anti-Westernism, linking this position to a long-standing debate between "Westernizers" and "Slavophiles" in Russian political thought, with Slavophiles insisting on Russia's special path distinct from the West. In contrast, others see the "dominance of the state" as the core idea, which Putin acquired while working in the KGB in the Soviet period. In my view statism has been the central and dominant strand of thought from the very beginning, whereas both anti-Westernism and conservatism have been more contested and grown in strength over time. Together, though, they represent a distinct ideational core at the heart of Putinism.[37]

Putinist Habits

It is common in political analysis to attribute someone's behavior to things they believe; it is much less common to claim people act politically based on things they do without really thinking. Indeed, referring to it as a "habit" could be misleading, because the issue is not whether someone smokes or bites her fingernails. Rather, when Weber emphasized the importance of "traditional" behavior "determined by ingrained habituation," he was referring to an "almost automatic reaction to habitual stimuli." As the political scientist Ted Hopf puts it, habits are "unreflective reactions . . . to the world around us," including "perceptions" and "attitudes." We get these perceptions and attitudes from our social surroundings, such as our family, our friends, and our colleagues. Habits, Hopf continues, "simplify the world, short-circuiting rational thought." For example, Hopf notes that in the world of international politics the leaders of the United States don't even think about whether Canada might attack the United States militarily—it just goes without saying (and thinking).[38]

A potential pitfall of trying to decode the habits of a small group of people, specifically in this case Putin and his team, is that the analysis could lapse into what would derisively be called armchair psychologizing—the adjective "armchair" clearly meant to imply shoddy and unsupported analysis. This is a real concern, but, like the discussion of Putinist ideas, our study of Putinist habits gains greater confidence by studying the decades of statements and actions by Putin and others. Further, many experts, including scholars and journalists, have tried to discern the essence of Putinism, and point to aspects of his character and the attitudes of other close associates, basically what we are calling habits. Relying on this evidence to single out some key habits improves our confidence that we are on the right track. Further, the opposite danger must also be noted—that by relying only on post hoc efforts to explain any action by Putin as motivated by a rational response to circumstances, we ultimately take individuals out of the equation entirely. After all, if anyone would have rationally done the same thing, what difference does it make who holds the top jobs?[39] The importance of analyzing habits is particularly strong in the case of a system like Russia's, where much depends on a small group of top officials. As Hopf notes, when a state's executive branch is the key actor in politics, it matters a great deal what the habits of that small group of individuals are.[40]

One key impulse of Putin and his team, which fits our understanding of a habit, is the desire to establish *control*. This habit of control includes a distrust of spontaneous action and a sense that most human acts are driven by others, rooted in a rather pessimistic view of human nature that sees the average person as weak and easily led. This view of individuals is often attributed also to states, so most states outside the great powers are subject to manipulation by more powerful states.

For Putin and many of his close associates, this habit is at least in part an attribute either acquired or strengthened by time working for the Soviet secret police, the KGB. Of course, to attribute Putin's action to his KGB past is somewhat of a cliché; the first suggestion in a satirical essay for "lazy journalists" working in Russia recommends that they always remember to remind their readers that Putin worked for the KGB. But clichés often capture an important truth—that's how they become clichés. Putin dreamed of joining the KGB from the time he was a teenager, and famously went to the KGB in ninth grade to ask how one became an agent. He chose law as a major based on the advice of a KGB officer, and he served in the KGB from the time he graduated from college until the collapse of the Soviet Union. Many of his closest associates are people he met while working in the KGB, including Security Council Secretary Patrushev and Sergey Ivanov, his former minister of defense and chief of staff. It would be surprising indeed if this experience did not somewhat shape his worldview.[41]

This desire for control probably also was influenced by Putin's experience with the martial arts, which he studied from his youth, rising to the level of black belt in judo and winning a local championship in Leningrad. In his campaign biography in 2000 he declared, "judo is not simply a sport, but a philosophy," and his personal website discusses the positive results from studying judo, including learning "self-control." The study of law, the academic track suggested to a young Putin, reinforced this tendency. As one biographer puts it, "The law appealed to Vladimir as martial arts did. It imposed rules and order, which he came to respect more than any ideology."[42]

Many observers have noted this emphasis on control. One journalist, a Putin critic and a specialist on the KGB, wrote in 2004, "by training, Putin is a man of control.... The KGB taught its soldiers well; its institutional culture has not been easily thrown off." A Moscow think tank director and former military officer claimed that "controllability" is one of the most important things to Putin. This springs from a "cold, cynical" outlook on people and the belief that people in principle are weak and easily manipulable—"he doesn't believe in people who aren't controlled." This expert noted that this is not just a characteristic of Putin—many in power think the same way. Similarly, an academic study of elite political culture in Russia found that Russian elites see the people as "inert," "manipulable," and "ignorant."[43]

This attitude toward the masses leads to the more general attitude that if those in power loosen control, they will lose control of the country. As a renowned Russian sociologist put it, "What is 'disorder' in the eyes of a man in uniform? It's the absence of control. If there is not control, there is the possibility of independent influence. And *siloviki* [people with backgrounds in the security services, law enforcement, and the military] perceive the presence of alternative centers of power in the country as a threat to the country's integrity." Putin argued in 2007 that Russia was not stable enough to allow legal and economic institutions to work without "manual steering," a position endorsed by sympathetic analysts.[44]

Very closely related to this attitude about control is a commitment to *order*. As someone who spent his entire career prior to 2000 as a bureaucrat, not a politician, and who only ran for public office after being thrust into the role of acting president by Yeltsin, Putin is used to hierarchical organizational structures. Indeed, Putin's closest associates throughout his time as Russia's leader are people who have made their careers as officials in a bureaucratic hierarchy, not in electoral politics, whether as a legislator or a governor. This preference for order is likely to be most pronounced among the *siloviki*. Putin, a Russian journalist observed, thinks that a military hierarchy is the best system of administration, with higher-ups giving orders and subordinates carrying them out. As the Russian authors of a major book on the Russian secret police observe, "If the FSB has an ideology, it is the goal of stability and order." This habitual orientation was evident in the first slogan adopted by Putin to explain his goals as president, the "vertical of power."[45]

Stanislav Belkovskiy, a prominent and perceptive analyst of Putin and Putinism, describes Putin as having a "guardian" personality type, referring to the scheme of the American psychologist David Kiersey. This personality type is conservative by nature and distrustful of change. Stability of the state order is of primary importance, Belkovskiy argues, and Putin "hates revolutions as a class." Like the conservative Russian tsar Nicholas I, who ruled in the mid-nineteenth century and sent Russian troops abroad in 1848 to suppress revolution, uprisings even in neighboring countries are a threat to be resisted. For Putin, revolutions are not spontaneous domestic uprisings brought on by popular dissatisfaction but events that are instigated by someone, often outsiders. Similarly, a well-known St. Petersburg journalist who has followed Putin's career closely, emphasized that Putin "HATES revolutions." Putin thinks revolutions don't happen on their own, and, believing that people in general are stupid, thinks they are manipulated by someone, like the United States.[46]

As early as his 2001 state of the nation speech, Putin called for an end to revolutions in Russia, and the "stability" of the 2000s compared to the chaos of the so-called wild 90s under Yeltsin, became a signature rhetorical device. Putin's hatred of revolution was on fullest display in his March 2014 press conference after the Ukrainian Maidan Revolution. Putin made clear his view that the events in Kiev were not a revolution at all, but an externally sponsored coup, and warned about the danger of unlawful protests, which inevitably lead to "chaos" (a word he used seven times in the press conference), "anarchy," "disorder," "pogroms," "terror," and "bacchanalia."[47]

Habits favoring control and order also lead into a preference for *unity*, or what more politically might be called *antipluralism*. Ideationally this is

connected to conservative and antiliberal ideas, ones that stress the importance of national unity and downplay the importance of individual freedoms
and expression. This impulse toward unity was also there from the beginning. As acting prime minister, Putin addressed the Duma in August 1999,
emphasizing the importance of "all branches of power being subordinate
to one goal—maintaining the unity and integrity of our state." When Putin
maintained in his 2003 state of the nation speech that Russia's "strategic goal"
was to return to the ranks of the great powers, he emphasized that this was
only possible with "consolidation . . . mobilization . . . the uniting of forces."
It will be impossible for Russia to defeat the threats it faces in the world,
Putin continued, "without consolidation at least around basic national values
and objectives." Similarly, after the 2004 Beslan attack he stressed, "the main
thing is the mobilization of the nation in the face of the common danger."
Dmitriy Medvedev, at the time the head of the Presidential Administration,
went further, maintaining in 2005, "if we cannot consolidate the elite, Russia
could disappear as a single state."[48]

Of course, pleas for national unity are the bread and butter of politicians
everywhere, democratic and authoritarian alike. One of Barack Obama's
signature campaign lines proclaimed, "There's not a liberal America and a
conservative America; there's the United States of America." What elevates
unity or antipluralism to a habit that is part of the Putinist code is the way
that these calls are linked to mobilizational efforts that emphasize that those
who are not with us are against us, and potentially dangerous. This came
out most clearly in the aftermath of the military annexation of Crimea in
2014. Putin observed in the national speech marking the event that "certain
Western politicians" had argued that sanctions might lead to greater internal
problems in Russia, and stated, "I want to know what they have in mind: the
activity of some kind of fifth column, some sort of 'national traitors'?" Putin
reiterated the danger posed by internal disagreements in 2015: "The lessons
of rebellions, revolutions, the civil war, serve as a warning about how destructive any divisions are for Russia. Only the unity of the people and social
agreement can lead to success, secure the state's independence, and help re-
buff powerful and treacherous enemies."[49]

There is a general connection between habits favoring control, order, and
unity and ideas that are statist, antiliberal, and anti-Western. Further, the
synthesis of these ideas appeared long before 2014. One Russian scholar
analyzed all of Putin's state of the nation speeches from 2000 to 2007 and
concluded that the two main ideas he emphasized when talking about

Russia's past were a "strong state" and "unity." Another Russian academic has demonstrated that it is standard practice for electoral campaigns under Putin to emphasize the need to unite against foreign and domestic enemies for the good of the country. Putin and his supporters made clear that these enemies were in league with each other, as in the December 2007 speech mentioned earlier in which Putin called Russian oppositionists "jackals." This continual linking of domestic critics and foreign adversaries represented a return to a "besieged fortress" image of Russia, a tendency that resonated naturally with the Putinist team.[50]

Another habitual tendency that has marked the Putin era is personal *loyalty*. This is a feature that clearly applies specifically to Putin himself, but it can also be seen as a feature of the system. This aspect of Putin's personality has been noted by many observers. A St. Petersburg journalist who has followed Putin's career closely describes Putin as "a friend to his friends," which is both a "strong and weak point" of his personality. This journalist compared Putin's background as a kid and teen growing up in 1960s Leningrad as being similar to that of the nineteenth-century Lower East Side in New York City, in which loyalty to "the guys" and sticking together was a key part of the social code. Later, while working for the KGB, Putin saw himself as a "loyal servant" of a very special agency. A sense of the honor of an officer applies to how Putin deals with personnel issues, with loyalty being very important. This emphasis on loyalty, as we see in chapter 3, helps explain the longevity of many top personnel under Putin. One Putin biographer emphasizes "a fierce sense of personal honor and loyalty" as a key personality trait.[51]

Most commentators agree that Putin's demonstration of loyalty to two key patrons explains his rise to the top of Russian politics. The first key demonstration of loyalty was to Anatoliy Sobchak, the mayor of St. Petersburg in the early 1990s. After Sobchak lost his reelection bid in 1996 to Vladimir Yakovlev, who like Putin had been one of Sobchak's deputies, Yakovlev offered Putin a job. Putin, however, saw Yakovlev as a "Judas" for running against his boss and declined, maintaining, "it's better to be hanged for loyalty than for betrayal." The following year Putin helped spirit Sobchak out of the country, ostensibly for health reasons but in reality to protect Sobchak from corruption charges. The second key demonstration of loyalty was to Yeltsin. In 1998 Russia's chief prosecutor was investigating people close to Yeltsin for possible corruption, and Yeltsin pushed to have the prosecutor, Yuriy Skuratov, fired. Yeltsin faced resistance until a video of "someone who looked like Skuratov" in bed with two prostitutes was shown on Russian

TV. Putin, at the time the head of the FSB, vouched for the authenticity of the tape, and Skuratov was forced from power, which effectively ended the corruption investigation. This act of loyalty was perhaps the key moment paving the way for Putin's rise to the presidency.[52]

Putin's notions of loyalty and honor influence how he classifies his opponents and determines who deserves special contempt. Aleksey Venediktov, the editor of the prominent *Ekho Moskvy* radio station, seen as one of the few remaining bastions of free speech among prominent media, says that Putin told him that he has two kinds of opponents, "enemies" and "traitors." Venediktov quotes Putin as saying, "Traitors are those who were part of the same team, and then unexpectedly stab you in the back. To them I show no mercy." Putin emphasized his attitude toward disloyalty in a speech to high school students in 2015. Recalling his teenage years and the informal education he received on the streets and courtyards of Leningrad, he said, "treachery and betrayal were for us the worst, most despicable thing."[53]

Loyalty is not just a personal characteristic, however, but also a more general feature. The sociologist Alena Ledeneva, who interviewed many top elites for a study of how power really works in Russia, contends loyalty is "the key value in Putin's *sistema* [system]." Another academic study similarly found that loyalty to the "clan" or "team" is a key part of elite political culture. The importance of loyalty is related to a general feature of Russian politics historically, which is that formal institutions tend to be rather weak, thus heightening the importance of informal networks and connections. As one Siberian journalist put it, "the key question in Russian politics is—'this is whose person?'" In such a system, demonstrations of loyalty are vital. Putin's decision to designate Medvedev as his presidential successor in 2007 was clearly linked to Putin's faith in Medvedev's personal loyalty—a faith rewarded in 2011, when Medvedev stepped aside so Putin could return to the presidency.[54]

The importance of loyalty as a habit has been a constant under Putin. However, in recent years there has been a noticeable shift in how he interprets loyalty. In the 1990s, as a junior official, he exhibited firm loyalty to his boss, whether Mayor Sobchak or President Yeltsin. From 2000–2015, he expected loyalty from his team of allies, and repaid the favor with long and stable appointments. Since 2015, however, he has replaced several of his closest allies and peers, inserting former assistants and bodyguards into top positions. It appears that Putin now rewards personal loyalty to *him*, rather than collective loyalty to the team.[55]

The final habit that is part of the code of Putinism is *hypermasculinity*. This feature, above all others, is the one that is most specific to Putin himself. Probably even the most casual observer of Russian politics is familiar with Putin's penchant for macho displays: demonstrations of his judo prowess, fishing and riding horseback bare-chested, flying in a fighter jet, tranquilizing a tiger, hanging out with a biker gang, and so on. A St. Petersburg journalist observes that those who knew Putin well from his past say that one of the things that Putin has been able to do as president is "realize his childhood dreams" in such macho stunts. In fact, it is a mistake to think of them simply as "stunts"—they really do reflect Putin's own hypermasculine outlook. A former Putin adviser also maintained that such episodes are only in part about image-making, they are also "personal" for Putin, and that he likes these macho pursuits. Putin himself portrays his own childhood as being marked by his "pugnacious character" and a tendency to get in courtyard fights, calling himself a "hooligan" and a "punk"—it was martial arts that helped him control these tendencies.[56]

This tendency toward masculine posturing, to the point of outright sexism, sometimes seeps into Putin's speech. He once famously threatened a French journalist with circumcision after the reporter asked a question about Russian military behavior in Chechnya that Putin considered provocative, and on another occasion he crudely joked that Israeli President Moshe Katsav was a "mighty man" and an object of envy of other men because "he raped ten women" (Katsav was accused and convicted of raping women on his staff). Many observers have noted how Putin has a tendency to use criminal slang to emphasize his toughness.[57]

Why are hypermasculine habits politically salient? Valerie Sperling, in the brilliantly titled *Sex, Politics, and Putin*, describes how Putin's macho image became an important legitimation strategy for the Kremlin. This image resonated well among average Russians, according to Sperling, because of the prevalence of sexist and homophobic norms among the Russian population, as well as popular feelings of lost national pride after the Soviet collapse. The Kremlin believed that Putin's macho toughness could serve to bolster support for a resurgent Russian state. Although Sperling acknowledges that some of this promotion of hypermasculinity may be personal and a reflection of Putin's background, for her it is primarily about image-making.[58] Without denying the importance of that component, I would also suggest that Putin's hypermasculinity was not just a PR construction but also a habit that affected how Putin sees the world, and the policy importance attached to reclaiming Russian power and greatness.

To summarize, these are the key habits of the Putinist code:

+ control
+ order
+ unity/antipluralism
+ loyalty
+ hypermasculinity

Some of these habits seem to be fairly widely shared among the Putinist elite, such as control and order, and others seem more specific to Putin himself, especially hypermasculinity. Like Putinist ideas, to a certain extent these habits can be seen as reinforcing each other. For example, loyalty is so important at least in part because of the necessity of maintaining unity and order, especially among the ruling team. Similarly, in many ways these habits also reinforce the set of dominant ideas. Hypermasculinity, for instance, fits well with elite views about rebuilding the strength of the Russian state, both internally and vis-à-vis other states, because, as Putin put it, "the weak are beaten." Putin doesn't believe in showing weakness, and, according to one biographer, thinks that giving in to opposition protests is tantamount to negotiating with terrorists.[59] In general, this group of habits is a powerful influence on the behavior of Putin and his closest associates, because they represent the automatic or instinctive impulses that often drive decision-making.

Putinist Emotions

The fourth basic motivation for what Weber calls "social action," besides rationality, ideas, and habit, is emotion. Weber refers to this type of action as "affectual," saying it is determined by "feeling states." Emotions, like habits, are often disregarded by social scientists trying to explain political behavior, especially that of elites. Feelings are things to be ignored or suppressed or controlled, to allow the rational part of the brain to do its work. Biological and psychological research, however, shows that emotions don't just cause problems but also help solve them, and that emotion is fundamental to decision-making. Indeed, brain researchers have discovered that it is necessary to have feelings to prefer one thing to another, and thus make any decision at all. Moreover, emotions are not simply individual biological experiences but also can be shared by groups—being part of a group helps bring about shared interests, ideas, and, yes, feelings. Emotions like fear, pride, respect, and hatred are central to domestic and international politics.[60]

Of course, all of us experience a vast range of emotions. For our purposes, the important emotions are those that have been highlighted as central to the identity of Putin and his close associates, relying on the evaluations of experts. Further, some emotions that might be salient are hardly worth mentioning, like love of country—a feeling that is presumably widely shared both by Russian proponents and detractors of Putin. Similar to the discussion of ideas and habits, there are several emotions that are both prominent and closely related, helping to make up a relatively coherent code or mentality.

The first emotion of central importance to the Putinist code is *respect*. More specifically, the Putinist elite feels that it has been disrespected, offended, even humiliated, in particular by the West. In his 2014 speech to an international audience, Putin returned repeatedly to the theme of respect, arguing that the most important thing in international relations is "respect for your partner and his interests." Much of the speech was a recitation of the many ways that Putin felt the West in general and the United States in particular had disrespected Russia. One Russian journalist emphasized that Putin's feeling of having been "offended" was the central theme of the speech, in which Putin with "maximum openness" conveyed how he felt Russia had been disrespected over the years. The journalist noted that the feeling was not new, but had increased recently and that Putin no longer tried to hide it. Similarly, a Russian think tank director close to Prime Minister Medvedev states, "both Putin and his closest circle are overcome with feelings of humiliation and betrayal."[61]

Indeed, there is at least some evidence that Putin feels that Russia has not been afforded proper respect for some time. A British historian recalls how he witnessed Putin in 1994, while deputy mayor of St. Petersburg, talking about how Russia's interests as a "great nation" needed to be respected after the Soviet collapse. In another instance, while campaigning for president for the first time in February 2000, Putin interrupted a journalist asking about whether the International Monetary Fund was "offending" Russia by not issuing credits to interject: "Anyone who offends us will not last three days." Others who have observed Putin throughout his career emphasize that the desire for respect, and a tendency to be easily offended, are key components of Putin's character. This became clear very early in Putin's presidency, when the Russian television station NTV portrayed acting President Putin as an ugly dwarf in its satirical puppet show *Kukly*. Putin reportedly was very offended and NTV executives were told that "the Kremlin would never for-give us." NTV's parent company was raided by armed tax police only four days after Putin was inaugurated, its owner was forced to flee the country, and NTV was taken over by the media arm of the state gas company Gazprom.[62]

Although there may be personal aspects to feelings of disrespect, it seems to be a much broader phenomenon. The theme of disrespect, offense, and humiliation has been particularly pronounced since the annexation of Crimea, the attack on Ukraine, and the Western response of sanctions. Sergey Karaganov, one of Russia's most prominent foreign policy analysts who for many years has been a good bellwether for elite opinion (pro-Western under Gorbachev and Yeltsin, becoming increasingly anti-Western under Putin), noted a "feeling of humiliation and a desire for revenge" on the part of "a significant part of the elite and the population as a whole." Sergey Medvedev, the political scientist/"moron" discussed earlier, says that Putin and the rest of the elite harbor a deep humiliation complex, with Russia in the role of the "great loser" that has been offended.[63]

Closely related to this feeling of disrespect is the emotion of *resentment*. Webster defines resentment as "a feeling of anger or displeasure about someone or something unfair." The social scientist Roger Petersen, an expert on the po-litical effect of emotions, observes that a rapid loss in social status of a group can lead to powerful feelings of resentment. It is not surprising that Vladimir Putin would feel resentment about the collapse of the Soviet Union and the en-tire communist bloc, and the rapid change in Russia's international status; one biographer states that Putin saw these events as "a humiliating, chaotic, and catastrophic retreat." Equally important was his own personal loss of status; he had joined the powerful and respected KGB, only to see the organization vilified for its terrible crimes and disbanded in 1991. He had to scramble for a new career at middle-age, and according to one account he briefly considered becoming a cab driver after returning to Leningrad from East Germany.[64]

The fancy/pretentious way this emotion is discussed in academic litera-ture is to use the French term *ressentiment*, often traced to the philosoph-ical writings of Soren Kierkegaard and Friedrich Nietzsche. The basic idea in scholarly writing on ressentiment is that one group takes another group as an example or model, but then feels angry and frustrated when it is unable to meet the standards, whether objectively or subjectively, of the exemplary unit. Two Russian scholars, applying the concept to post-Soviet Russia, char-acterize this ressentiment as being a form of "frustration, developing into an aggressive hostility to the state that formerly was a model."[65]

Resentment/ressentiment is all the rage among Russian scholars of national identity and elite and public opinion. Relying on two decades of surveys of the Russian political elite, two experts trace this feeling of resentment to the 1990s, when it became obvious that Russia, although the main successor to the superpower Soviet Union, would not be able to quickly and easily catch up with its former competitor and new model, the United States. The Russian political scientist Olga Malinova points out that Russian feelings of resentment toward the West can be traced back at least as far as the debate between "Westernizers" and "Slavophiles" in the nineteenth century, and that multiple distinct episodes have taken place since then, most recently as a result of the westernizing reforms begun in the Soviet Union in the late-1980s and continuing after the Soviet collapse in the 1990s. It is worth quoting Malinova at length:

> After 1991 Russia officially adopted the "Western" values of market economy, democracy and the rule of law as its aims, which dooms it to a long and difficult period of "pupilhood." At the same time it is not ready to give up on the idea of "equalness" to the Western great powers. The tension between these two aspirations should become a source of negative emotions even if the transition to democracy had been successful. While it is not, the situation becomes even more *ressentiment*-prone.[66]

Asking who is to blame for these feelings of resentment is somewhat beside the point, and certainly plenty of mistakes were made both by Western and Russian policymakers.[67] The point of the notion of ressentiment is that these feelings were somewhat inevitable, given that the West simply was richer and more democratic than the Russia that came out of communism as a newly independent state. Thinking about the issue as one of emotions and identity also helps explain the somewhat conflicting attitudes toward the West described above, in which Russian elites both strongly identify with and resent the West.

Arguably one manifestation of this resentment is the apparent belief of Putin and others that Western promotion of democracy and human rights is basically lies and hypocrisy. As one of Putin's former advisors put it, "He [Putin] looks at those people in the West, here's what they say, and here's what they do in reality.... Putin doesn't believe that there is real competition between the political parties in the West. He thinks of it as a game." A Russian scholar put it much the same way, noting that Putin thinks the whole world says one thing and does another, and that the people don't decide anything, despite "pretty words." From this perspective, elections in the West are "crap," as one Russian observer characterized Putin's views. Elections give voters a chance to blow off some steam and change the faces now and then, but the basic policies remain the same, including hostile and unfair Western policies toward Russia.[68]

Another manifestation of this feeling of resentment is the desire for "revenge" mentioned earlier by the foreign policy expert Karaganov. He actually used the term "revanche," which in politics is a type of revenge related to the recovery of lost status or territory. Former Kremlin insider Gleb Pavlovskiy pointed to revanche as a key motivation not just for Putin but "a very extensive . . . unseen layer of people," including Pavlovskiy himself:

> Putin was one of those who were passively waiting for the moment for *revanche* up till the end of the 90s. By *revanche*, I mean the resurrection of the great state in which we had lived, and to which we had become accustomed. We didn't want another totalitarian state, of course, but we did want one that could be respected. The state of the 1990s was impossible to respect.[69]

A final emotion that is an aspect of the Putinist code is *vulnerability* or even *fear*. This claim probably sounds dubious, given the amount of power wielded by Putin and his government, and the degree of popularity Putin has enjoyed over the last eighteen years in Russia. But close observers of Putinism insist that this feeling is genuine. One biographer calls it "a profound fear of disorder." This feeling is connected to other pieces of the code, such as ideas about how the West is out to get them, or the habits of order and control. Putin apparently fears his fall from power or even his own overthrow, and this feeling intensified after the Arab Spring, especially the murder of the Libyan leader Muammar Gaddafi by opposition fighters, which made an "indelible impression" on Putin.[70]

Pavlovskiy spoke at length about this issue after his dismissal as a key Putin advisor in 2011. Pavlovskiy agrees that the Arab Spring intensified this feeling of vulnerability among the Russian political elite, but he traces it back much further. He mentioned the violent 1993 confrontation between Yeltsin and the Russian parliament; the power transition in 1999, when Yeltsin sought guarantees about the freedom and safety of his family both from his opponents and from Putin; the Orange Revolution in Ukraine in 2004, when the sitting

Ukrainian president failed to transfer power to his chosen successor; and even the struggle within the Kremlin in 2011 about whether Medvedev would run for a second term as president or Putin would return to the top job. Pavlovskiy describes this long-standing fear among the elite as follows:

> An absolute conviction that as soon as the power center shifts, or if there is mass pressure, or the appearance of a popular leader, then everybody will be annihilated. It's a feeling of great vulnerability. As soon as someone is given the chance . . . they will physically destroy the establishment, or we'll have to fight to destroy them instead.[71]

According to Pavlovskiy, this feeling of vulnerability is connected to habits of control and a lack of faith in institutions to work without "manual steering." Putin does not believe that Russia is capable of having elite rotation of power without the new group settling scores with the previous rulers. Pavlovskiy states, "Putin always said, we know ourselves, we haven't reached that stage yet; we know that as soon we move aside, you will destroy us. He said that explicitly: you'll put us up against the wall and execute us."[72]

To summarize, these are the key emotions of the Putinist code:

+ respect, specifically feelings of disrespect and humiliation
+ resentment, which is closely related to the issue of respect
+ vulnerability or even fear

Once again, emotional components of the code overlap with other aspects of it. The desire for respect is connected to habits of hypermasculinity, because one quality of perceived "manliness" is not being humiliated. Feelings of vulnerability further ideas about the need for a strong state at home and abroad, and habits of order, unity, and hypermasculinity (real men are not supposed to feel vulnerable or afraid). The ways in which emotions, habits, and ideas combine and overlap is what gives the code of Putinism a greater coherence beyond any one element.

Putinism or Russianism?

Where does the code of Putinism come from? The code is made up of the values, emotions, and habits that, in addition to circumstances and rational calculation, drive decision-making under Putin. This mentality is first and foremost the product of Putin's psychology and life experiences, given his centrality to the system. Many components of the code are shared by his team, the close collaborators who have been with him for decades, come from the same generation, and usually have overlapping professional experiences with Putin, such as working in the KGB in the Soviet period or in the St. Petersburg mayoral office in the early 1990s (on Putin's early professional experiences, and his team from the KGB and St. Petersburg, see chapter 3). It is not surprising that Putin would surround himself with people he has known for a long time, who share a common background and worldview. This is especially important in Russian politics, where informal ties are often more important than formal rules and titles. The tight-knit nature of Team Putin may lead to a form of "groupthink," in which it becomes even harder than usual for members of this group to see things from a different point of view or contradict the code.[73]

Perhaps, though, Putinism has broader roots? For some, Putin is simply a reflection of Russian society, or even a manifestation of centuries-old Russian traditions of one-man rule in which the state dominates a passive society. Russians, so the story goes, always crave the rule of a strong hand, a tsar. Feelings of resentment, habits of order and control, ideas of statism and anti-Westernism—these are not the code of Putinism, but the essence of being Russian. The Belarussian winner of the Nobel Prize for Literature, Svetlana Alexievich, has endorsed this view, observing, "In the West, people demonize Putin. They do not understand that there is a collective Putin, consisting of some millions of people who do not want to be humiliated by the West. There is a little piece of Putin in everyone."[74]

This view represents a strong challenge to the notion of a Putinist mentality, and is seductive in its simplicity. In its simplicity it actually shares something in common with the rational choice school described previously. According to rational choice theory, Putin is just like any other leader, or indeed any other human being, seeking to always advance his own interests the most efficient way possible; ideas, emotions, and habits can be ignored as a guide to his actions. According to the view that Putin is a traditional Russian leader, one in tune with Russian society and Russian culture, there is also something inevitable about his authoritarian rule. Social scientists call this type of explanation a "culturalist" one; Russian political culture is the source of the code of Putinism. History repeats itself, or at least rhymes quite strongly.

The political culture argument, however, is not only simple, but too simple. Cultures are not completely static, nor are they completely uniform. They change over time, and are internally complex and contradictory. There is not one Russian political culture, but many. Several decades of public opinion research have shown that contemporary Russians are not authoritarian by nature, and that majorities support many democratic rights and freedoms.[75] They want both democracy and a "strong hand," rather than seeing them as irreconcilable alternatives. Although Russians tend to be less democratic in their political views than citizens of long-established democracies, it seems just as likely that the experience of living in a democracy led to more democratic values, rather than the other way around. In short, Russian culture is not in itself a barrier to democracy or a guarantee of authoritarianism. Furthermore, autocracy has been the modal form of government for most of human history everywhere, so Russia is hardly unique in this respect. Many countries that were once declared inhospitable terrain for democratic institutions—including such prominent examples as Germany and Japan—now have them.

The code of Putinism, then, is not simply the twenty-first-century version of eternal Russian truths. However, there is a more limited version of the Putinism-equals-Russianism argument that carries more weight. Rather than seeing Russian societal attitudes as the inheritance of some long-distant past, a more plausible account finds their source in the collective experience of the last several decades. Russians were shaped by the revolutionary trauma of the late-1980s and early-1990s: the failed reforms of the last Soviet leader, Mikhail Gorbachev; the collapse of not just communism but also the communist bloc as a whole and the Soviet Union itself; the political and economic reforms of Boris Yeltsin, which overturned the existing order known to Russian citizens and introduced profound uncertainty and, for many, considerable hardship. They experienced disorder and sought order. They felt humiliation and desired respect. They were tired of revolutions and grand experiments and feared further state collapse. They leaned on their friends and relatives for support, because none of the formal laws and institutions worked the way they were supposed to. They resented the triumphalism of the West, and the Americans most of all, with their blue jeans and bubble gum and fast food and Hollywood blockbusters. Putin, according to the journalist Anna Arutunyan, "acted as a mirror of society, a product of his times, reflecting what was desired of him on a subconscious level."[76]

Two iconic Russian movies, *Brother* (*Brat*) and *Brother 2*, released in 1997 and 2000, captured well this social mood. The hero of the two films, a young man named Danila, makes his way from his small village to St. Petersburg, where he gets drawn into the world of the Russian mafia by his older brother Viktor, a hitman. Viktor has been seduced by money, thinking that this makes him strong. But the mafia assassin turns out to be fundamentally weak. Danila, who always keeps his word and retains his loyalty to his brother and his country, even though they have either literally or metaphorically betrayed him and strayed from the correct Russian path, proves to be the stronger one and beats the bad guys. Danila, unlike other young Russians in the movie, has not been seduced by American fast food or pop culture or drugs, telling one bewildered Frenchman at a party, "American music is shit. . . . America is going to bite it." In the sequel Danila and Viktor travel to Chicago to settle scores with an American businessman who is swindling a Russian pro hockey player, the brother of one of Danila's friends. Danila confronts the businessman, telling him that truth is stronger than money. In the most famous line of the movie, Viktor responds to the query "Are you gangsters?" with a curt "No, we are Russians."

Social demand for Putinism, then, existed long before Putin ever appeared on the scene in 1999, talking tough and threatening, after a series of apartment bombings, to "snuff out [the terrorists] in the outhouse." Indeed, as early as the summer of 1992, six months after the Soviet collapse, Russians saw an early glimpse of a Putin-like figure. I was living in Moscow at the time, a young graduate student working on a dissertation on the role of the military in politics; contrary to conventional wisdom, I intended to argue, the Russian military was not a particularly powerful political actor, and Russia faced no risk of a military coup. So I remember vividly the June 1992 appearance on Russian TV of a gruff, powerfully built and stone faced Russian general, Aleksandr Lebed, who among other things, denounced the efforts of Boris Yeltsin to secure economic support from the West: "Enough going around the world cap in hand, like a goat after a carrot. Enough." In 1995 Lebed published a memoir, *Za Derzhavu Obidno*, which can be translated loosely as *The Humiliated Great Power* or *I Feel Pity for the Great Power*, a line from a classic Soviet movie of the late 1960s about the Russian Civil War. The following year Lebed ran for president and finished third. Yeltsin appointed Lebed the secretary of the Security Council and implied that he might someday be a worthy successor. Lebed and Yeltsin quickly fell out, however, and Lebed lost his post. He was elected governor of a major Siberian region in 1998 before dying in a helicopter crash in 2002.[77]

Although the experiment with Lebed failed, Yeltsin continued to search for a similar figure. The number of *siloviki* in and around the Kremlin began to grow, including in such key positions as prime minister and chief of the presidential staff. Yeltsin was looking for a successor, trying out various options. He wrote in his memoirs, reflecting on his views in 1998, "Already at that time I felt a demand growing in society for a new type of state, one with a steel core, which would strengthen the entire political structure of power. Demand for an intelligent, democratic, new-thinking, but at the same time firm military man. After a year such a man really appeared—I am talking, of course, about Putin." Yeltsin decided in August 1999 to appoint Putin as prime minister and set him up as successor. Yeltsin wrote, "I intuitively felt the power and strength of Putin. . . . And also the atmosphere rising up in society. Society was ready for a new figure, and a quite tough and strong-willed figure." Once Putin became prime minister, leading the resumption of the war in Chechnya that autumn, he "stopped the fear" and "instilled hope . . . providing a feeling of order and being defended."[78]

There is undoubtedly considerable truth in this linking of Putinism to broader Russian societal values, emotions, and habits. This social demand for order and respect and a strong state was undoubtedly real, and may partially explain Putin's enduring popularity. But it also explains too much, because it implies that Russia would have followed the exact same trajectory even under a different president with a different team, an implausible claim. This is not to say that such features of Putinist rule, including authoritarianism and corruption, would not have happened without Putin. Rather, the point is that both the specific outcomes and the path to them were powerfully shaped by the code of Putinism. Further, although the revolutionary changes of the 1980s and 1990s did affect everyone, they did not affect everyone in the same way. For example, Russian sociologists have shown that anti-Americanism appeared earlier and was more widespread among the elite than the masses; they felt the loss of status, and corresponding resentment, much more acutely than average Russians.[79] In other words, Putinism spread from the top down—it is not just a reflection of Russian culture and society. Indeed, to the extent that average Russians show aspects of the Putinist mentality, it is partially because these ideas and emotions have been promulgated by Putin and his allies, especially through the media.

Moreover, Putin's background in judo and Soviet law, and the KGB and bureaucratic background of most of his closest associates, shaped this circle in a distinct way. As we will see in the rest of the book, the code of Putinism was central to a whole series of momentous decisions and policies pursued by Putin. The ruling elite chose a particular course, it was not foreordained. Putinism and Russianism are not the same thing.

Because Russia is a highly centralized, hyperpresidential autocracy, the ideas, habits, and emotions of the top leader matter a great deal. Further, because many of Russia's top political elite are old associates of Putin's, come from a similar background and set of experiences, and interact quite frequently, many of them have a similar complex of thoughts, tendencies, and feelings. This is the code of Putinism, summarized in Table 1-1. Evidence for this code comes from statements of Putin and other top leaders and observations of many experts, most of them Russian, some of them former insiders or with channels to insiders.

Is Putin a pragmatist or an ideologue? He is both and neither, sometimes one and sometimes the other. His politics and decisions are motivated by a combination of circumstances, rationality, ideas, habits, and emotions. He has a mentality and certain goals, but not a detailed road map. He is, in short, a human being. Reducing the motives of him and his ruling team to just one thing means missing a lot of the story.

It is a key claim of this book that this code is real, and does influence policy. This contention is in opposition to accounts that attribute Russian behavior under Putin to either pure, rational pragmatism or the inevitable pull of Russian culture and traditions. Some observers treat the elements of the code, whether resentment or anti-Westernism or unity, as simply devices to mobilize the population and pump up the government's legitimacy. Such a stance, although attractive, is ultimately too simple and thus unpersuasive,

Table 1-1 **The Code of Putinism**

Ideas	Habits	Emotions
+ statism, including great power statism	+ control	+ respect/disrespect and humiliation
+ anti-Westernism and anti-Americanism	+ order	+ resentment
	+ unity/antipluralism	+ vulnerability/fear
+ conservatism/antiliberalism	+ loyalty	
	+ hypermasculinity	

failing to grapple with the complex nature of human motivations. Obviously Putin and other elites are occasionally insincere, and they will sometimes spout platitudes and lies as circumstances require. But the core of the code outlined here has been articulated too often (including in unscripted settings) by too many Russian elites for too many years to simply ignore. Further confidence that this description of the Putinist mentality is correct will come from showing how it shaped not just what Putin and his team said, but what they have done during their eighteen years in power.

It is true that the boundaries between the components—ideas, habits, emotions—is not always clear. Some aspects of the code that I treated as habits could just as easily be seen as emotions; for example, one biographer contends that Putin has "an emotional attachment to discipline, order, command, and control."[80] Importantly, the elements can reinforce one another. The idea of Russia as a strong state at home and abroad is connected to habits of control and order and feelings of resentment and disrespect. The overlap and blurring between the elements is what makes it a cohesive code or mentality.

Having a code is neither good nor bad, and the components of it can be either positive or negative. Loyalty is usually a virtue, and a strong state is definitely better than a weak one. All of us have felt disrespected or fearful at some point. That said, a code also can be counterproductive. In the case of the Putinist code, whether one thinks the code has led to positive results depends to a large extent on what one believes about Russia's current situation and how Putin has led the country for the last eighteen years. If one believes that Russia's domestic and international situation is quite precarious, that strong centralized "manual control" is necessary to hold the state together, and that the West is out to get Russia and makes common cause toward this end with Russia's domestic opposition, then the Putinist code is indispensable. As one Russian pro-Kremlin journalist puts it, "living without enemies and having a besieged fortress mentality is indeed stupid. But living in a besieged fortress and not having a besieged fortress's mentality is downright idiotic."[81] In contrast, a different evaluation of Russia's situation—less precarious, less threatened, more possibilities for development with the West, not in opposition to it—would lead to different judgments. Either way, the code helps explain the essence of Putinism, including the move from a frail but functional semidemocratic system in 2000 to the authoritarian hyperpresidentialism we see today.

2

Leashes and Clubs

Russian authoritarianism has a long and distinguished history. Ivan the Terrible, ruling Muscovy in the sixteenth century, was an autocrat. Peter the Great and Catherine the Great in the eighteenth century were autocrats. The various Nicholases and Alexanders of the nineteenth century were autocrats too. When the Soviet Union replaced the Russian Empire in the early twentieth century its new leaders changed many things, but not the tradition of authoritarian rule—tsars were replaced by general secretaries of the Communist Party, equally as dictatorial as their predecessors.

Then, in the late 1980s, something unusual happened. The general secretary of the Communist Party, Mikhail Gorbachev, decided that "normal" was not authoritarianism but democracy, and launched policies of "restructuring" (*perestroika*), "openness" (*glasnost*), and "democratization." Gorbachev's reforms led to the collapse of the communist bloc in Central and Eastern Europe and ultimately to the collapse of the Soviet Union itself. Gorbachev's one-time rival and sort-of successor, Boris Yeltsin, even more vehemently declared that Russia would be a "normal country" (Yeltsin was only a sort-of successor because he was president of Russia, one of fifteen independent states formed after the Soviet collapse). For Yeltsin, "normal" meant Russia would become a wealthy capitalist democracy, like countries in the West. This was nothing short of a revolution, but a peaceful one.[1]

At the time it looked like authoritarianism, the traditional mode of rule in Russia, had been unceremoniously tossed off. Authoritarianism had never been so threatened in Russia as it was in the early 1990s. This was true because democracy seemed to be sweeping the globe, with authoritarian regimes falling in southern Europe, Latin America, Asia, Africa, and, yes, Eastern Europe. Moreover, never had the conditions for democracy in Russia seemed so auspicious—unlike earlier periods of brief liberalization, such as during the 1917 Russian Revolution, Russia was now an urban, literate, educated, and relatively wealthy country, just the sort of place where democracy has the best chance of succeeding.

Who saved Russian authoritarianism? Vladimir Putin did. Since coming to power in Russia in 2000, he took a political system that had significant elements of freedom and democracy, such as competitive elections at multiple levels and a relatively free press, and made it considerably less free and democratic. Elections at all levels—municipal, regional, and federal—are now generally uncompetitive, boring affairs. The four major political parties are to varying degrees completely loyal to the Kremlin (by which I mean the president and the Presidential Administration, the highly important administrative organ), as are the two branches of parliament, the Duma and the Federation Council. Regional governments—both governors and legislatures—are also to a considerable extent controlled by Moscow. The three main national TV channels are generally subordinate to the Kremlin. The Constitutional Court enables rather than constrains executive power grabs. The freedom to organize and protest has been severely limited.

The code of Putinism played a central role in this authoritarian turn. It is not so much that the code is explicitly hostile to democracy. Rather, the ideas, habits, and emotions of the Putinist elite, and especially Putin himself, meant that at key turning points other things were valued more highly than democracy. Higher values included building a strong state and making Russia a great power. Traditions of order, control, stability, and unity led to a desire to concentrate power in the presidency and weaken other political actors. Feelings of resentment and vulnerability, similarly, meant that Western hectoring about democracy was dismissed as hypocrisy and organized political opposition often was perceived as an intense threat to the very system. Under these conditions, democracy was given short shrift.

As a result, Putin and his team constructed a political system of two unequal parts. The system of rule includes a formal set of institutions that I call "hyperpresidentialism" and an informal arrangement of clan networks. The Constitution gives considerable power to the president—it is often described as "superpresidential." At the same time, the Constitution also established both a horizontal separation of power—between executive, legislative, and judicial branches of government—and a vertical separation of power, with meaningful powers at the regional and local level. As we will see in this chapter, by making these vertical and horizontal separations of power largely fictitious, Putin has created a system that is not just superpresidential but hyperpresidential. Russia now has an authoritarian regime within the formal shell of democracy—what political scientists call electoral authoritarianism.[2]

The day-to-day management of Russia's system of hyperpresidentialism depends on a system of leashes and clubs. The notion of leashes comes from the Russian political analyst Maria Lipman, who quipped that the Kremlin under Putin has a good system of "leashes of all sizes—long, short," and so on, as the case requires. If these leashes prove inadequate to ensure the Kremlin's control over the political process, "the state holds a club," as Putin remarked in 2000, adding "if we get angry . . . we will use the club without hesitation." Scholars of electoral authoritarianism have cataloged the ways in which rulers can manipulate parties and elections and the media to ensure the "right" outcomes—these are Lipman's leashes, what scholars call "the menu of manipulation." Relatively less attention has been given to the use of clubs, or what I call the "menu of repression"—the use of law enforcement and the courts to marginalize and weaken the opposition, and to repel possible threats to the powers that be.[3]

This chapter traces the evolution of Russia's political system under Putin's rule, in particular the way in which alternative centers of possible power were weakened and brought under his control. This authoritarian direction was not some inevitable byproduct of culture or history or circumstances, but the product of human decisions. Moreover, these decisions are explained not simply as a rational pursuit of power but as a product of the code of Putinism. This code led to a series of decisions that tightened the political space in Russia over the past eighteen years.

The neutering of the formal checks and balances in the political system meant that informal clans became the only real counterweights under Putinism. Although hyperpresidentialism and informal clan networks are thus logically connected and interrelated in one system of rule, these two parts of the system deserve separate discussions, with this chapter focused on the former and chapter 3 dealing with the latter.

Yeltsin's Ambiguous Legacy

By giving Putin credit for saving Russian authoritarianism, I don't mean to deny the important role played by others, especially his predecessor, Boris Yeltsin. Yeltsin did much both for efforts to build a democratic Russia and to create conditions that enabled the return of authoritarianism. He left his successor a political system with many flaws, but one that was much more open and democratic than was typical for Russia historically, and compared to the current Putinist form.

Russia's post-Soviet constitution came into being only after a violent constitutional struggle in October 1993 between Yeltsin and the old parliament, in which more than 100 people died, was won by Yeltsin.[4] The new Constitution declared Russia a "democratic, federal, rule-of-law state," but this was more an aspiration than a reality. It established, as noted, both horizontal and vertical separations of power. At the federal level, it recognized a Constitutional Court with the power of judicial review, the ability to declare acts of the executive and legislative branches unconstitutional. It established a bicameral parliament, the Federal Assembly, composed of a State Duma of 450 elected members and a Federation Council with two representatives for each region (currently 85, according to Russian law).[5] The executive branch is technically "semipresidential," like that in France, with a directly elected president as well as a prime minister who heads what Russians call the government—the ministries and other executive branch agencies. Unlike in France, however, the constitutional rules make the prime minister largely dependent not on the majority in the parliament but on the president; for this reason and several others, many analysts consider the system to better fit the label "superpresidential" than "semipresidential." The 1993 Constitution also established a federal system of rule, in which the central government has some powers, the regional governments have others, and many powers are shared; local self-government is also a core constitutional principle. For a large, multinational country like Russia, federalism represents the best political system for establishing democratic rule.[6]

The Duma elections that took place under Yeltsin—in 1993, 1995, and 1999—were competitive, with a relatively level playing field. They were far from perfect, but there was no concerted effort on the part of the Kremlin to systematically distort or falsify the results. For that reason the Duma throughout most of Yeltsin's presidency was dominated by his political opponents, with the Communist Party holding the most seats throughout Yeltsin's second term from 1996 to 1999. The other house of parliament, the Federation Council, also was not controlled by Yeltsin, and represented a strong check on his power. Yeltsin was reelected in 1996 in a deeply flawed election, with vote rigging in some regions and an unfair television and spending advantage for Yeltsin. Even so, it was the closest and most competitive presidential election post-Soviet Russia has experienced, with

Yeltsin forced into a second round by the communist challenger Gennadiy Zyuganov. In other respects as well, politics under Boris Yeltsin were more open and democratic than under Putin. There was considerable diversity and pluralism of opinion on the major national television channels, whether state or privately controlled, not to mention the vibrant print media.[7]

Other aspects of politics under Yeltsin made a departure from authoritarianism more difficult. The war in Chechnya, an ethnic republic in southern Russia, led to massive human rights violations and increased the voice of security and military personnel in national politics; a particular problem was the failure to subject the so-called power ministries (such as the Federal Security Service and the Ministry of Defense) to more reliable forms of civilian and parliamentary control. A system of crony capitalism took root in which wealthy tycoons—"oligarchs" is the standard term in Russia—wielded considerable influence on government decision-making and the media. Most importantly, perhaps, Yeltsin chose a successor—Vladimir Putin—who could be expected to protect him and his family from corruption inquiries or political reprisals, but whose conservative and antipluralist instincts would lead him to rebuild an authoritarian system that had been weakened during the more open and democratic 1990s.[8]

The extent to which Russian politics has moved in an authoritarian direction under Putin is demonstrated in multiple ratings of democracy around the world. A useful and illustrative rating is the World Bank's "Voice and Accountability" measure from their Worldwide Governance Indicators (WGI) project, which began in 1996. They define "Voice and Accountability" as "the extent to which a country's citizens are able to participate in selecting their government, as well as freedom of expression, freedom of association, and a free media," which reflects basic understandings of the meaning of democracy. Rather than relying on one measure, the WGI aggregates multiple measures from different sources, which should somewhat lessen concerns about bias in the measures. Figure 2-1 shows Russian performance on the Voice and Accountability measure for the period from 1996 to 2015; the WGI scale runs from 2.5 (most democratic) to -2.5 (least democratic).[9]

The WGI "Voice and Accountability" measure shows Russia becoming increasingly authoritarian after 2000, when Putin takes power. This result is consistent with other international measures of democracy. For example, the well-known democracy ratings by Freedom House, a Washington-based nongovernmental organization (NGO), listed Russia as a "partly

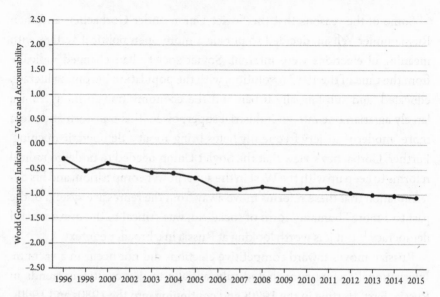

Figure 2-1 Russia Voice and Accountability, 1996–2015

free" country from 1992 to 2003, and "not free" after that. The year 2004 was the last in which Russia appeared on Freedom House's list of "electoral democracies." Similarly, the most detailed academic study of Russian electoral fraud contends that it was only under Putin that a national pattern of electoral fraud took hold, as opposed to scattered fraud in a few republics. Thus, there are good reasons to agree with the dominant view that Russia was on the whole an electoral democracy in the 1990s, albeit a quite flawed one, and an electoral authoritarian regime since around 2003–2004.[10]

Was Authoritarianism Inevitable?

Why does Russia bother with elections anyway? For centuries tsars received their mandate to rule from heaven and relied on dynastic succession, and general secretaries drew their legitimacy from the Communist Party's claim to be in the vanguard of history, not from the ballot box. It was not until Gorbachev's reforms that competitive elections, as opposed to communist-style sham elections, were seen as the source of a mandate to rule. Even then, Gorbachev himself never submitted to a national election; it was not until 1991, when Yeltsin was elected president of the Russian Federation, still one of fifteen Soviet republics at the time, that Russia had a national leader chosen in a democratic ballot.

Some of the reasons that the Soviet Union under Gorbachev, and then Russia under Yeltsin, decided to pursue a more open political system with meaningful elections were internal. Soviet society had changed radically from the time of the 1917 revolution, with the population becoming literate, educated, and substantially urban and the economy transforming from a largely agrarian one into an industrial superpower. This transformation to a more "modern" society frequently helps bring about a democratic opening. Further, Gorbachev's view that the Soviet Union needed to undergo radical reforms to keep up with the West in the superpower competition, and his determination that these reforms move away from the repressive system of the past to a more "humane" form of socialism, was critical to the move toward democracy.[11] But it is worth looking at Russia in a broader context.

Russian moves toward competitive elections did not occur in a vacuum. International factors contributed substantially to democratizing trends in Russia. First, starting in the 1970s and continuing into the 1980s and 1990s, a "wave" of democracy swept across the globe, transforming political systems in Europe, Latin America, Asia, and Africa. According to Freedom House, the percentage of countries in the world that were electoral democracies increased from less than 30 percent in 1974 to around 60 percent by the mid-1990s. Second, the end of the Cold War gave a further boost to democratizing pressures, with Western states more inclined to insist on multiparty elections for good relations, and the rise of an entire global industry of democracy promotion and election monitoring. The most important international change was the ideational hegemony of liberal democracy after the collapse of communism, with democracy seen as a better political system than various forms of authoritarianism. This shift in values was reflected in Gorbachev's and Yeltsin's pronouncements indicating that democracy and capitalism were the new "normal" for Russia.[12]

This ideational hegemony of democracy as the most legitimate form of government still holds sway in Russia, despite the return to authoritarianism, at least at the rhetorical level. For example, in his 2012 annual address to parliament, Putin stated, "For Russia there is not and cannot be any political choice other than democracy." He emphasized that Russia adheres to "universal democratic principles," but it will not accept "standards imposed on us from outside." This formulation is consistent with the notion of "sovereign democracy" that was promoted in the mid-2000s by Vladislav Surkov, often referred to as the Kremlin's "chief ideologist." Although the adjective "sovereign" was more important than the noun "democracy," stressing the need

for Russia to pursue its own conception of democracy without outside interference, the very presence of the word "democracy" was indicative of the
hegemonic status that democracy holds among official political discourse in
Putin's Russia. Some proregime writers have argued that authoritarianism is
the correct path for Russia, but Putin himself has never made that argument
or said that Russia was not democratic. Some analysts have suggested that
China and Russia represent a new wave of authoritarian great powers, but at
the ideological level Russia has not positioned itself as a defender of authoritarianism, and is unlikely to do so.[13]

Thus, there remain clear reasons why Russia will not simply abandon multiparty elections, and so the adjective "electoral" is likely to remain, even if
the elections are far from free and fair. What about the authoritarian part
of electoral authoritarianism? Most of the literature on Russian electoral authoritarianism seeks to explain not why Russia has elections at all, but why
it has become authoritarian after the so-called democratic transition of the
early 1990s. The simple answer, which I defend later, is that Putin made it
authoritarian. But perhaps we should first turn the question around: why
should we be surprised that Russia is authoritarian? This is, after all, what it
has been for most of its history.

The most obvious variant of this line of argument is the political culture
one. According to this view, discussed briefly in chapter 1, Russia has an authoritarian political culture, with the population preferring a "strong hand."
Some versions of this argument contend that, given Russia's size, climate, and
remoteness, only a powerful authoritarian government can hold it together.
Without denying completely these influences, it is an overstatement to say
that Russia is somehow doomed to authoritarian rule. First, and most importantly, lots of countries that were once authoritarian, and allegedly cultur-
ally predisposed to autocracy, are now democratic. Similarly, there is nothing
about Orthodox Christianity that has stopped countries like Greece and
Bulgaria from adopting democracy—Russia is actually *less* democratic than
any other Orthodox Christian country in Europe except for neighboring
Belarus. Big countries with difficult climates—too cold in Canada, too hot in
Brazil—also have succeeded as democracies.[14]

Furthermore, we no longer need to speculate on what Russians think
about what the best political system is—there is now a wealth of public
opinion data on the political views of Russian citizens, and a considerable
academic literature based on these data. The most persuasive effort to make
sense of the sometimes contradictory findings is that of the political scientist

Henry Hale. Hale contends that there is little support for the view that most Russians hold authoritarian beliefs. Russians are democrats, but "delegative democrats"—Russians want a strong leader to try to solve national problems, but one who is chosen in free and fair multicandidate elections. They want both democracy and a "strong hand," and see no contradiction between the two. Russia's recent authoritarian turn is not primarily about culture.[15]

Why have many countries successfully transitioned from authoritarianism to democracy over the last several centuries? The dominant explanation among political scientists, often called modernization theory, links political change to economic development. Some scholars connected Gorbachev's reforms to the modernization of Soviet society, which went from being predominantly rural and illiterate at the time of the 1917 revolution to overwhelmingly urban and literate. Russia remains highly literate and urbanized today, and was classified by the World Bank as a high-income economy from 2012 to 2014, although the subsequent recession (see chapter 4) knocked Russia down to the upper-middle-income category starting in 2015. Still, the most recent figures show Russia with a gross domestic product (GDP) per capita of 23,000 dollars. Countries this wealthy tend to be much more democratic than Russia is today.[16]

Or consider a different comparison, one that Russia is apt to invoke and one we return to throughout the book—that of the BRICS countries. The original BRIC countries were Brazil, Russia, India, and China, so designated by a financial analyst due to their status as large, developing economies. The BRICS countries are now a formal organization, joined by South Africa. Of these five countries, Russia is by far the wealthiest on a per capita basis (the next closest are Brazil and China, at around 15,000 dollars), but the second-least democratic, followed only by China; India, Brazil, and South Africa all do much better on democracy measures than Russia. Russia has become much richer under Putin, but also more authoritarian.

One possible reason that modernization theory might do poorly in explaining Russian authoritarianism has to do with a different theory linking economics to political outcomes: the resource curse. The resource curse argument contends that countries that are heavily dependent on hydrocarbons (oil and gas) for their economy are less likely to be democratic; this might be because they are not dependent on taxing their population for revenue (no taxation, no representation), or because they can buy the loyalty of state repressive organs like the military and police, or because they don't go through the broad-based social changes other countries go through when they become rich (as described by modernization theory). Most of the world's undemocratic high-income countries are petro-states such as Qatar and Saudi Arabia. Although there are oil-rich democracies, such as the United States, Canada, and Norway, they have been democratic for a long time. More relevant comparisons for Russia might be Mexico and Nigeria, both of which are major oil producers and have democratized in the last several decades. Although the resource curse might not be an iron law, it seems likely that Russian dependence on oil and gas exports (which account for about 25 percent of GDP and about half of annual budget revenues) made authoritarianism more likely, regardless of who occupied the Kremlin.[17]

Besides culture and economics, another factor that influences what type of regime a country has—democratic, authoritarian, or "hybrid" (a mix of democratic and authoritarian)—are its institutions. Institutions are the basic "rules of the game" of the system. As noted earlier, the 1993 Constitution put in place by Yeltsin had ambiguous effects. Although it set out a long list of rights and freedoms and established vertical and horizontal separations of power, it also gave a great deal of power to the president. This "superpresidentialism" arguably contributed to enabling Russia's authoritarian system. Henry Hale argues that Eurasian (that is, post-Soviet) political systems with strong presidents have a tendency toward "single-pyramid" presidential rule, in which political and economic elites line up behind the ruling president in order to maintain their position in the system. Only institutional reform to divide power among multiple positions, such as strengthening the prime minister so s/he is more equal to the president, can break this tendency toward single-pyramid systems that are likely to be authoritarian. Hale would point out, correctly, that many of Russia's post-Soviet neighbors with strong presidencies are also authoritarian, so Russia is hardly a major exception.[18]

Hale's approach assumes that political elites are rational power-maximizers motivated by roughly identical motives. Thus, contrary to the conventional story, Russia moved from electoral democracy to electoral authoritarianism not because Putin replaced Yeltsin but simply because Putin had more resources at his disposal—political, economic, coercive, and so on. In the rest of this chapter I want to stand up for the conventional wisdom: Russia is authoritarian because Vladimir Putin made it so. In this case, at least, the simplistic answer is the correct one, or at least a pretty good starting point. Authoritarianism was one possible outcome after Yeltsin, but it was not inevitable. Some factors favored more democratic outcomes—the general worldwide and European trend toward democracy, the wealth and "modernity" (urban, literate, educated) of Russian society—whereas others—the resource curse, the superpresidential political system, and arguably Russia's own traditions—tended to favor a more authoritarian direction. Putin had choices to make, and authoritarianism was not inevitable.

This is not to suggest that Russia could have easily been remade into a flourishing liberal democracy with a different leader. Rather, it is a claim about the direction of Russia's political evolution. Here the comparison to its post-Soviet neighbors is instructive. The three Baltic states of Estonia, Latvia, and Lithuania have become stable democracies, whereas other countries have firm dictatorships—such as Azerbaijan, Belarus, and Uzbekistan. Countries like Armenia, Georgia, Kyrgyzstan, Moldova, and Ukraine are somewhere in the middle, combining elements of democracy and authoritarianism. Russia, given its circumstances, was unlikely to turn out as democratic as Estonia, but under different leadership it could look more like Georgia, Moldova, and Ukraine in terms of its political regime, all of which have faced civil war (like Russia in Chechnya) and are poorer than Russia, but have more democratic political systems than Russia's.[19]

In contrast, then, to versions of the Putin story that stress either the gravitational pull of what social scientists call "structural constraints" (economics, geography, and so on), or the grim logic by which all leaders are driven to become dictators due to rational self-interest if circumstances permit, this account of Putinism and hyperpresidentialism stresses how the code of Putinism pushed Putin and his team in the direction of authoritarianism over time.[20] There was no grand plan at the beginning to build an authoritarian regime; rather, the values, habits, and feelings of Putin and other elites meant that, at each possible decision point, Putin chose the option that reinforced control. He and his team used the leash, and occasionally the club, to rein in other political actors, whether the parliament, the media, political parties, or civil society.[21]

Leashes: The Menu of Manipulation

Vladimir Putin, at the time of writing, had been elected president of Russia three times—in 2000, 2004, and 2012. This was perfectly consistent with the Russian Constitution, which limits presidents to two *consecutive* terms. After serving two four-year terms, Putin stepped aside for his hand-picked successor, Dmitriy Medvedev, who served as president for four years while Putin served as prime minister. Perhaps the most significant action by Medvedev as president was to amend the constitution so presidential terms were extended from four to six years (and parliamentary terms from four to five years). This means that Putin's third term lasted from 2012 to 2018. By the time you are reading this it is basically preordained that he will have been re-elected easily to a fourth term. If this is correct, his fourth term lasts until 2024 (at which point he would be 71 years old).

The ease with which the constitution was amended—flying through the Duma with a massive majority (392 to 57), an almost-unanimous Federation Council (144 to 1), then all 83 regional legislatures, all in less than two months—is indicative of the nature of Russian electoral authoritarianism, in which formal democratic procedures are observed while democracy is undermined in practice. Putin and Medvedev's elections as president are also telling examples. Neither of them has conducted anything that resembles an election campaign in a real democracy. In August 1999, when Yeltsin offered Putin the prime ministership and proposed that Putin be his designated successor, Putin responded, "I hate campaign battles. A lot. I can't conduct them and I hate them." Since then Putin has largely been true to his word. In 2000, when Putin ran for public office for the first time in his life, he refused to do traditional campaign events such as debates or television commercials, stating, "These videos, their advertising, I will not be trying to find out in the course of my election campaign which is more important, Tampax or Snickers." Putin has never engaged in a public debate with a political rival, and almost certainly never will.[22]

One reason that competitive elections don't matter that much to Putin and others in his circle is that they think Western promotion of democracy and free elections is all hypocrisy, a way to pressure adversaries. The code of Putinism, with emotional resentment of being treated as a pupil of the West when it should be afforded the respect of a great power, as well as habits of control and unity, makes genuinely democratic competition in which the outcome is truly uncertain something to avoid. A pro-Kremlin journalist explains that the Russian elite doesn't believe Western elections are meaningful contests; rather, Western elites use elections as a way to let the population blow off steam, which can lead to a change of faces at the top but doesn't really change policies in a substantive way. Russian elites also feel that there should be a change in faces, this journalist suggests, "but haven't found a way to make [this change] dependent on votes." This observation brilliantly sums up the logic of Russian electoral authoritarianism under Putin—elections are a good idea in principle, but in reality it's more important to make sure one gets the "right" outcomes.[23]

Given these feelings and ideas about democracy, the tendency over time has been in an authoritarian direction. This is not because Putin set out to build authoritarianism per se; it was more a matter of establishing control and promoting the more important goals of building a strong state and great power than any conscious embrace of dictatorship. To this end, the Kremlin has manipulated both the rules of the game (institutions) and the players. Political scientists have detailed the various ways in which electoral authoritarian regimes can render the playing field uneven. For example, authoritarian rulers can restrict access to the ballot or the media, interfere in vote procedures or vote counting, and change the rules to favor the ruling party. Moreover, elections, even manipulated ones, may deliver genuine benefits, including information about sources of support and opposition, co-optation of other elites and potential rivals, and some measure of legitimacy (even if partially tarnished), both domestically and internationally.[24] In the following two sections I review the ways in which both the rules of the game and the players have been manipulated under Putin, first with respect to formal state institutions and then as regards nonstate actors.

Formal State Institutions

The Russian Constitution, while giving a great deal of power to the president and the executive branch, also distributes power among different branches of government—the legislature and the judiciary—and levels of government (federal, regional, and local). Under Yeltsin, these countervailing institutions made the realization of superpresidentialism difficult in practice, regardless of Yeltsin's intentions. From the beginning, Putin made clear with his actions and his slogan about building a "vertical of power" that he intended to make superpresidentialism a reality. As an American political scientist put it in 2001, "Putin did not inherit a superpresidential order, he sought to build one."[25] Over time, particularly after the December 2003 parliamentary elections and the 2005 cancellation of governor elections, the other branches and levels of government have become more dependent on the president and presidential administration. In effect, Putin shot straight past superpresidentialism and on to hyperpresidentialism.

The Federal Assembly

Russia's bicameral legislature, the Federation Council and the State Duma, had been a thorn in Yeltsin's side for much of the period from 1994 to 1999, and Putin had witnessed some of this needling firsthand while working for

Yeltsin. For example, in 1998 the Federation Council had stood in the way of the dismissal of the procurator general (similar to the US attorney general, but more powerful), and in 1999 the Duma came within seventeen votes of passing an impeachment resolution against Yeltsin.

The Federation Council proved to be the easier chamber to bring under Kremlin control, which Putin was able to do in his first year as president. A key reason it was easier is because most of the Russian political elite, and many independent observers as well, agreed that the way the Federation Council had been formed in Yeltsin's second term was problematic at best and positively harmful at worst. Governors were simultaneously executive heads of their regions and members of the national legislature—in American terms, combining the office of governor and senator. Shortly after becoming president, Putin successfully pushed for a change in how the Federation Council was formed. Although in theory "senators" were now to be chosen by the regional governor and the regional legislature, in practice Putin and the Presidential Administration often played the key role, and it became common for members of the Federation Council to have no connection to their supposed home region.[26]

It took a little bit longer for Putin to bring the Duma under control, but not much longer. A pro-Putin party was cobbled together at the last minute in fall 1999 to contest the December 1999 Duma elections and prevent Yeltsin's and Putin's rivals from winning and possibly taking power. This new party, Unity, managed to finish second in the voting behind the Communist Party. Still, the Communists had the biggest share of seats, 113 out of 450, although considerably fewer than they had under Yeltsin. With the support of several smaller parties, Putin was able to push key legislation—including a series of liberalizing economic reforms that had been stalled under Yeltsin—through the Duma.

The key step in bringing the Duma under firm control took place during Putin's first term, when Kremlin aide Vladislav Surkov helped engineer the unification of the Unity bloc with another party controlled by several powerful governors. This new superparty, United Russia, became the "party of power" that has dominated the Duma since 2001. United Russia is a centrist party motivated more by loyalty to Putin than any coherent ideology. In parliamentary elections in 2003 and 2007, United Russia captured 38 and then 64 percent of the vote. In the controversial elections of 2011, which led to mass protests, United Russia officially received 49 percent of the vote, although independent experts estimated that the true result was closer to

35 percent of the vote. United Russia received 54 percent of the voting based on party lists in the 2016 Duma elections. As with previous elections, there were credible allegations of considerable fraud on behalf of United Russia.[27]

The menu of manipulation is clearly evident in how Duma electoral rules have been changed over time to benefit Putin and the Kremlin. When United Russia was strong and growing in power, small electoral districts (like in the US House of Representatives) were eliminated in favor of party list voting, in which voters select their favorite party (like legislative elections in many European parliamentary democracies). This had the effect of getting rid of difficult-to-control independents who could otherwise make it into the Duma based on local popularity. When United Russia support declined after the fraudulent 2011 elections, the electoral system was changed back to a combined party-list and single-member-district electoral system, which was believed to offer the best opportunity for United Russia to dominate the Duma. This gambit worked out perfectly in the 2016 Duma elections. United Russia won 54 percent of the party-list vote but captured 76 percent of the Duma seats because of its dominance in single-member districts, where opposition votes were scattered across multiple candidates and the United Russia candidate could capture the seat with a mere plurality of votes.

Other changes enacted over the years limited electoral participation to major parties having the status of national political parties and prohibited electoral blocs of multiple parties. Registration rules were tightened and parties became more dependent on the government for financing and media access. All of these changes meant that only Kremlin-approved parties were able to make it on to the ballot. The three other parties sitting in the Duma are also parties deemed acceptable by the Kremlin, and these parties frequently vote together with United Russia. Russia has an ostensibly democratically elected parliament in which only Kremlin-approved parties are allowed to participate.[28]

The creation of a subordinate Federal Assembly, with the Federation Council and Duma answering less to the voters than to the executive branch, completely changed the lawmaking process. Under Yeltsin, the legislative process depended on bargaining and ad hoc coalitions of legislators on an issue-by-issue basis, and the government often failed to get its way on important legislation. Between 1994 and 1999, Yeltsin used his veto power 438 times, vetoing over 30 percent of laws. Under Putin (and Medvedev), the executive branch decided which laws would pass and played the central role in drafting the text of the majority of laws. Most of the bargaining about the content of laws took place not inside the legislature, but inside the executive branch—for example, the Presidential Administration might work out the text in negotiations with the relevant ministry. Between 2004 and 2011, Putin and Medvedev only needed to use the veto 10 times total, less than 1 percent of the time. United Russia had become a reliable instrument of parliamentary control.[29]

By Putin's third term, which started in 2012, the Duma became known as a "mad printer"—mad as in crazy, not angry—rushing through a variety of laws to tighten the political space in response to initiatives of the Kremlin. Sometimes, it is true, entrepreneurial legislators would try to anticipate the will of the executive branch and put forward some conservative initiative, but it needed executive branch okay to have a chance of passing. The changed role of parliament was reflected in an iconic quote of the Putin era, when the Duma Speaker Boris Gryzlov, a Putin ally from St. Petersburg, declared, "The State Duma is not a place for political battles," a remark later satirized with the expression "the Duma is not a place for political discussion."[30]

The Judiciary

The judiciary represents the third branch of power, in addition to the legislative and executive branches. The 1993 Constitution, as noted, established the principle of the separation of powers and recognized a Constitutional Court endowed with the power of judicial review.[31] In reality, however, the Constitutional Court has been unwilling to challenge a dominant executive, so it represents a feeble restraint on authoritarian tendencies, despite the many political rights elaborated in the Russian constitution. Moreover, the criminal courts, as we will see below, are an important part of the "menu of repression."

In general, the judicial role in the construction of Russian electoral authoritarianism is more passive than active. Even in established democracies, and especially in new democracies, high courts often avoid direct challenges to the other branches of power, especially the executive. With the legislative branch firmly under Kremlin control, one of the main sources of potential legal conflict requiring the Constitutional Court to take sides has been eliminated. In terms of the vertical separation of powers, the Russian Constitutional Court has been a firm proponent of strong central power. Its most consequential decision under Putin allowed the center to end governor elections between 2005 and 2012, reversing an earlier Constitutional Court decision and, according to many analysts, the clear logic of the Constitution itself, which according to its declared federal structure gives the regions the power to create "organs of state power." Constitutional Court deference to the Kremlin, in general, is primarily a product of caution and deference on the part of the high court, which fears having its rulings ignored if it confronts the executive directly.[32]

Thus, despite its potential status as a counterweight to presidential power, in reality the Constitutional Court has not played that role. Manipulation has been less important than meekness. Some manipulation has nevertheless taken place. The Constitutional Court was moved from Moscow to St. Petersburg, which former Deputy Chair Tamara Morshchakova referred to as an "exile" and a blow to the "prestige" of the Court. More directly, one of the two judges who issued "blistering" dissents in the governor elections decisions was forced from the bench in 2010, and the other one was censored and removed from the Council of Judges but kept his seat on the Constitutional Court. The tendency has been to nominate judges to the Constitutional Court who went to St. Petersburg State Law School, not coincidentally the alma mater of both Putin and Medvedev. As Morshchakova put it, "the main trend is to approve everything proposed by the leadership of the country." A Siberian newspaper editor expressed the same thought, observing that "the Constitutional Court can explain any decision of the Kremlin as being in line with the Constitution."[33]

Western legal experts on Russia generally give the Constitutional Court good marks for beginning the process of establishing constitutional jurisprudence that elaborated some of the civil and political rights of citizens as laid out in the Constitution. Certainly in comparison to the Soviet past this was a new and welcome phenomenon. But it also should be noted that the Court has done little to oppose state limitations on freedom of speech, freedom of assembly, freedom of the press, and other basic rights. Tens of thousands of Russian citizens have sought help from the European Court of Human Rights (ECHR), which has frequently ruled against the Russian government, a source of some embarrassment to Russia. In December 2015 Putin signed a law formalizing the ability of the Constitutional Court to reject rulings of international courts that pertain to Russia. These moves are consistent with the code of Putinism's stress on the importance of maintaining Russian sovereignty as a great power, even though the Constitution explicitly establishes the supremacy of international treaties and agreements over domestic law.[34]

The Regions

The constitutional separation of powers at the national level has not been a major impediment to building hyperpresidentialism under Putin. What about the horizontal separation of powers under Russia's federal system? Under Yeltsin the regions had acquired considerable power, and governors were formidable officials not only in their regions but also often at the national level. Russian electoral authoritarianism actually got its start at the regional level in the 1990s, with rigged elections, neutered legislatures, compliant courts, and weak opposition in some regions. The federalism expert Alfred Stepan asserted in 2000 that the "territorial dispersion of constitutional, political, budgetary and coercive power in Russia . . . has greatly complicated the tasks of a centralizing dictatorship."[35]

"Greatly complicated," perhaps, but not made impossible. Consistent with the Putinist code's belief in order, unity, and a strong state, Putin and his team set out to "restore vertical power." As he put it shortly after becoming president in 2000, "Everyone was saying that the administrative vertical had been destroyed and that it had to be restored." He immediately launched a series of federal reforms that changed the Federation Council and made it more dependent on the Kremlin, changed the fiscal formula so more tax money remained with the central government rather than going to the regions, and created seven "federal districts" as an administrative layer between the central government and the regions. These federal districts had the job of regaining control over the regional branches of federal ministries and "harmonizing laws" to make sure regional laws were consistent with federal ones. A series of bilateral treaties that Yeltsin had negotiated with many regional governors were phased out.[36]

Leonid Smirnyagin, Yeltsin's regional affairs adviser, told me in 2001, Putin "does not need or understand federalism." Indeed, Smirnyagin noted, the very idea of building "vertical power" is inconsistent with the logic of federalism. I saw Smirnyagin again in the summer of 2015, and he recalled a long-ago meeting with Yuriy Trutnev, currently a deputy prime minister but at the time the governor of the Perm region near the Ural Mountains. Trutnev invited Smirnyagin to give a presentation on federalism, and Smirnyagin used a framework similar to the one used here to describe both the horizontal and vertical division of power, a series of checks and balances, that is intrinsic to democratic federalism. Trutnev's advisers were appalled by the presentation, exclaiming, "He is telling us how to weaken power—we need to know how to strengthen power!" The point of federalism, Smirnyagin added, is to make elected governors answer to voters, not to the central government. For the code of Putinism, leaving it up to the voters leaves too much to chance and weakens the powers of the center. Power is zero-sum, either belonging to this or that actor, not something that can be positive sum, with both strong regions and a strong Russia.[37]

There is little doubt that in important ways the pendulum in Russian federal relations had swung too far toward the regions under Yeltsin, and that some rebalancing was necessary. Although some of Putin's federal reforms arguably were necessary to restore a center-regional balance, once gubernatorial elections were canceled in 2004 Putin had returned Russia to a form of "sham federalism" more similar to Soviet federalism than democratic federalism. When governor elections were restored in 2012 as part of a concession to anti-Putin protests that broke out in late 2011, they were only restored with a series of "filters" that made it difficult to impossible for a candidate not approved by the Kremlin to get on the ballot, let alone win. Another proviso allows some regions to skip governor elections altogether, a loophole that has been applied particularly in the volatile North Caucasus, but in other regions as well.[38]

Putin's moves away from meaningful federalism, justified as strengthening the state, was also a move toward authoritarianism. As one Russian analyst explained, the path of real federalism and democracy from Putin's point of view was the more complicated and risky path, with the possibility of separatism and conflict. Seeking control was easier, and in Putin's eyes was the best way to maintain state integrity, which was more important than democracy.[39]

Thus, with respect to the checks and balances on presidential power in the 1993 Constitution—the legislative branch, the judiciary, and regional governments—Putin and the Kremlin manipulated the rules to strengthen the executive branch. Control, a strong state, and unity—key elements of the code of Putinism—were more important than the constitutional separation of powers.

Nonstate Actors

Within the institutions of the state, the Kremlin has been able to strengthen the position of the central executive vis-à-vis other branches of power, arguably beyond even the considerable powers afforded by the Constitution. Putin turned superpresidentialism into hyperpresidentialism in his bid to establish control and build a strong and unified system of rule. What about nonstate actors? The nature of a political regime is explained not just by what government officials and organizations do but also by the connections between society and the state. Many people have claimed that the power of the modern state is on the decline, with non-state actors like NGOs and the media on the rise. Within this context, Putin's Russia would seem to be a cautionary tale, showing the power of the state to manipulate and dominate key branches of civil society in the interests of state rulers. We can see this with respect to three important nonstate actors: political parties, the media, and NGOs.

Political Parties

Political parties are a fundamental part of all democracies, an intermediary connecting citizens to politics and government, and often play a similar role in hybrid and authoritarian regimes as well. Under Soviet rule the Constitution affirmed the "leading and guiding" role of the Communist Party, but democratization brought a flourishing of political parties. Analysts agree that under Yeltsin political parties were weak and unstable. Some were dominated by prominent flamboyant leaders, some were generally failed efforts by the Kremlin to create a centrist "party of power" under its control, and many were mocked as "couch parties," so small that they might fit on a single couch. Only the Communist Party of the Russian Federation (KPRF) had a reasonably strong brand and decent grassroots infrastructure, both legacies of the Soviet period. But its leader, Gennadiy Zyuganov, inspired little excitement and its most loyal voters were pensioners, which seemed to doom the party to eventual decline. Surveys showed that citizens didn't trust political parties in general, or have strong and enduring party loyalties.[40]

Putin and his team sought to change this reality, and probably surprised even themselves at how spectacularly they succeeded. The chief conductor was Vladislav Surkov, whose title as deputy chief of staff of the Presidential Administration for the period 1999–2011 somewhat obscures his true importance in domestic Russian politics for much of the Putin epoch. The Russian journalist and analyst Maria Lipman describes Surkov as a unique figure among hybrid regimes around the world, given the way he was a top state official who also wrote postmodern novels and liked to hang out in intellectual circles. Lipman likened Surkov to a "sculptor," playing with parties like clay. He was also the mastermind of United Russia, the successful "party of power" based on loyalty to Putin, and its chief monitor.[41] The air of mystery about Surkov and his manipulation of the system extended to an apparently (?) fake Twitter account, leading to speculation about whether the account @SurkovRussia was really Surkov, a fake, or Surkov himself having fun by pretending to be a fake Surkov.

Surkov the "sculptor" also fashioned other parties as the circumstances required. In 2003 the nationalist Rodina ("Motherland") party was used to siphon votes from the Communists, whose vote share was cut in half compared to the previous election, and then abandoned when its leaders proved difficult to control. Then in 2007, the pro-Kremlin Just Russia (sometimes called Fair Russia) party was promoted as a "center left" party to balance the "center right" United Russia. Just Russia was headed by Sergey Mironov, another Petersburger who ran for president in 2004 but endorsed his ostensible opponent Putin anyway. In 2011 Surkov tried to promote a liberal party called Right Cause, recruiting the billionaire oligarch Mikhail Prokhorov to lead the party. Prokhorov, best known to American basketball fans as the 6'8" owner of the Brooklyn Nets, rebelled at Surkov's attempt to control his campaign and was forced from the party leadership. Prokhorov denounced Surkov as "a puppet master who long ago privatized the political system," declared Right Cause to be a "puppet Kremlin party" and declared the whole affair a "farce."[42]

In one respect, at least, the situation from 2007 forward with parliamentary parties is an improvement over the past—the same four parties won enough votes to enter the Duma in 2007, 2011, and 2016. This electoral stability in different circumstances would suggest a maturation of the party system, but since these four parties—United Russia, Just Russia, the Liberal Democratic Party of Russia, and the Communist Party—were all to varying degrees reliable supporters of Kremlin laws and initiatives, what it really indicated was the stability of Putin's hyperpresidentialism. The leaders of these parties understand that crossing the Kremlin on important issues will lead to a sharp yank on the leash (potential restrictions on funding and access), and even perhaps a blow from the club (trouble with law enforcement). One anecdote, relayed by a long-serving political journalist for a major Russian newspaper, reflects the way in which even supposed "opposition" parties toe the Kremlin line, with party leaders pushing their own members to keep quiet. Dmitriy Gorovtsov, a member of Just Russia, mentioned to the journalist that he was going to make a strong anticorruption speech on the floor of the Duma. When Gorovtsov didn't do so, the journalist called to ask him what had happened. Gorovtsov, who according to the journalist sounded hung over, said that Just Russia leader Mironov had told him to drop the issue, indicating that he had "asked up" (meaning the Presidential Administration) and was told not to do so.[43]

After 2011 Surkov was no longer the Kremlin "puppet master" controlling the political parties. This responsibility was taken over for the next five years by Vyacheslav Volodin, who famously stated in 2014 that there is no Russia without Putin. It was the idea of Volodin and his staff in the Presidential Administration to shift the 2016 Duma elections from December to September, in the belief that this would be a more auspicious time for United Russia to deliver a convincing win. All parliamentary parties except the Communists easily approved this change, which was also approved in a hasty fashion by the Constitutional Court. Furthermore, electoral laws continue to be tweaked to provide the basis for electoral commissions to refuse the registration of "undesirable" parties, even for regional legislative elections. Volodin's manipulation gave United Russia a commanding victory in September 2016, and Volodin was rewarded with the post of Duma speaker.[44]

The Media

Unlike many important steps taken on the road to consolidating hyperpresidentialism, the perceived need to control major media was there from the very beginning. Putin understood well the important role television had played in building his popularity in the autumn of 1999 after Yeltsin named him prime minister, and the equally vital role it had played in cutting down to size his potential opponents at the time. As one former Yeltsin advisor observed, Putin understood that if the media could make him president, it could make anyone president. According to one prominent Russian journalist, the presidential press-service changed radically when Putin came to power, dividing the "Kremlin pool" of journalists into the loyal and disloyal, dishing out favors to the loyal and restricting the accreditation of those perceived as disloyal.[45]

Two very prominent Yeltsin-era oligarchs, Boris Berezovsky and Vladimir Gusinsky, controlled major national TV channels and thus were a particular obstacle to Putin's vision of vertical power and were dealt with immediately. Putin played a central role in this drama, although he publicly insisted that all of the investigations into Gusinsky and Berezovsky were the work of "independent" prosecutors. Putin's chekist (former KGB) allies encouraged this hard line. But Putin also found tacit support from Yeltsin-era holdovers among the oligarchs and the Kremlin staff, according to one former journalist. Oligarchs decided that it was better to solve their problems directly with the Kremlin behind the scenes, rather than using their media holdings to fight it out in public. Chief of Staff Aleksandr Voloshin, a key insider under both Yeltsin and Putin, suggested privately that being too soft was what allowed the Bolsheviks to overthrow the tsars, and that harsh methods were needed to prevent another revolution. Less than a year after Putin's inauguration both Gusinsky and Berezovsky had fled the country and the Kremlin had a firm grip on the major national television stations.[46]

The new attitude toward the press was encapsulated in early 2001 by a former Putin aide, who remarked, "Putin is no enemy of free speech. He simply finds absurd the idea that somebody has the right to criticize him publicly." This remark, while both illuminating and funny, was also a bit of hyperbole. In a manner fitting of an electoral authoritarian regime, it was still quite possible to criticize Putin in the Russian media, but for the most part the critics were confined to newspapers, magazines, one prominent radio station called "Moscow Echo" (*Ekho Moskvy*), smaller TV stations, or, on occasion, late-night talk shows on a major channel. To use Lipman's metaphor, the nightly network news was on a very short leash, while small-circulation newspapers were on much longer leashes. Many people have reported the existence of a "black list," made up of prominent opposition figures who are not allowed to appear on the major state-controlled television channels, with some experts being told directly that they are on this list and thus banned from appearing on the major networks.[47]

Manipulating TV extends beyond efforts to ban certain people or themes (such as Putin's health or corruption among Putin's close associates); it also involves steps to shape coverage. This is particularly important for the evening news. Insiders have explained how the system worked in the 2000s. Most important were Friday meetings at the Kremlin for television officials, hosted by Surkov and the so-called political technologist Gleb Pavlovskiy. These meetings outlined the agenda and key talking points for the week, and were an "instrument of control" over TV, according to one participant. The Presidential Administration staff also paid attention to print and online media, which became embarrassingly clear in early 2015, when hacked communications between a Kremlin official and various editors uncovered prewritten articles that were planted in the media. Equally significant, the enormous and influential National Media Group, with many television and newspaper holdings, is controlled by Putin's close friend Yuriy Kovalchuk, with other Putin-associated billionaires also partial investors in the holding. Thus, even ostensibly private media are controlled by people close to Putin.[48]

For most of the Putin era the established media equilibrium persisted, with national TV stations on a short leash and other media on longer leashes. The Russian Internet, which developed rapidly during Putin's rule, was very free indeed, and opposition media and activists used this freedom to explore issues that would never appear on Russian television. However, over time the Kremlin has sought to extend more control over the Web. The return of Putin to the Kremlin in 2012 after the street protests of that winter and spring led to a more aggressive campaign to control all forms of media. Television began to run pseudodocumentaries attacking the opposition for being under foreign control and working to undermine Russia from within, consistent with the "besieged fortress" component in the code of Putinism. A liberal cable TV channel, *Rain TV*, was forced out of its studio and off cable networks, reducing it to a Web presence, while the editorial board of Russia's most popular online newspaper was also forced out; its editor and many of their journalists moved to neighboring Latvia and opened a new online paper there. A prominent online opposition newspaper and the blogs of two opposition politicians were blocked inside Russia, and popular bloggers were required to register as journalists, making it easier for the authorities to regulate them. Another law was passed limiting foreign ownership content in the media, which undermined the independence of some of Russia's most professional papers and magazines. Publications known for their careful investigations into state corruption found themselves under attack by law enforcement—leashes were giving way to clubs.[49]

Nongovernmental Organizations

The Soviet Union didn't really have "NGOs," with even apolitical social and cultural activities taking place under the auspices of the state or the Communist Party or the Young Communist League. For example, when rock and roll started to develop underground in the 1970s and 1980s, the KGB (State Security Committee) decided it should monitor and control it by informally sponsoring the creation of "rock clubs" in Moscow and Leningrad. Post-Soviet Russia, in stark contrast, allows the creation of autonomous groups in which citizens can pursue a large variety of social, cultural, and political goals, from charitable support for the disabled to human rights organizations. In developed democracies these NGOs are seen as helping develop the tools of democracy among citizens, sometimes partnering with the state to pursue common objectives and sometimes resisting the state and fighting for environmental protection, human rights, or other group goals.

Although NGOs were allowed to develop without much state interference under Yeltsin, the economic depression of the 1990s, and the Russian tendency to rely on personal networks rather than social and political activism to solve their problems, meant that civil society remained relatively weak, despite the proliferation of groups. External support from Western governments and foundations helped nurture some new groups, but in line with their overall funding priorities, with the most successful organizations based in Moscow and possessing more professionalized staff who spoke English and were good at writing grants.[50]

Under Putin there have been positive developments for certain types of NGOs. In particular, the improved economic conditions have made it easier to work and have attracted more interest from citizens who can think beyond mere survival now. State funding for NGOs has increased dramatically. At the same time, it has become clear that the code of Putinism envisions a certain type of relationship between the state and NGOs. Personal conversations with many NGO representatives over the past 15 years have shown a clear distinction between those who work on apolitical goals, such as provision of social services to veterans or orphans, and those who have political objectives that are seen as undesirable by the state, such as opposing state human rights abuses or monitoring elections. Those groups who work for state goals are welcomed and can develop a positive relationship with official bodies, including state funding. Given Putinism's commitment to state control and unity, and suspicion of Western motives and money, those groups who criticize the state and rely on foreign funding have seen their political space progressively tightened.[51]

The first major initiative to crack down on suspicious NGOs took place in Putin's second term in 2006, when a new law substantially increased the reporting and registration burdens for NGOs and gave the state considerable authority and discretion to investigate and shut down NGOs for violations of this law. This was in the period after the Beslan terrorist attack and the Orange Revolution in Ukraine, both of which occurred in 2004, when the code of Putinism achieved its mature form. Putin increasingly spoke out against groups who served "doubtful interests" and relied on foreign funding, referring to them as "jackals" in 2007; other officials accused them of being foreign spies. The St. Petersburg NGO Citizens' Watch, which in the late 1990s and early 2000s had several successful projects with the local police, were told in 2008 that all joint projects with international funding had to stop and that "America is now enemy number one!"[52]

This Putinist policy of dividing NGOs into "good" and "bad" groups was escalated dramatically in Putin's third term that began in 2012. A new law was adopted requiring all NGOs that receive foreign funding and engage in vaguely defined "political activities" to register as "foreign agents." As implemented, this law was more a club than a leash, so its impact is discussed in the next section. But long before 2012, while still serving as head of the FSB in 1999, Putin suggested that foreign intelligence services "very actively" use Russian NGOs as a cover for spying, so the "interests of the state" require close monitoring of their activities. Given this long-standing view, it is not surprising that as president Putin has sought to closely scrutinize and control NGO activity.[53]

"Presidential" grants to civil society groups, as well as Ministry of Economic Development support for social services, were greatly expanded—more the carrot than the stick. Activists in NGOs from around the country, whom I spoke to in June 2015, were rather critical of the lack of transparency and strange decision-making of the presidential grants—a noteworthy example was a grant to publish the collected works of Anatoliy Sobchak, the former mayor of St. Petersburg and Putin's political mentor. The biggest recipient of presidential grants was the Russian Orthodox Church, and pro-Kremlin youth groups and groups promoting anti-Western ideology also were big winners. In contrast, the Ministry of Economic Development grants were well thought of, although they seemed most designed for groups who could contract for the provision of social services to disadvantaged populations like orphans and the disabled.[54]

Overall, the approach to NGOs under Putin is consistent with that toward other nonstate actors, and a strategy of creating a "vertical of power" and protecting Russian "sovereignty." Parties, media outlets, and NGOs that play by the rules are fine, and allowed to prosper or at least do their own thing. There remains plenty of political space to operate, as long as your profile is not too big or your stance too critical. But there must be some degree of control over parties allowed into the Duma and major media outlets, and NGO or media with foreign support are potentially problematic and must be monitored, controlled, and if necessary closed down. The menu of manipulation extends beyond elections to nonstate actors that touch on politics, like the media and NGOs. All of this has the effect of creating a tilted playing field in which genuinely competitive political alternatives to the ruling group are not allowed to mount a serious challenge. And if leashes weren't enough to manage the political arena, there were always clubs that could be pulled out and used.

Clubs: The Menu of Repression

The Soviet Union had a famously repressive regime that killed millions of its own citizens. After Stalin's death, however, the system did moderate its use of violence internally, creating what the political scientist Mark Beissinger called a very robust "regime of repression," which was based on "the predictable, consistent, and efficient application of low level and moderate coercion." This regime broke down under Gorbachev due to liberalization from above and democratic and nationalist mobilization from below, as was evidenced most dramatically during the failed August 1991 hardliner coup attempt, when state repression was no match for a mobilized citizenry. The September–October 1993 events in Moscow, in which Yeltsin only with great difficulty mobilized coercive power to save his government, showed that a new regime of repression had not yet been built. This was further confirmed in March 1996, when the head of the national police told Yeltsin that he doubted the ability of the army and police to implement a possible order closing down the Duma and canceling presidential elections.[55]

Under Putin, starting in his second term, a more concerted effort was made to rebuild a regime of repression. Putin described the issue in stark terms: "in the first half of the 1990s our armed forces and special services were in a state of 'knock-out,' a half-decayed condition." To reverse this situation, he placed the FSB (Federal Security Service) and Ministry of Internal Affairs (MVD) under the control of close allies and increased the security services' budgets substantially. The so-called colored revolutions in Eurasia, especially the Orange Revolution in Ukraine in 2004, made Putin and his team wary of the spread of the "Orange plague" to Russia. Subsequently the MVD increased the number of riot police, providing them with higher budgets and enacting closer coordination. The MVD also expanded its ability to monitor the political opposition with the 2008 creation of the Department for Countering Extremism ("Center E").[56]

In general, the government increased the use of "low-intensity coercion" to harass actual or potential regime opponents. Low-intensity coercion includes such tactics as surveillance, harassment, investigations, and detentions. High-intensity coercion, in contrast, involves violent suppression of mass protests or targeted assassinations and death squads.[57] Besides the FSB and the MVD, law enforcement and judicial bodies such as the Investigative Committee, the Procuracy, and the courts play a key role in using low-intensity coercion against actual or potential opponents, from both the political and economic spheres. Surkov's leashes were used to manipulate the political sphere by rearranging parties, controlling television, forming and funding pro-Kremlin NGOs, and changing election rules to favor proregime candidates. The menu of repression, in contrast, involved using state clubs to arrest and harass opposition figures and "bad" NGOs, control public demonstrations, and intimidate potential challengers.

Experts on electoral authoritarianism often emphasize how ruling groups manipulate the elections through such means as electoral commissions. That certainly happens in Russia as well.[58] Equally important, however, has been the use of low-intensity coercion on the part of the police, prosecutors, and the courts to control elections. When Putin wanted his ally Valentina Matviyenko elected as mayor of St. Petersburg in 2003 (she is now the chair of the Federation Council and a member of the Security Council), law enforcement was there to lend a hand, seizing opposition campaign materials, detaining opposition campaign workers, and opening a criminal case against a printing company that had printed materials critical of Matviyenko. In other cases opposition campaign events are called off by the police at the last minute due to "bomb threats" or other pretexts, and courts and electoral officials declare signatures needed to get on the ballot invalid; in one memorable case in Moscow in 2014, even the candidate's own signature was declared bogus.[59]

The menu of repression is even more evident when it comes to public demonstrations. Although the Russian Constitution recognizes "the right to assemble peacefully, . . . hold rallies, meetings and demonstrations, marches and pickets," for much of the Putin era the right of the opposition to hold demonstrations has been constrained in various ways by the authorities. Between 2007 and 2011, the authorities in Moscow and St. Petersburg routinely denied permission for protest rallies and aggressively policed demonstrations that went ahead without official sanction; in smaller cities, the police would often detain organizers in advance and disperse any protesters at all. Pro-Kremlin groups, in contrast, had no trouble getting permission for public rallies. Prime Minister Putin declared with characteristic macho bravado in 2010 that those who participate in protest marches without formal permission can expect "to get a nightstick to the noggin" (*poluchite po bashke dubinoy*).[60]

The large Moscow protests of 2011–2012 after the fraudulent December 2011 Duma elections arguably represented the biggest challenge yet to the stability of Putin's hyperpresidentialist system. The elections were a proximate trigger for the protests, but were hardly the sole cause. Protests in Russia, which in the 1990s were primarily driven by economic concerns and located in the provinces, had become more political and centered in the capital under Putin. Moreover, a key source of political grievance for the opposition in 2011–2012 was not just electoral fraud but also the prospective return of Putin to the Kremlin as president. Although Putin was and remains the most popular politician in the country, many of the opposition protestors in Moscow—young, well educated, in touch with the outside world—saw the possibility of 25 years of Putin as national leader (2000–2024) as an embarrassment and farce, a possibility made all too real by the ham-handed September 2011 announcement that Prime Minister Putin and President Dmitriy Medvedev would trade offices.[61]

Initially the regime made several concessions to the protestors, and the Moscow authorities granted permission for several large opposition rallies that passed largely without incident; this showed some flexibility compared to earlier practice. The protests that greeted Putin's inauguration on May 6, 2012, however, erupted in violence. Thirty-three people were arrested or charged with crimes due to the May 2012 protests, with more than a dozen sentenced to multiyear prison terms, five more spending more than a year in detention, several given suspended sentences, and twelve amnestied. One of those imprisoned, Sergey Udaltsov, was one of Russia's best known oppositionists, leader of the "Left Front" movement, who was convicted of organizing mass uprisings with foreign money, an accusation first broadcast on a pro-Putin television channel. But other targets for repression were seemingly random, such as the 20-something former marine who went to the protests with some friends simply to see what was going on, and ended up being arrested and serving over three years in prison for participating in "mass disorder" and "using force against a representative of the state." A human rights lawyer later complained, "The relative guilt or innocence of any particular defendant was irrelevant. It was intended as a deterrent to the whole society, and the message was clear: go to a protest rally, and this can be you." The state was using its club to send a broader signal.[62]

In the aftermath of these events, the regime of repression was bolstered considerably. The crackdown has been carried out mainly in parliament, the courts, and law enforcement offices. There were three major prongs of this tightening of the screws: legislative, law enforcement, and public relations.

The legislative crackdown began in 2012, after the beginning of Putin's third term, and continues to unfold. New laws increased penalties for participation in unauthorized protests, broadened the definition of treason, required that NGOs receiving foreign money and engaged in "political activity" register as "foreign agents," and created the category of foreign "undesirable organizations," which can be banned from working in Russia. In 2013 Putin made a speech to the FSB in which he criticized "structures financed from abroad and serving foreign interests" and insisted that the foreign agent law be vigorously upheld. By 2016 there were more than 100 groups on the list, including electoral watchdog groups, human rights organizations, and even charitable foundations supporting Russian scientists in an effort to keep them in Russia to prevent "brain drain." Some of these groups shut down, unable to work under these conditions. Even seemingly nonpolitical organizations are suspect if they receive foreign money, according to one pro-Kremlin analyst, because "their paymasters may well give them the order, at some moment, to stop what they were doing and go over to revolution."[63]

Law enforcement and the courts are also important actors in the general crackdown. Criminal cases were designed to imprison or otherwise limit key oppositionists and to send a signal to the broader public both about the dangers of participating in protests and the alleged "true goals" of the protestors. A prominent example was the infamous Pussy Riot case, in which three members of the feminist punk collective were sentenced to several years in jail for their "punk prayer" in Moscow's Church of Christ the Savior. Pussy Riot was singled out not because they were particularly dangerous opposition leaders—they were not—but to paint the opposition in general as antireligious sexual deviants (the judge singled out Pussy Riot's professed feminism as a subversive ideology).[64]

More consequential were the series of criminal cases against the opposition leader Aleksey Navalny, who heads a small political party, publicizes official corruption, and finished second in a spirited campaign for mayor of Moscow in 2013, despite having no access to prominent TV channels. Putin himself seems unable even to utter Navalny's name, even when asked a direct question about Navalny, apparently out of fear of legitimizing Navalny as an opposition figure. Navalny has been convicted of embezzlement in two different cases, both of which were routine business deals in which he was basically convicted for selling something at the wrong price, according to the prosecutors. The Russian legal expert Vadim Volkov observed that the prosecution's argument in the Navalny's cases would allow them to uncover a crime in "any entrepreneurial activity," adding that "it is hard to think of something more destructive to legal institutions and the court system" than the Navalny cases. The ECHR agreed, ruling that Navalny was convicted for "acts indistinguishable from regular commercial activity." After the ECHR ruling, Navalny and his business partner were retried and found guilty again. In both cases against Navalny he was given a suspended sentence, rather than being put in prison, although his business partner and his brother both received prison sentences as part of these cases. The criminal cases against Navalny seem designed not only to harass him, and intimidate other opposition figures, but also to make it impossible for him to run for president in 2018, because Russian law prohibits those serving criminal sentences from running for office. Although Navalny announced his candidacy for president in December 2016 and commenced campaigning, basically daring the authorities to ban his candidacy, the Central Electoral Commission ruled in December 2017 that he was ineligible to run.[65]

One reason the law enforcement organs and the courts are such effective instruments of any political crackdown in Russia is that much of their activity is so routinized. Grigoriy Okhotin is a young activist who works with the group OVD-Info tracking state repression of political activity. Okhotin explained to me that, although after 2012 there was a change in the media and from the Kremlin in terms of how it dealt with the opposition, from the point of view of law enforcement and the courts nothing important had to change. Courts in Russia are part of a bureaucratic structure, whose job it is to make sure that the police and the prosecutors have done all the procedures correctly—they are not seeking some kind of abstract "justice." If the forms are procedurally correct, then the judicial decisions just rewrite what is on the police protocol. This attitude toward cases is part of the more general nature of the criminal court system, in which the police, the prosecutors, and the courts work as part of one system and in which acquittals are extremely rare. Although some articles of the criminal code have been applied more expansively since 2012, the system is using the same repertoire it has always used. Indeed, on the eve of major planned protests, a fax will go out to police precincts with preprepared arrest protocols for officers to use. For middle-class and educated people who are caught up in this system, they are shocked when they get to court and discover that judges are not interested in their testimony, simply rubber-stamping the materials brought by police and prosecutors.[66]

The public relations component of all of these legal changes and criminal cases had two goals. The first was to demonstrate the risks in opposing the powers that be, both to those in the active opposition and those who might be sympathetic. A variety of opposition-minded journalists and activists have moved abroad in the last several years, which suits the authorities just fine. But the broader campaign is equally important—to convince the average Russian that the opposition is some kind of alien, anti-Russian force. This goal can be seen in the Pussy Riot case, and in laws that criminalize "abusing the religious feelings of believers" and propaganda of "nontraditional sexual relations" among minors. This fits with a broader narrative, which became particularly pronounced after the annexation of Crimea, that painted the opposition as what Putin in March 2014 called "national traitors." It also was quite consistent with elements of the code of Putinism, including antiliberalism, anti-Westernism, hypermasculinity, order, loyalty, and antipluralism.

The Future of Hyperpresidentialism under Putin

Vladimir Putin became president when Russia was in the "gray zone" between democracy and authoritarianism—a common place for countries in the twenty-first century. During his first term as president, as one St. Petersburg journalist put it, Putin managed to "fix the mistakes" of the Yeltsin period, bringing the Federal Assembly (Duma and Federation Council) and television under control.[67] In his second term from 2004 to 2008 we saw the consolidation of developed Putinism, with the regions also subdued and a more robust "regime of repression" restored. In this way Putin saved Russian authoritarianism.

It is important to understand that Putin did not and does not see himself as the savior of Russia's glorious authoritarian traditions. Rather, he is the savior of Russia's status as one of the world's great powers, and Russia cannot be a great power without a strong, centralized state. Each step in building hyperpresidentialism was undertaken not with the explicit goal of killing democracy, but with the goal of establishing the necessary control to restore Russia. At first it was called "managed democracy" and then, after Beslan and the Ukrainian Orange Revolution in 2004, a growing sense of a Russia under siege among the ruling elite fostered the idea of "sovereign democracy."[68] If it is necessary to end gubernatorial elections, or more tightly regulate NGOs, or establish greater control of political parties, or restrict opposition demonstrations, these were necessary sacrifices, especially since the Americans are hypocrites who wish us ill. Over time, the code of Putinism pushed the domestic political order into a narrower set of confines, one that felt more comfortable than the unruly semidemocracy that Yeltsin had tolerated. As the Russian sociologist Olga Kryshtanovskaya put it in 2007:

> What is "disorder" in the eyes of a man in uniform? It's the absence of control. If there is not control, there is the possibility of independent influence. And *siloviki* [power ministry personnel] perceive the presence of alternative centers of power in the country as a threat to the country's integrity. The Duma is not subordinate to the presidential administration? Disorder. . . . Political parties wanted something, the mass media talked about something? All of this is disorder that must be liquidated. And they liquidated it. In seven years the chekists [former KGB officials] have completely changed the political system in the country, not changing one letter of the Constitution.[69]

The Medvedev interregnum from 2008 to 2012 was a curious period. Many knowledgeable observers thought in 2007 that some way would be found for Putin to stay on as president, perhaps by amending the constitution, but Putin transferred power to one of his most loyal subordinates and moved to the prime minister's office, while keeping control over the United Russia party. Extending the presidential terms to six years seemed a clear signal that Putin would return to the top job in 2012, but as late as summer 2011 many insiders still thought it was possible that Medvedev would stand for a second term. The Putin-Medvedev partnership was called a "tandemocracy" by Russian pundits, and like a tandem bike it didn't always move smoothly, particularly because Medvedev was sitting in the front seat but Putin seemed to be doing the steering. At the same time, the differences in style and image between the younger and seemingly more liberal Medvedev and the older, more conservative ex-KGB tough guy were important. Putin's decision to return, perhaps until 2024, greatly disappointed those who hoped that Russia under Medvedev might partially liberalize, opening up more space for political activity and debate. Chief Kremlin ideologist and "puppet master" Surkov, who played a central role in creating and managing Putin's hyperpresidential system but allegedly favored a second Medvedev term as president in 2012, responded to the large anti-Putin Moscow demonstrations of December 2011 by declaring that the existing system was indefensible, suggesting that the protests were "real and natural," and stating that those protesting were the "best... [and] most productive" part of society whose "reasonable demands" should be embraced.[70] The hardline policies pursued since Putin's return in May 2012 strongly suggest that Putin and other more conservative elements blamed Medvedev and Surkov for unleashing forces that threaten the regime.

The menu of repression continues to work as well. One manifestation of this turn to repression was the 2016 creation of a new, powerful National Guard of several hundred thousand armed personnel under the direct control of Putin's longtime associate and former bodyguard, Viktor Zolotov. This force brought together the riot police and the Internal Troops, a heavily armed force available for internal repression if the ordinary police and the riot police were ever to falter. The creation of the National Guard seemed to indicate that Putin, despite his enormous popularity, still feels that his position is vulnerable and that the state's club must be ready to impose order if necessary. A top military advisor to the National Guard argued that its creation was necessary to prevent American efforts to bring about a "colored revolution" in Russia.[71]

The need for Putin to swing this club is at the moment very far-fetched. Vladimir Putin has maintained consistently high approval ratings for the past eighteen years, albeit with some occasional minor dips, and public support has been stratospheric since the annexation of Crimea in 2014. He is credited with raising living standards, restoring order, and improving Russia's international position. Earlier in his tenure economic growth and higher standards of living drove his approval rating, while in recent years his perceived international achievements have been particularly important to Russians. It is quite possible that in a genuinely free and fair election Putin and United Russia would win, although probably by smaller margins. But it's hard to know, since in a real democracy we would have not just an accurate ballot count but a completely different media in which the president and his party would be subject to daily criticism by opposition parties and politicians, a court system that didn't always rule with the executive branch in important cases, and a parliament that debated, amended, and frequently rejected executive branch proposals, rather than rubber stamping them. A vitally important difference between Putinism and the Gorbachev and Yeltsin periods is that, as one Russian analyst put it, "no striking political leaders" have been allowed to rise under Putin; ones that might have that potential, such as Navalny, are dealt with. One reason the opposition is so small, according to a Russian journalist, is that they don't have "a Yeltsin"—not the enfeebled President Yeltsin of the late 1990s, but the upstart populist of the late 1980s and early 1990s who eclipsed Gorbachev and created a new Russia. "Putin," this journalist remarked, "made sure there is no Yeltsin."[72]

This state of affairs, in which there is no alternative to Putin, and no one can imagine such an alternative, is a direct consequence of the hyperpresidentialist system and Putin's commitment to what he once called "manual steering." Dmitriy Trenin, the head of the Carnegie Moscow Center, aptly summarized the current state of Russia's political system in a long discussion in 2014. He noted that there is an effort to create some formal legality, but that this is strictly organized from above. Thus there is a Duma that is not a real parliament, but it still makes laws. There are four political parties, but they are not real parties. There are elections that aren't real elections, but they still serve to legitimize rule. There are courts that are pressured politically, but they still uphold the law. Putin doesn't believe in self-regulating institutions, because he thinks that without manual steering he would lose control of the country, which could lead to conflict, even civil war, that other great powers would exploit. So the form of organized legality that exists doesn't lead to the creation of functioning institutions, which in essence gives Putin unlimited power. The result of this, according to another Russian political expert, is that Putin can dismiss anyone at any time, including not just in the executive branch but also the other branches of power—the Duma, the Federation Council, the courts, and even the media (the so-called fourth branch of power).[73]

A crucial question going forward, after the 2018 presidential elections, is whether this type of hyperpresidentialism can provide sustained legitimacy for Putinism. For eighteen years, Putin has been able to garner at least passive support from the masses and elites, while at the same time moving Russia in a definite authoritarian direction. This legitimacy comes not from divine right, as for the tsars, nor from Marxist-Leninist ideology, as for Communist Party leaders. It ostensibly comes from the ballot box, but the unlevel playing field of Russian elections makes this dubious; however, survey research shows that elections are far from the most important thing associated with the word "democracy" for average Russians, with political rights and freedoms, the rule of law, and even economic well-being rating higher. Russians also tend to say that Russia needs a "special" form of democracy consistent with "national traditions," rather than the type found in the West. Thus, to a certain extent Russia's "sovereign democracy," which is really a form of electoral authoritarianism, does provide some legitimacy for Putinism.[74]

More important for Putinism, however, is "performance legitimacy"—the perception that Putin is delivering the goods that Russians want. For many Russians, greater prosperity (at least until 2014), a perceived sense of stability, and return to great power status are associated with Putin. Relying on performance legitimacy, however, rather than the procedural legitimacy associated with real electoral democracy, can be unstable and fleeting. If this source of legitimacy breaks down, then maintaining power through coercion is always a possibility, but the resilience of Russian police and security bodies in "high intensity coercion" scenarios is untested and uncertain.

Most important, perhaps, is the recognition that Putinism works not just because of the formal institutions set out in the Constitution, which work poorly or are frequently subverted anyway. Central to Putinism is the ability of Putin to balance between competing elite groupings in a way that keeps key players satisfied and cements his position at the center of the system. Hyperpresidentialism is bound together with an interconnected and overlapping system of informal clan networks.

3

Clans and Networks

Vladimir Putin has ruled Russia for the last eighteen years (as of 2018), but only for fourteen of those has he been president. This simple fact tells us something especially important about how Russian politics works under Putin. How could Putin remain the key person on the political scene without being president, the central position in Russia's "superpresidential" Constitution? That Putin was able to be the top dog without holding the top job, and decide to return as president while the sitting president obediently stepped aside, indicates that the formal rules of the game are not necessarily the most important thing driving Russian politics.

Real political power in Russia depends not just on the formal rules and the way they are subverted under electoral authoritarianism but also on relations among a set of informal clan networks that fight over access, resources, and power. Political and economic power is based as much on these dealings between groups as they are on so-called parchment institutions like the Constitution. Putin is simultaneously the president of the formal state and the "boss" of the informal network state.[1]

This informal network state of jockeying individuals and clans is another key component of Putinism. It is not unique to Putin—far from it. Informal clan networks have been an important feature of political life in Russia historically, and are found in many places around the world. In any political system, questions of friendship, loyalty, and personal ties can be highly important in politics. When Barack Obama replaced George W. Bush as president, no one was shocked when the number of Texans in the White House went down and the number of Chicagoans went up.

But these informal ties among small groups of elites, ties that cross divides between the public and private sector and bureaucratic divisions within government, are particularly important under Putinism. Key aspects of the code, such as the importance of control and loyalty, and feelings of vulnerability, favor a system in which friendship and personal ties matter a great deal. Putin's rapid ascent to the top after his move to Moscow in 1996 meant that he felt particularly compelled to draw on his friends and acquaintances from St. Petersburg and the KGB, given his relative lack of connections in the capital.

The code is not the only reason that informal clan networks are so important to how Putinism really works.[2] For starters, such relations have been important in Russia and throughout Eurasia for centuries. Additionally, the sudden collapse of communism as an ideology and Communist Party rule as a mechanism of control left the elites with few reliable guideposts to orient their behavior; in this environment, personal connections were more dependable sources of support and direction than the formal rules. Finally, under electoral authoritarianism the formal democratic system is predominately for show and does not serve as a mechanism of competition and elite rotation, meaning that these crucial political processes take place in behind-the-scenes battles between informal clans. As the Russian sociologist Olga Kryshtanovskaya observed, the key difference between the Russian and American system is that both depend on a system of weights and counterbalances, but the American one is based on institutions, whereas in Russia there is a "hybrid state" of both institutions and clans. In Russia there is a big divergence between the legal rules that explain how institutions are supposed to work, and a de facto system in which clans dominate.[3]

This chapter explains how informal clan networks work in Putin's Russia. Like the last chapter on hyperpresidentialism, it describes both the rules and players of the system. Putin acquired considerable skill as a dealmaker or "fixer" while working for the KGB and in the mayor's office in St. Petersburg—he could have given Machiavelli lessons—and he has drawn on these talents and experience to manage the different groups jockeying for power and resources.[4] A central point, as with other aspects of Putinism, is that this system has changed over time. The period 2003–2004 was a key break point, the turn toward mature Putinism. Entering his second term as president in 2004, Putin was able to shed two of the most important figures he inherited from Boris Yeltsin and more firmly solidify the position of various St. Petersburg groups that he had elevated to prominence. Further, the system has moved toward greater personal dominance over time, with Putin becoming a more tsar-like figure less dependent on various elite groupings or even his long-time allies. This has been particularly notable since the annexation of Crimea in 2014.

The combination of hyperpresidentialism in the formal institutional sphere and clan networks in the informal sphere is a widely recognized feature of Russian politics. Fiona Hill and Cliff Gaddy refer to the two aspects as "two parallel universes," but that is not quite correct—these two features are not separate realms but interlocking pieces of a single whole. Some prominent terms succinctly smash the two parts together, with labels such as "dual state," "network state," or "patronal presidentialism." Others have gone one better, reducing the idea to the single Russian word *Sistema* ("The System").[5] I call it simply Putinism. This chapter shows how the code of Putinism has shaped the structure and operation of this system of clan networks.

Of Clans and Networks

What is a clan, and what is a network? Both of these terms have been used to describe key features of Russian politics, but used in ways that may be different from what people normally mean. In Russian politics, a clan is not, as Webster's dictionary would have it, "a number of households whose heads claim descent from a common ancestor," and it obviously has nothing to do with the Scottish Highlands. In Russian politics clans are a close-knit group of individuals who share a common history, are bound together by both common interests and a shared sense of loyalty, and work to advance both individual and clan well-being. One could just as well use words like "team," "group," or even "gang," but Russians are more likely to use the term "clan." The key fact about clans is that they are not dependent on, nor limited to, more formal boundaries between the public and private sector or between different government agencies or political parties. They may have started in a particular city or region, or particular bureaucratic agency or company, but they outgrow their original roots and spread throughout the system. Family ties do sometimes exist among members of a clan, but unlike the way the word is often used in other places, it is not a defining feature of Russian clans.

One of the most important points about Russian clans is that they lack the high degree of stability of traditional clans. Although there is some disagreement about this issue among Russian experts, most of them stress in interviews the flexible nature of clans. One think tank director calls them "conditional," noting that people don't have "party member cards," and that relations change and people partner for a while and then fall out. Another analyst doesn't like the word "clans," because even though they are an obvious and important feature of politics, in the Russian context they are more overlapping, more volatile, and more ad hoc than in a real clan system. One journalist observed that clans are "flexible" and that people sometimes change clans, while stressing that knowing these informal connections is a crucial issue in Russian politics.[6]

This point takes us to networks. The most famous network in the world is of course the Internet, in which multiple smaller networks (belonging to businesses, governments, universities, and so on) are all connected together to create the world's greatest ever time-wasting device. The illusion of the Internet is that everything is connected to everything else, although of course governments and corporations go to great lengths to keep some stuff secret from even the most determined hackers. But interconnectedness is the key to the way we often think of networks, like webs spreading outward. A network, then, seems to be the opposite of a clan, which is supposed to be compact and insular.

If clans are fundamental to Russian politics, and clans are the opposite of networks, why do so many people describe Russian politics in terms of networks? Leading scholars build their analyses around concepts such as "power networks," "economic-political networks," and "network state."[7] Usually the term network is used to describe informal relations that cross formal institutional lines, such as those between business and the state, or between different parts of the state. Rather than seeing "clans" and "networks" as opposites, then, they really are two different terms for the same basic idea, but one stresses the insularity of these groups ("clans") whereas the other stresses interconnectedness ("networks"). In fact, both insularity and interconnectedness matter. Those who use the term "networks" are thinking of what in the computer world are called "local area networks," which are interconnected computers in a limited area such as within a business or a school.

It is the combination of clan and networks that best describes the patterns of power in Russia. Clans are informal groups of "our people," individuals with some common history and sense of loyalty that work together to advance their interests. Boundaries are elastic and shifting, and membership is not fixed, but there is some coherence and stability. Clans are not atoms—they are connected to other clans through personal ties and short-term alliances and deals. These connections spreading out from one clan to members of another clan help network elites together. That is, individuals are networked tightly *within* their clan, and loosely to other clans. At the same time, major clans often compete with each other for power and resources. The clan metaphor is useful because, just as in the Highlands of Scotland and the computer game "Clash of Clans," rival clans do battle with each other. If some people are "ours," then other people are outsiders to the team, and perhaps part of a rival group. Russian politics is characterized by these periodic clashes that are high-stakes battles determining the fortunes of political and economic elites. And because these networks connecting different clans are informal, they are not easily reduced to battles between, say, the parliament and the president or Party A versus Party B. Henry Hale's notion of "patronal networks" captures the core idea well:

> Patronal networks tend to take on a hierarchical character, though they also typically include many connections among equals. . . . The most powerful people in these relationships can be called *patrons*, and more subordinate ones *clients*. Politics in patronal societies therefore revolves chiefly around personalized relationships joining extended networks of patrons and clients, and political struggle tends to take the form of competition among different patron-client networks.[8]

For Hale and others, this reliance on clan or patronal networks is the way Russia has always been ruled.[9] There is a substantial degree of truth in this, and plenty of evidence for the importance of these informal groupings at different times in Russian history, including under the tsars and during communism. The declared "transition to democracy" under Yeltsin was supposed to mark a break with the old way of doing things. In the new democratic order, the formal institutions of democracy were supposed to determine how power flowed. Similarly, with the creation of a modern capitalist system, private property rights and contemporary standards of corporate governance and state regulation were supposed to allow the winners and losers to be decided by the market. Undergirding this new political and economic system was going to be the rule of law, where all were equal before the law and the state itself was subject to the formal rules of the game.

Of course, it did not turn out that way. American diplomat Thomas Graham went public with this open secret in one of Moscow's major newspapers in 1995, arguing that focusing on battles between "reformers" and "conservatives," or President Yeltsin and the Duma, obscured the true nature of Russia's political system, which was based on battles between political and economic clans. He highlighted four key ones that existed under Yeltsin at the time, headed by the prime minister, the mayor of Moscow, the liberal economic reformer in charge of privatization, and Yeltsin's chief bodyguard. For example, the mayor of Moscow was allied with one of the leading new class of businessmen known as "oligarchs," a banker with a powerful media empire, and the mayor's wife became a billionaire in construction and manufacturing.[10]

Experts have identified several key characteristics of Russian clan networks, some of which have already been mentioned. Six features—informality, shared background, porous boundaries, competition, fluidity, and multilevel structure—seem the most salient.[11]

1. *Informality.* Clans coexist with, and are in many ways more important than, the formal institutions of state power as well as the legal structures of capitalism. In an idealized version of modern polities and economies, politicians and parties succeed based on their ability to attract votes; bureaucrats get ahead based on their formal qualifications, technical skills, and administrative experience; and businesses prosper based on their ability to attract customers to buy their products or services because of their quality or competitive pricing. In reality, of course, informal ties often matter more than formal rules and procedures. This is definitely the case in Russia, where who you know often matters much more than what you know and connections matter more than competence. The term "informal" implies a set of unwritten rules and understandings that are widely held but not codified in any legal fashion. One Russian official I know mentioned that he got his job in the government through someone he knew from his hometown, and that it was easy to fudge the formal rules on civil service hiring to make sure he was the chosen applicant.[12] This is the "parallel universe" of clan networks.

2. *Shared background.* As the previous anecdote suggests, having a shared history is a key feature for building and holding clan networks together. Sometimes this tie is in fact reminiscent of clans in the Scottish sense, in which family members are brought into an elite clan—who better to protect your interests than your daughter or son? Further, the practice of cementing elite alliances through marriage, familiar from medieval European history or *Game of Thrones*, is quite common in Russia. For example, one top law enforcement official who was seen as part of Yeltsin's team cemented his new alliance to Putin when his son married

the daughter of one of Putin's closest allies.[13] More frequently, the shared background involves being from the same city, or studying together, or working together early in one's career.

3. *Porous boundaries.* Clans cross formal boundaries between the state and business, and administrative divisions within the state. Gulnaz Sharafutdinova, in her book on "crony capitalism" in Russia, uses the label "economic-political networks" to refer to these clans, because of the close connections between businesspeople and state officials. For example, Sharafutdinova describes how in the region of Tatarstan in the 1990s the major business conglomerate in the region was connected to the region's leader directly through his son, who worked for the company. At the national level, all of the major oligarchs in the 1990s under Yeltsin sought to develop close ties with a major political sponsor. Under Putin, this crony capitalism, in which state connections matter more than market forces, became more centralized and based on loyalty to the state and Putin himself.[14]

4. *Competition.* Clans are formed to advance the political and economic interests of their members. They are trying to get good jobs, win lucrative contracts, and promote their members—they are vehicles for acquiring additional wealth and power. They also may be united by a certain set of political ideas, although in general those are usually considered secondary to the overall interests of the clan and its members. In pursuing these interests, clans will necessarily come into conflict with other groups who also are seeking that plum position or sweet deal. If he is not one of "our guys," then he must be one of "them" (most, but not all, of the key players in Russian clans are men).[15] This competition can take many forms, from lobbying to leaking compromising information (what Russians call *kompromat*) to criminal cases; even murder is not unheard of. Although Putin has established himself as the boss of this system of clan networks, competition continues below the very top level.

5. *Fluidity.* The notion of "clan" in general usage suggests some kind of family origin, a fixed and unchanging identity. However, as noted above, it would be a mistake to think of Russian clan networks this way. Although some personal relationships of mutual support may last for decades, and even extend to the next generation of children, there are also many examples of people being allies and working together at one point in time and then being enemies at a different time. For young officials or businesspeople trying to make their way in Russia, finding reliable patrons and peers to advance

one's career is essential. But one doesn't have to stay in the same team forever. Although long and stable ties, based on common backgrounds, represent the most common way of organizing clan networks, circumstances often lead to shifting groupings and connections.

6. *Multilevel structure.* Clan networks are not just peer-to-peer connections, although this is certainly a key component. They also involve patrons and clients, bosses and underlings. These positions are not fixed, and they change over time. These relationships are not just horizontal but vertical. The key clans that attract the most attention in Russia are those that are influential in and around the Kremlin, seeking to shape state policy at the highest levels. But journalists and scholars have detailed the workings of clans in Russia's regions as well. For example, experts in Novosibirsk, Russia's third-largest city, suggested that the reason a Communist Party candidate won the mayoral election in April 2014 was because infighting between two major clans in the region opened up space for a candidate not associated with United Russia to make a strong showing. One journalist observed that it was very difficult to know how regional clans in Novosibirsk are connected to Moscow groupings; he quoted the song "Puppets" by one of Russia's most famous rock groups, Time Machine (*Mashina Vremeni*), with the line "the strings run up and into the dark."[16]

These six features of Russian clan networks capture the essential elements of how the system of informal politics works. It is important to bear in mind that this informal system of clan networks is unique neither to Russia nor to Putin. A former student in my class on Russian politics used to marvel aloud in class, "this sounds so much like Indonesia!" Clan networks were an important part of politics under Yeltsin as well, and the political scientist Henry Hale has argued that "patronal politics" of this type are the key to understanding both Russian history and politics in the entire region of Eurasia, which encompasses Russia and other post-Soviet states.[17]

There are several features of the code of Putinism, however, that make clan networks particularly important today. In particular, habits that emphasize control, order, and loyalty have led Putin, even more than most previous Russian leaders, to rely on a close circle of trusted friends and associates. Putin's view of humans as weak and easily manipulated means he placed great priority in having "his" people in the key power nodes.

Another crucial factor explaining the importance of clan networks to Putinism is Putin's meteoric rise to the top. In 1996 he was a briefly unemployed deputy mayor of St. Petersburg after his patron, Mayor Anatoliy Sobchak, lost his reelection bid. Brought to Moscow with the help of a group of government officials who also came from St. Petersburg, Putin climbed rapidly, so that within two years, by the summer of 1998, he was the director of the powerful Federal Security Service (FSB). Thirteen months later he was prime minister and on his way to the presidency. Given this ascent and Putin's limited tenure in Moscow, he had a narrow circle of colleagues to draw on in creating his own patronage machine. As we will see, he thus reached back to his associates from the KGB and St. Petersburg to build his ruling networks. This was all the more important to Putin because he wanted to free himself from the clan that had made him president, the so-called Yeltsin "Family."

Putin's Rise and Clan Networks

Vladimir Putin had his eyes set on a stable and prestigious career from the time he was a teenager, planning on a future with the KGB. He went to law school at Leningrad State University with this goal in mind, and his childhood dreams came true when we was given a position in the KGB in 1975. He was stationed in his hometown Leningrad for a decade, and then in 1985 he was sent to serve in Dresden, East Germany, a Soviet communist bloc ally. The year 1985 was also coincidentally the year Mikhail Gorbachev came to power in the Soviet Union and vowed fundamental *perestroika* (restructuring). Stationed in Dresden, drinking German beer—photos of Putin from this period show a conspicuous beer gut, definitely out of character given his later macho sportsman image—Putin largely missed out on the drama of Gorbachev's reforms, and the palpable sense of optimism in the late 1980s amid a society tasting new freedoms. Rather, Putin's strongest impression of this time period came at the very end, when the November 1989 East German revolution overthrew the communists and a small crowd in Dresden nearly stormed the KGB building. When he called a nearby Soviet military base for assistance, he was told that nothing could be done without approval from Moscow, and "Moscow was silent." This "paralysis of power," as Putin called it, made a big impression on him.[18] According to Putin's code, any demonstration of weakness can be fatal to the state.

Returning to the USSR in its last two years of existence, Putin encountered a country transformed and considerable uncertainty about his own future. One prominent St. Petersburg journalist recalls that it was a "big cultural shock" for Putin to return to a Soviet Union in which there was no longer respect for men in uniform, in which the KGB was "nothing," and the new mafia "bandits" were on the rise. In navigating this shift from the hierarchy and order of the KGB to the revolutionary political and economic transformation of early-1990s Leningrad—soon to be rechristened St. Petersburg— Putin quickly learned the importance of informal ties and established connections. Putin took an administrative job at Leningrad State University, remarking later that he "reestablished ties with his friends" in the law school. According to Putin's version of events, it was one of these friends who set up a meeting between Putin and Anatoliy Sobchak, the chair of the Leningrad City Council and the man who would become Putin's patron for the next six years. Connections from his time at Leningrad State helped Putin get reestablished in his hometown after returning from Dresden. According to one source, Putin's childhood judo friends, Boris and Arkadiy Rotenberg, also helped Putin out in this time frame, although this is not confirmed in biographies of Putin.[19]

Putin spent the next seven years working for Sobchak, who became the elected mayor of St. Petersburg in 1991. Putin was Sobchak's deputy and headed the city's Committee for Foreign Relations. To some observers, Putin was at least as important to running the city as the nominal mayor Sobchak. A democratic activist from the St. Petersburg League of Women Voters called Sobchak "superfluous," stating that he was a poor manager who couldn't cope with the day-to-day work of governing and delegated poorly. A member of the city council later wondered aloud, "who was No. 1 and who was No. 2?" [Sobchak or Putin], observing that Putin served as a sort of gatekeeper in the early 1990s, running interference for Sobchak in his outer office. More cruelly, one local journalist described Sobchak as "naïve" and "a baby," whereas Putin "was never a baby." He quipped that the Sobchak-Putin relationship was like that between the British fictional duo of Wooster and Jeeves— Wooster being a rather dim upper-class gentleman easily manipulated by his cunning valet Jeeves. More charitably, another local journalist described the Putin of this period as a "literate, precise bureaucrat" who was responsible for translating Sobchak's political promises into reality, the rational manager to balance the flamboyant mayor.[20]

Putin's stint as deputy mayor is sometimes treated as his school of democracy, but it is more accurate to see this period as his education in the art of the deal. Although it is debatable to what extent democracy came to St. Petersburg in the 1990s, capitalism—at least of a particular sort—definitely did. Putin was at the center of this transformation. One of his key tasks as deputy mayor was working with local and foreign businesses getting established in the city. His experience with the KGB in East Germany was seen as a useful asset for this work. Putin described his job as solving "problems" of "various business structures." Coincidentally or not, this terminology of "solving problems" for businesses is the exact phrase that the new mafia structures in St. Petersburg used to describe their role—"violent entrepreneurs," in the memorable phrase of a St. Petersburg sociologist. The circumstances of nascent capitalism meant that courts and regulatory agencies often were not up to their new tasks, so various fixers were needed—someone like Vladimir Putin working inside the system to decide who was allowed to conduct business in the city under what terms, or a bandit working illegally to get the same results. As the Putin biographers Fiona Hill and Clifford Gaddy observe, "Capitalism, in Putin's understanding, is not production, management, and marketing. It is wheeling and dealing. It is not about workers and customers. It is about personal connections with regulators. It is finding and using loopholes in the law, or creating loopholes."[21]

Given this context, it is perhaps predictable that Putin's tenure as deputy mayor was controversial, with multiple accusations of corruption, insider dealing, mafia connections, and other forms of malfeasance. Karen Dawisha has collected all of the dirt in one place in her blockbuster *Putin's Kleptocracy*, pulling together material from Russian and Western journalists, Russian opposition politicians, and disgruntled former state employees who believe their investigations into corruption by Putin were smothered due to his prominence. There is a certain catch-22 about investigations into allegations of corruption among Putin and his close circle—it is true that none of these accusations have ever been proven in court, but it is equally true that there is no chance that law enforcement or the courts in today's Russia would be allowed to make such allegations a matter of public investigation, let alone uphold them. Some of the charges seem plausible and reasonably well supported—for example, it would almost be more surprising if an official in Putin's position in the early 1990s *didn't* use his connections to acquire a better apartment in a more prestigious part of the city, bending if not breaking the rules in the process. Other allegations, such as ones about Putin's personal wealth, are impossible to prove either way; those interested in sifting through the available evidence should consult Dawisha's book.[22]

What is undisputed is that this period in the St. Petersburg mayor's office marked a critical phase in the building of Putin's networks. To the extent there is such a thing as a Putin "clan," it took shape in the early 1990s in his home city. His association with many of the key officials of the era—including Prime Minister (and former president) Dmitriy Medvedev, chief of the state oil company Rosneft Igor Sechin, former finance minister Aleksey Kudrin, head of state gas company Gazprom Aleksey Miller, and many others— dates from this period. Other key associates also come from St. Petersburg, with even older connections to Putin, dating to his childhood, law school, or his decade working for the KGB in Leningrad. His five years in the KGB in Dresden, East Germany, also produced valuable connections that he later drew on as president.

Expanding his circle beyond his KGB past, however, was crucial for building and advancing Putin's career. It was in the early 1990s when Putin developed relationships with individuals who would later become known as clans of "Petersburg economists," "Petersburg lawyers," and "Petersburg businessmen." Leningrad in the late-Gorbachev era was a hotbed of young, reform-minded economists, many of whom would go on to great promi- nence, and occasional notoriety, while working for Yeltsin or Putin. This group of young economists—including Yeltsin's privatization tsar Anatoliy Chubais and Putin's finance minister Kudrin—were initially the economic team of the Leningrad City Council, but they subsequently moved into the mayor's office under Sobchak. They were joined by Sobchak's graduate stu- dent German Gref and another young economist, Aleksey Miller. Gref later played the lead role in drafting Putin's initial presidential program, became Putin's minister for economic development in 2000, and is currently head of the largest state bank Sberbank, while Miller, as noted, was put in charge of Gazprom by Putin.

The Petersburg lawyers included Medvedev, the man entrusted with the presidency when Putin stepped aside after two constitutional terms as pres- ident. Medvedev also attended law school at Leningrad State and studied under Sobchak, although he is thirteen years younger than Putin. Dmitriy Kozak is another law school alumnus who worked both in St. Petersburg City Hall and the Russian government under Putin; among Kozak's responsibilities over the years was making sure Sochi was ready for the 2014 Winter Olympics.

Last and certainly not least are a group of businessmen from St. Petersburg who became well acquainted with Putin when he was deputy mayor of St. Petersburg and managing relations between the mayor's office and foreign and local business. Of course, the job of "businessman" or "entrepreneur" did not exist in the communist Soviet Union; those who engaged in private entrepreneurial schemes were "speculators," "mafia," or, if caught, prisoners. Therefore, those who got started in business in the 1990s came from a wide variety of professions. A perfect example for our purposes is the Bank of Russia (*Bank Rossiya*), which was founded in 1990 in Leningrad. Key players in the Bank of Russia included Yuriy Kovalchuk (a physicist), Vladimir Yakunin (a former KGB agent), Nikolay Shamalov (a dentist), and Sergey Fursenko (an electrical engineer). There were many routes into business in Russia in the early 1990s. What unifies the group of people just listed is that they all got to know Putin in the early 1990s, bought property together with him in 1996 by establishing a dacha (country house, or, in this case, lake house) cooperative, and have remained close to him in subsequent years. For example, Yakunin ran Russian Railways, Russia's largest employer, for ten years under Putin, and Kovalchuk heads National Media Group, one of Russia's largest media companies. Bank of Russia was sanctioned by the US government after the Russian invasion of Crimea in 2014, and was described as a "crony bank" by a US official, with Kovalchuk labeled as Putin's "personal banker." Other major businesspeople who subsequently became billionaires were also connected to Putin in the early 1990s.[23]

Putin was able to begin bringing together connections from various phases of his life and career, especially previous secret service colleagues. Viktor Cherkesov was head of the St. Petersburg FSB from 1992 to 1998, and was an acquaintance of Putin from at least the 1980s, if not from law school in the 1970s (they overlapped but were not in the same class). Nikolay Patrushev, with whom Putin had served in the Leningrad KGB, was head of the FSB in the neighboring region of Karelia in the 1990s. Both Cherkesov and Patrushev went on to important positions when Putin became president, and Patrushev is the highly influential secretary of the Security Council. Other KGB colleagues were brought into the mayor's office or became business partners of the city government. An East German secret police colleague from Dresden headed the St. Petersburg branch of a German bank starting in 1991, even before the Soviet Union collapsed.[24]

It would be a mistake to see this as a coherent team or clan, or even series of clans, at this point. But many of the hallmarks of Russian clan networks are evident in these early days in post-Soviet St. Petersburg, including informality, shared backgrounds, and porous boundaries. Some prominent figures combined official positions with business ventures. Personal connections mattered a great deal in finding jobs in the state sector or launching private companies. More to the point, these various network connections helped

Putin make his national political career in the late 1990s and served as his personal Rolodex—for the younger crowd, his smartphone contacts list—when he became president.

Putin's well-established position in St. Petersburg was undercut in 1996, when Sobchak lost his bid for reelection. Putin took this defeat quite badly for at least three reasons. First, he had been designated Sobchak's campaign manager, even though electoral politics was far from Putin's forte, so he bore personal responsibility for the loss. Second, the victor in the race was one of Sobchak's own deputies, Vladimir Yakovlev, whom Putin considered a "Judas" for running against his boss. Third, Yeltsin associates in Moscow instigated corruption investigations against Sobchak prior to the election—according to one Petersburg politician, "Yeltsin hated Sobchak"—which Putin later denounced as "direct interference of law enforcement organs in a political struggle."[25]

Yakovlev, the new mayor, offered Putin a job in his administration, but Putin declined, contending, "it's better to be hanged for loyalty than for betrayal." Although this left him temporarily unemployed, it was consistent with Putin's particular distaste for those whom he considers traitors. Instead of finding another position in St. Petersburg, Putin took a job with the federal government in Moscow. In hindsight, this move to Moscow seems to echo that of the hero of the iconic 1990s Russian movie *Brother* (*Brat*), who, after vanquishing the bad guys in St. Petersburg, which is "provincial," follows his older brother's advice and goes to Moscow, where "all the power is." Of course, Putin did not really leave St. Petersburg as a conquering hero, given Sobchak's defeat and what two biographers call "a string of failures and dubious successes" during his time as deputy mayor.[26]

Putin's ability to find a job in Moscow depended a great deal on his connections to "our guys" from St. Petersburg. In particular, Putin's former colleague under Sobchak, Aleksey Kudrin, helped Putin secure a job in the Kremlin Property Office, relying also on the intercession of another Petersburger who worked in the central government. Although Putin's boss in Moscow was not from Petersburg, Putin had done him a personal favor once while working for Sobchak, so he thought positively of Putin. None of the sources on this pivotal move to Moscow mention a formal job application process. This is consistent with academic research that found that 85 percent of those in state service in Russia got their job through either direct personal connections or a recommendation from a friend or relative. Rather, the entire story of how Putin moved to Moscow is based on a series of personal connections built in Petersburg. State Duma Deputy Vyacheslav Nikonov, from the ruling United Russia party, told me that Kudrin still has a pivotal role as the "guru" of the liberal economists close to Putin, and that this status continues "for very personal reasons"—namely, Putin is grateful to Kudrin for helping him get a job when he was unemployed.[27]

In the next three years, Putin's career rapidly took off. Certainly much of the credit is to Putin himself, the "literate, precise bureaucrat" described earlier, who also seemed to have a talent for establishing relationships with people in different political and economic circles. But it is a fact that his previous connections helped him move to Moscow and then to the Presidential Administration, where he caught Boris Yeltsin's eye. Six months after taking a job with the Kremlin Property Office, Putin was able to move to the Presidential Administration after his friend Kudrin was promoted to the Finance Ministry, and Kudrin recommended Putin be given his former job. After holding several important jobs in the Kremlin working on financial monitoring and relations with Russia's regions in 1997 and 1998, Putin was appointed by Yeltsin to head the Federal Security Service.

Not only did Putin benefit from his established Petersburg networks in building his career in Moscow but also he was able to bring various colleagues with him up the career ladder. Igor Sechin asked to come along to Moscow, and he deputized for Putin in several positions. Former KGB colleagues Sergey Ivanov and Nikolay Patrushev, described by Putin as among his most trusted colleagues (along with Kudrin and Medvedev), were also promoted on Putin's initiative. When Putin became prime minister in August 1999, Patrushev succeeded him as director of the FSB. Ivanov also became a deputy in the FSB under Putin, and then succeeded Putin as secretary of the Security Council in 1999. Other KGB colleagues from either Leningrad or East Germany also followed Putin to the FSB. Although he did not know it at the time, Putin was putting in place many of the core group of officials that he would most rely on as president. Putin understood from watching clan politics around Yeltsin, in which various groups fought with each other for influence, that he needed his own team on whom he could rely.[28]

Putin's move to Moscow, then, was a spectacular success within a few short years. Although the help of friends like Kudrin was very important, the critical thing that happened was that Putin gained the trust of Yeltsin. Indeed, in 1998–1999 Putin was seen as one of the leading members of the Yeltsin "Family" clan. The clan came by its name honestly: key figures in the group were Yeltsin's daughter Tatyana, who served as his adviser, and her future husband Valentin Yumashev, who was head of the Presidential Administration. To continue the family theme, Yumashev's daughter married the billionaire oligarch Oleg Deripaska as well. Other prominent oligarchs were also linked to the "Family."

As head of the FSB, Putin played a key role in successfully blocking a prosecutor's investigation into corruption around the "Family" (see chapter 1). This act of loyalty to Yeltsin was both consistent with Putin's code and potentially a huge gamble, since Yeltsin was politically weak and unpopular at the time. In the end it worked out spectacularly well, but it would be a big stretch to say that Putin planned it that way. Putin's loyalty was interpreted not just as a pro-Yeltsin move, but as a pro-"Family" move, taking sides in the war of clans heating up over the coming Yeltsin succession, whose term as president was to expire in 2000. Regardless of Putin's motivation in 1998, within a year and a half he was in a position to take the central role in managing clan conflicts, and promoting trusted people from his networks.[29]

Putin's Clan Networks

Mapping the ups and downs of various clans under Vladimir Putin, and the shifting loyalties of leading elites as alliances break down and new ties are forged, has been a leading preoccupation of Kremlinologists since his rise to power. This clan cartography, bordering on an obsession especially for some Russian experts, is an understandable consequence of a political system in which informal clan networks matter more than formal bureaucratic structures. Although different Kremlinologists promote different schemes, the one constant is Putin's place at the center of these shifting clans.

Another key feature of Putin's clan networks has been a top group of considerable stability around him. Habits of control and loyalty, and feelings of vulnerability, have made it very important to Putin that he have a trusted team around him. Even when these clans fight, sometimes viciously, with each other, their personal commitment to Putin has held the system together. In the last few years, however, Putin has begun to dismantle this core group of allies. Personal loyalty to him is replacing loyalty to the team. I first document the stability of the core group from 2000 to 2015, then briefly describe its partial dismantlement in 2015–2016. Putin seems to be elevating himself above the team he once relied on, becoming a more tsar-like figure.

The stability at the very top was particularly noticeable from 2003–2004 until 2015–2016. As noted in chapters 1 and 2, 2003–2004 was a key turning point in the development of the code of Putinism, and the building of hyperpresidentialism. It also marked an important phase in the development of clan networks. In 2000 Putin relied on his St. Petersburg and KGB networks to bring in many top officials who would remain part of his team. At the same time, during his first term as president some of the key players were not from these groupings, but belonged to the Yeltsin "Family" that had elevated him to the presidency in 1999–2000. Both his first prime minister and first Kremlin chief of staff were inherited from the "Family," and several of the top oligarchs were connected to this clan. By 2004, however, Putin had appointed a new chief of staff and prime minister. Allegedly, Putin's close associate Sechin told the previous prime minister Mikhail Kasyanov, "Thanks for showing us how to run the country. Now we can do it ourselves." The "Family," at least as a powerful clan, was no more.[30]

It is striking how many of the people who were key members of Putin's team at the beginning have remained members of the team, nearly two decades later. Duma deputy and Putin ally Vyacheslav Nikonov noted that this is a big contrast with Yeltsin. Under Yeltsin, Nikonov observed, there was a lot of turnover of key personnel, and none of the people he started with at the beginning in the early 1990s were there at the end of his presidency. In contrast, Nikonov noted in 2014, there had not been much renewal under Putin. Personal loyalty is very important, and there has not been much effort to distribute key jobs around by region or administrative background. Some of Putin's key allies from Petersburg—such as Medvedev (prime minister), Sergey Ivanov (former chief of staff), Valentina Matviyenko (speaker of the Federation Council), and Sergey Naryshkin (former speaker of the Duma, now head of the Foreign Intelligence Service, and another former KGB official from Leningrad)—were all still in top positions when we spoke. Nikonov, whose grandfather Vyacheslav Molotov was Stalin's foreign minister, related an illuminating quip: "The great struggle between communists and liberals ended with the victory of the St. Petersburg KGB." In mock disappointment, Nikonov lamented, "We poor Muscovites are on the outskirts."[31]

The one major downgrading that Nikonov could think of at the time was Viktor Cherkesov, a Leningrad KGB colleague of Putin's who held two different key posts during Putin's first two terms as president. Cherkesov fell out of favor for two basic reasons. First, he was on the losing side of a clan struggle about what was then called the "2008 problem"—what would happen at the end of Putin's second constitutional term as president? In 2006–2007 there was a major political battle about whether Putin would step down or amend the constitution to allow a third term, and if he stepped down who might succeed him. The *siloviki*—people with backgrounds in the so-called power ministries, such as the KGB, the police, or the military—who are often simplistically described as one coherent clan, were divided into several competing groups. Cherkesov was widely believed to be a member of the "third term" faction among the competing *siloviki* clans. Allegedly, another source of conflict was over which law enforcement agency would control oversight of the highly lucrative smuggling business. The second reason for Cherkesov's downfall is that he took his complaints public after losing the struggle, publishing a remarkable article in one of Russia's top newspapers called "Warriors Should Not Be Traders." The implication of the article was that the involvement of security and law enforcement agencies in various economic schemes to enrich themselves was undermining their ability to protect Russian sovereignty and security. Cherkesov was removed from his top post, proving that the only thing worse than losing an internal Kremlin power struggle under Putin is subsequently airing the dirty laundry about it in public.[32]

Aleksey Makarkin is one of Russia's most prominent Kremlinologists. The author of an early study of "political-economic clans" under Putin, Makarkin also emphasized the considerable stability among the top elite under Putin, with almost all of the top people in the system being those that Putin brought with him. The one exception he highlighted was Defense Minister Sergey Shoygu.[33] Shoygu is the great survivor of Russian politics, having served as head of the Ministry of Emergency Situations from 1991 to 2012—through two Yeltsin terms, two Putin terms, and Medvedev's one term. He became defense minister in 2012 and is routinely rated among the top ten most influential political figures in Russia.

How did Shoygu do it, given he did not have KGB or St. Petersburg connections to Putin? Makarkin maintained that Shoygu always played by the system's rules, not showing political ambitions of his own and not objecting when one of his key subordinates was charged with corruption— unlike Cherkesov, who went public with his disagreements. Shoygu also is widely believed to be an effective manager. Finally, and certainly not least, Makarkin contends that Shoygu did himself a big favor when he gave Putin a dog as a present in 2000. Putin's dog Konni was a faithful companion for fourteen years, regularly seen at his side. Given Konni's loyalty to Putin, several commentators waggishly (pun intended) suggested that Konni could be put forward as Putin's successor as president in 2008. Konni has her own Wikipedia page that chronicles her great adventures. Although Makarkin was somewhat joking, his basic point is quite serious—close personal relations matter a lot to Putin in choosing top officials, and Shoygu successfully established that relationship with this well-considered gift, even though he came from a different background and set of networks than Putin. One additional factor not mentioned by Makarkin, but highlighted by others, is that Shoygu helped arrange several adventure vacation outings for Putin, including the famous ones where a bare-chested Putin went fishing and horseback riding. Whether Shoygu is really a trusted insider, however, remains a matter of dispute. Some well-informed observers stress Shoygu's "maximum loyalty" to Putin, whereas others think that from Putin's point of view Shoygu still remains "one of them"—that is, not "one of us."[34]

The importance of being "one of us" was made clear in a 2011 study of Putin's networks and "who's who" in the Russian elite by two young Russian journalists, Viktor Dyatlikovich and Filipp Chapkovskiy.[35] They conducted a thorough analysis of the top figures in the Russian government, including the presidential administration and state-controlled corporations. They showed that Nikonov's lament that Petersburgers were taking all the top jobs and that "poor Muscovites" couldn't get a break had some basis in fact, although it wasn't so much Muscovites who were being disadvantaged as it was people from everywhere else in the country. In 2000, officials who came from the region around St. Petersburg amounted to 24 percent of state officials, more than double what one would expect if jobs were distributed evenly to people from around the country. By 2011 nearly 39 percent of all top jobs were held by people from the Petersburg area—more than four times higher than that region's share of the total population. People from Moscow and surrounding regions represented 32 percent of officials in 2000 and 30 percent in 2011. Muscovites were certainly holding their own, then, but since more than 25 percent of Russia's population lives in the area around Moscow, the share of top government employees from the area was roughly proportionate to the overall population. It was the other regions of Russia that were really losing out by 2011, with people from the southern and eastern parts of the country grossly underrepresented. These regions contain almost two-thirds of Russia's total population but as of 2011 provide less than one-third of the top government officials. Not surprisingly, a growing share of officials under Putin also went to college in St. Petersburg. In 2011 half of the members of the Russian cabinet went to college in St. Petersburg, with a particularly strong contingent from the St. Petersburg State Law School—the alma mater of both Putin and Medvedev. Thus, in the battle between the "two capitals" of Moscow and St. Petersburg, St. Petersburg was winning. In 1713 Tsar Peter the Great moved the capital from Moscow to the new city of St. Petersburg to create a "window to the West." Now, instead of moving the capital to St. Petersburg, Putin was moving St. Petersburg to the capital.[36]

Dyatlikovich and Chapkovskiy also mapped the networks among top officials. From these network maps—see Figure 3-1, for one example—they conclude that most cadre (staffing) and political events under Putin can "easily be explained by personal connections." Consistent with the general notion of patrons and clients, they observe that the "administrative weight" of officials is explained both by their ability to influence those above them to whom they are connected, and their capacity to bring along lower level officials who are loyal to them. The more connections stretching up and down, the tighter they are woven into the "fabric of power" and the more influence they have. It will surprise no one to learn that they discovered one constant in the period from 2000 to 2011—Putin was at the center of the different network connections. Moreover, "Putin destroyed centers of power that were independent from him. And when the question of whom to appoint to replace a banished individual, the choice was made in favor of personal acquaintance or loyalty." They conclude, "The main and sole criteria for coming into power . . . was the trust of the president." [37]

The network map shows only connections among government officials, including people working for major state-controlled corporations; it does not show connections to oligarchs in the private sector. The lines show connections between different people, and the size of the cell is an indicator of "apparat weight." Cell size is not, to be clear, a measure of overall influence, or how much Putin listens to this or that person. It reflects, instead, how many connections a person has in the government, including to lesser figures not shown in the map. Thus, someone who managed to appoint a lot of previous connections to subordinate positions would have a greater "apparat weight." This definition of influence can therefore account for some obvious anomalies, like the fact that Sergey Ivanov, one of Putin's closest allies for most of his rule, is depicted as having little "apparat weight." This reflects the fact that for most of his KGB career he was stationed abroad and thus did not acquire a close circle of clients that he could promote with him.

One striking thing about this network map is that in 2011, three years into the Medvedev presidency, Medvedev had not only much less administrative weight than Prime Minister Putin but also less weight than two "St. Petersburg economists," Kudrin and Gref. Other very powerful figures are shown with much less "administrative weight" than their true political influence at the time. It would thus be a mistake to read too much into the network map, especially because it is a snapshot from 2011, but it does indicate the extent to which Putin at the time remained the key node of Russian

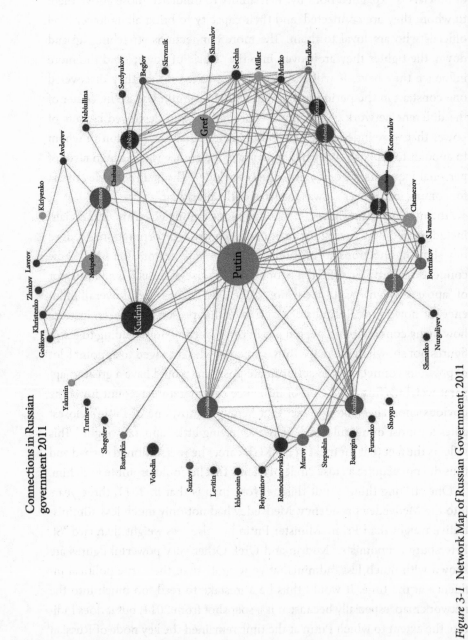

Connections in Russian government 2011

Figure 3-1 Network Map of Russian Government, 2011

Source: Viktor Dyatlikovich and Filipp Chapkovskiy, "Kto est' kto i pochemu v rossiyskoy elite," *Russkiy Reporter*, September 7, 2011. English version prepared by Mikhail A. Strokan

power, better connected and more influential than anyone else, including the actual president.

A second noteworthy feature of the network map is the extent to which the "Petersburg economists" played a central role in the government and were able to place a lot of their circle in key positions. Many members of the so-called economic bloc of the government were from the team of reform economists who formed in Leningrad in the 1980s. Key members of this group worked for Sobchak and with Putin in St. Petersburg in the early 1990s. Many of the other top economic officials under Putin are also connected to this group, including the current head of the Central Bank, Elvira Nabiullina. Putin might not have been connected directly to all members of the economic bloc, but he was connected by "one handshake" through someone like Kudrin or Gref. It was this group of Petersburg economists who helped Putin find work in Moscow in 1996.

There was another economic group of sorts from the city that has been at least as important to Putinism as the "St. Petersburg economists"—the so-called "Ozero group" (the Russian word *ozero* means "lake"). The members of this group were not professionally trained economists working in government, but businessmen from different walks of life who got their start in the rough-and-tumble capitalism of the early 1990s. They were connected to the Bank of Russia mentioned earlier, and formed a dacha (lake house) cooperative in 1996. There were eight members, including Putin. Most of them have had great success in business or politics or both since Putin became president. Some of the members, like former Russian Railways boss Yakunin, who started his career in the KGB, and Yuriy Kovalchuk, labeled by the US government as Putin's "personal banker" and the head of the powerful National Media Group, were long considered to be in the very closest circle to Putin, among the ten most powerful people in Russia, although Yakunin's influence has dropped in the last few years. It is widely believed, with quite good evidence, that one of Putin's daughters was married to the son of Ozero cooperative member Nikolay Shamalov, although this simple fact has never been confirmed by the Kremlin. Experts disagree about the influence of the Ozero group. One well-informed expert called Ozero the "key group" among Russian clan structures, while other, equally well-informed analysts think their influence has been overstated. Perhaps the best way to think about it, according to a political commentator, is that "Ozero doesn't run Russia—but their interests can't be offended." Thus, even if it's hard to know what role these people play in decision-making, everyone understands

that they are important people close to Putin, so it is easy for them to advance their business interests around the country.[38]

The key players of Putinism come from one of these earlier phases in his
career—from the KGB in Leningrad and East Germany, from St. Petersburg
city government, or from St. Petersburg business circles, like the Ozero cooperative. Experts disagree, however, about who the true inner circle is and
who the most important players are. The sociologist Olga Kryshtanovskaya
is the leading Russian scholar of the political elite. She is convinced that, although clans matter, it's the bureaucratic clans that dominate, and that one
must have an official position to have real influence. Informal lobbying, in
her view, is not a source of real power, and she thinks the influence of billionaire businessmen friends of Putin is overstated.[39] Other prominent analysts
disagree, contending that the most influential inner circle includes private
businessmen and heads of big state companies. For example, the Russian
political analyst Nikolay Petrov argues that several heads of state companies
are core figures, whom he calls the "shareholders," who take the key strategic
decisions. Close to the pinnacle of power, but not part of the inner circle, are
those Petrov calls "strategists" and "managers," who implement the decisions
taken by the shareholders.[40]

Looking across these different conceptions, some names come up repeatedly, whereas others are unique to one particular scheme. I compared
five different models that attempt to answer the question "who are the key
players?" at the top of Russian informal clan networks, and noted the fre-
quency with which certain people appeared.[41] Overall, fourteen people
appeared in more than one scheme.

Vladimir Putin, obviously, is the key player of Putinism—how could it be
otherwise? Only Putin overlaps with all the main networks: St. Petersburg,
KGB (Leningrad and Dresden), and the Ozero cooperative. Perhaps surprisingly to some, given his lightweight image, Medvedev is also considered a
key insider in all of the schemes. But since the early to mid-1990s, Putin has
entrusted Medvedev with key responsibilities, none more important than
serving as president from 2008–2012. Before being president, Medvedev
was chief of staff of the Presidential Administration, and now serves as prime
minister. Putin clearly values Medvedev, and trusts in his loyalty, even if they
have somewhat different worldviews—Medvedev is relatively more liberal
than the conservative Putin—and occasionally clash over policy. Still, it
does seem correct that Medvedev has always been the clear subordinate, the
younger brother figure, or, as a witty observer put it, Medvedev plays "Robin"

to Putin's "Batman." Kryshtanovskaya notes that, although Medvedev brought in some of his people in 2005–2011, none of them were elevated to the top level. Equally important, whether out of caution or loyalty, Medvedev never used the considerable powers of the presidency to try to get rid of other key members of the Putin team, or to challenge their clans.[42]

Next in the rankings, although obviously below Putin and Medvedev, were Igor Sechin and Yuriy Kovalchuk. Sechin has been close to Putin since the early 1990s, and has frequently served as Putin's deputy throughout Putin's career. Sechin, like Medvedev, was famous for his faithfulness. One Russian journalist describes Sechin's ability to follow "almost medieval rituals of demonstrating his loyalty to the boss," including meeting Putin at the elevator every morning at work and seeing him off and meeting him at the airport when Putin traveled.[43] Sechin played a central role in the 2003 criminal case against Russia's richest man at the time, Mikhail Khodorkovsky, and the subsequent takeover of Khodorkovsky's Yukos oil company by the state oil company Rosneft. In 2004 Putin named Sechin the chairman of the board of Rosneft, one of the largest oil producers in the world, and Sechin has been its president since 2012. Although Sechin did not serve in the KGB, he did work as a military translator in Angola and is considered one of the key *siloviki* in the Putin inner circle. Kovalchuk, as discussed earlier, has been close to Putin at least since the early 1990s, a physicist-turned-businessman who also was part of the Ozero cooperative with Putin. His significant media holdings and financial interests, many of which he acquired after Putin became president in 2000, demonstrate his critical position.

The remaining ten officials who feature as part of the inner circle in at least two prominent schemes are a more disparate lot in terms of background and current position.[44] Some have been connected to Putin for decades—since childhood, in the case of businessmen Arkadiy Rotenberg. Others are state officials who are arguably not true insiders, but officials who have shown great longevity at important positions, such as Foreign Minister Sergey Lavrov. Some are businessmen who have become billionaires due to their close links to Putin. In general, though, it is remarkable how for fifteen years Putin relied almost entirely on people from his old circles. The four people he mentioned in 2000 as his most trusted colleagues—Sergey Ivanov, Dmitriy Medvedev, Nikolay Patrushev, and Aleksey Kudrin—are all still part of his team, and two of them occupy the highly important positions of prime minister and secretary of the Security Council. The dominance of people from the KGB, St. Petersburg, or both in Russian politics was captured more than a decade ago in the following joke recounted by the journalist Andrew Jack: "Are you from the Kremlin? Are you from the KGB? Are you from St. Petersburg?" asks one man to another in a tram. "No? Then get off my foot."[45]

Clans arguably have become less important over time, particularly since Putin's return to the presidency in 2012. Although there is little question among most analysts that they exist in some form, Putin has been able to elevate his importance over any particular grouping. Some network alliances that were seen as important earlier seem to have diminished significantly. Although Putin considers the interests and opinions of other top players and their clans, ultimately he is in a position to get rid of anyone he wants at any time if they challenge him directly or display disloyalty. Rather than calling together all the key decision-makers, Putin is in a position to deal with them on a one-to-one basis. Thus, although top figures like Medvedev and Sechin may clash over policy, personnel, or different interests, both of them are smart enough to know the limits of conflict and not to do anything that would upset the boss.[46]

It is worth reiterating how different this informal network system is both from the formal institutional rules of the game described in the last chapter and from how power works in democratic polities. During his presidency Putin managed to place people he knew long before he was president in most of the important positions in the polity and economy. As of 2015, this included the prime minister, presidential chief of staff, secretary of the Security Council, speakers of the two houses of parliament, and the heads of three of the most important companies in the economy—Gazprom, Rosneft, and Russian Railways—as well as other key economic actors, such as the defense industry conglomerate Rostec and the media giant National Media Group. In American terms, imagine if during the Obama presidency that the vice president, speaker of the House, senate majority leader, national security adviser, and the CEOs of ExxonMobil, Lockheed Martin, and Time Warner were all close acquaintances of Barack Obama from, say, his days at Harvard Law Review or in the Illinois State Senate.

Even in Russian terms the longevity and stability of Putin's core team has been remarkable. Boris Yeltsin, as noted earlier, did not keep a stable team throughout his presidency, and he did not surround himself primarily with friends and professional colleagues from his childhood, his hometown, or his early career. None of Yeltsin's close associates became billionaire oligarchs while he was president; the 1990s oligarchs sought influence with Yeltsin once they became rich, they did not become rich because they had influence with Yeltsin. This difference between Putin and Yeltsin can be explained by the code of Putinism—the impulse toward control and loyalty, and the feelings of vulnerability, have made informal clan networks even more important than they have been historically in Russia. According to one Russian political scientist, channeling Putin, what matters to him "is that I'm not afraid. And the only way I won't be afraid is if I see a familiar face next to me."[47]

At the same time, in recent years there has been a noticeable shift in Putin's core team, and in his understanding of loyalty. Key members of his old team who lost top positions in 2015 and 2016 included no less than four former KGB veterans with ties to Leningrad/St. Petersburg: Sergey Ivanov, who served in a series of top posts, including minister of defense and presidential chief of staff, and was one of Putin's most trusted confidants; Vladimir Yakunin, who was part of Putin's dacha cooperative and headed Russian Railways for a decade; Viktor Ivanov, who served Putin both in the Presidential Administration and as head of a major law enforcement agency and who, according to rumors, was the man who initially recruited Putin into the KGB in the 1970s; and Yevgeniy Murov, who for sixteen years headed the Federal Guards Service, the Russian equivalent of the US Secret Service. Sergey Ivanov's replacement as presidential chief of staff was a forty-four-year-old functionary named Anton Vaino, who had worked himself up from the Kremlin protocol department, where he managed Putin's schedule and carried his umbrella. Other top positions were filled by younger men who had worked as Putin's bodyguards. One of them, Yevgeniy Zinichev, in less than a year and a half went from being one of Putin's bodyguards to head of the Kaliningrad FSB, acting governor of the Kaliningrad region, and deputy head of the national FSB. Another, forty-four-year old Aleksey Dyumin, had a similarly steep ascent from service as a bodyguard to deputy minister of defense to governor of the Tula region; allegedly, Dyumin played an important operational role in the military annexation of Crimea in 2014.[48]

Russian analysts were struck by a noticeable change in how Putin managed appointments to top jobs. Rather than surrounding himself with old friends and colleagues, who might see themselves as "corulers," he was gravitating toward "those who serve him," in the words of one commentator. Another Russian analyst observed, "The era of the collective rule of Putin's friends is coming to an end. . . . Instead of a 'prince' governing with his 'coterie,' a tsar has ascended, ruling with his 'serfs.'"[49]

The Boss of the Clans

.

Putin is both president of the formal political system and boss of the informal clan network system. In both roles, Putin has grown stronger over time. Calling Putin the "boss of the clans" makes him sound more like a mafia head than the president of a great power. Indeed, several highly respected Russian commentators have made the mafia analogy—not because they think Putin and his circle are literally an organized criminal group, but to call attention to the role that informal codes of loyalty and honor, and implicit understandings and unwritten rules, play in decision-making (some Western journalists have used the term "mafia state" in a more literal way, but that is not what I am talking about here). In this sense Putin is a "boss," as former adviser Gleb Pavlovskiy put it, the one who can be the arbiter of conflicts, taking into account the interests of different key players, and holding others to account, making sure they play by the rules and keep their promises. Olga Kryshtanovskaya pushed the analogy further, suggesting that during the Medvedev presidency he was playing the role of the mafia Don's consigliere temporarily taking charge, with the Don fading into the shadows temporarily, but still ultimately in charge. The point of the analogy is not to denigrate Putin, but to call attention to the priority of informal norms and understandings over formal institutions.[50]

Calling Putin the boss also suggests his centrality to the system. He is not simply the first among equals, he is the first, full stop. For a time, some commentators insisted that Putin was a "virtual" president and the product of clever public relations that masked the extent to which he was a weak and indecisive leader who was an attractive façade for the "collective Putin" of former KGB officials. More accurate, in my view, is the image of Putin as a powerful tsar, the ruler who can dismiss any other official at any time and to whom all top officials owe their position. This dominance was demonstrated most of all when Putin was prime minister by title but still the boss in reality. Clans still exist and compete with each other and try to influence him, but he is the main decision-maker, and it is very risky to openly cross him. Allegedly, Yuriy Kovalchuk remarked to a small circle of friends that there is nothing to be gained by contradicting Putin or giving him unpleasant news—that would only lessen Kovalchuk's access and make him worse off.[51]

Putin's status and the role of clans is also very different from that under Yeltsin. Under Yeltsin there was a system of what Gulnaz Sharafutdinova calls "fragmented cronyism," with multiple competing networks; under

Putin the system is one of "centralized cronyism," with the public "clash of clans" largely replaced by behind the scenes maneuvering in a noncompetitive system. With the Kremlin's control over media and key economic sectors under Putin, it is much easier to suppress clan battles and keep them largely out of the public eye, as compared to the very open skirmishes of the Yeltsin era. There also are objective reasons for Putin's ability to construct a more centralized crony system, such as better economic conditions and the related issue of Putin's considerable popularity compared to Yeltsin's; even the passing of time from the revolutionary era of the Soviet collapse played its role. But of utmost importance is the code of Putinism, its stress on order and stability, its distrust of pluralism, the primacy of loyalty to "ours" and distrust of "others," and the feeling of vulnerability among the elite about the potential of the whole system collapsing.[52]

Calling the Putinist clan system centralized does not mean that clan skirmishes have ended, of course. For example, when opposition leader Boris Nemtsov was assassinated within full view of the Kremlin in February 2015, it was impossible to hide the fierce battle that raged between the FSB and powerful Chechen leader Ramzan Kadyrov, whose associates were implicated in the murder. The confrontation, and Putin's ten-day absence from public view shortly after Nemtsov's murder, sparked speculation that Putin was going to have to choose between two favored groups, one responsible for stability in the country's most fragile region (Kadyrov) and one responsible for stability in the country as a whole (the FSB). In the end, Putin apparently decided not to give up Kadyrov to the FSB, and, as was the case in other high-profile murders, the shooters were caught and punished but the ultimate contractor for the murder was never identified.[53]

Overall, though, the tendency during Putinism has been toward tighter control over feuding clan networks, and those clans that were "others" from Putin's point of view, such as the Yeltsin "Family," have broken apart or lost considerable influence. As the code of Putinism has become progressively more conservative, emphasizing the degree to which Russia is embattled by various internal and external enemies, both the formal political system of hyperpresidentialism and the informal system of clan networks have become more centralized and more dominated by Putin himself. Putin now demands loyalty not to "our guys," but to him personally. How the code of Putinism—operating through the interlocking system of hyperpresidentialism and informal clan networks—has affected the economy, government performance, and foreign policy is discussed in the next three chapters.

4

Lawyers, Guns, and Oil

In his 1978 song "Lawyers, Guns, and Money," Warren Zevon sings about a ne'er-do-well young man who keeps getting into trouble—including once "with the Russians"—and pleads for his dad to bail him out by sending lawyers, guns, and money.[1] One or more of these things, he reasons, is sure to get him out of most tight situations. In Putin's Russia, lawyers, guns, and oil are the three pillars of the economy. The oil (and gas) provides the money that lubricates the system, and lawyers and guns keep it under control. Until 2015, they seemed up to the job of keeping the economy out of serious trouble.

The political economy of Putinism, or "Putinomics," follows from the code. Putin and his team believe in the importance of a strong state to manage the economy, and returning Russia to its rightful place as a great power is the central goal of economic development. Although they recognize the superiority of capitalism and free markets over the centrally planned communist economy, their conservative outlook on life makes them cautious about liberal ideas about economic and political freedom. Their natural impulses make them inclined to favor control and order, which in the economic realm has led Putin to put loyalists he trusts in charge of key parts of the economy, especially oil, gas, transportation, military industry, finance, and the media. Feelings of vulnerability, both domestically and globally, as well as resentment about Russia's reduced status in the world and suspicion of the world's richest countries, especially the United States, further solidify this tendency toward statism and control in the economic realm. More colorfully, one former Federal Security Service (FSB) officer described the economic ideology of his former colleagues in the following way: "if you control the chief economic assets, then you are essentially holding everyone by the balls."[2]

Putinomics has the same dualism as the political system. As in the realm of politics, there is a formal set of institutions, in this case those of market capitalism, that coexist with informal practices that dominate and over-shadow the formal rules of the game. At the center of this set of informal relations sits Vladimir Putin and his circle, who make the most important decisions and benefit from and sustain the system. The weakness of the formal capitalist institutions, such as the protection of property rights and the rule of law, creates opportunities for state officials to decide who wins and loses, outside the parameters of market competition. Lawyers and guns represent the state, lawyers standing for the courts and prosecutors and guns for the police and security services. These lawyers and guns are analogous to the leashes and clubs of the political system, ways to manipulate the rules of the game and punish those who step out of line. Good courts and law en-forcement are important parts of any well-functioning market economy. Bad ones, on the other hand, in the long run undermine economic performance.

The economic rules of the game differ somewhat at the top and bottom of the economy. The political scientist Gerald Easter refers to Russia's economy as an "upstairs-downstairs" one. Upstairs, Easter explains, are "strategic industries in the form of large corporations that remain directly or indirectly subordinated to the state." Downstairs, in contrast, are small and medium-sized companies, from supermarkets to local construction firms to small manufacturers.[3] Upstairs, in what Lenin called the "commanding heights" of the Russian economy, are the big firms of vital sectors such as oil, gas, banking, metals, and transportation; in these areas key decisions happen at the very top, in the Kremlin. State domination of the oil and gas industry, the dominant sector of the Russian economy, is critical to making Putinomics work. Indeed, Putinism could not have been built in its current form without Russia's energy abundance. For Putin, big business is built on special deals growing out of personal relationships and commitments. Perceived violators of the rules of the game can be targeted and brought in line using the legal and coercive power of the state. In the downstairs part of the economy, populated by smaller firms, the key state officials are police, prosecutors, and courts, often acting not as neutral arbitrators but as selfish individuals seeking their own enrichment. The behavior of the lawyers and guns downstairs mimics that of their counterparts upstairs, but they are not under the Kremlin's con-trol. Putin actually would prefer a more orderly downstairs economy, but the system he built tends to encourage state officials to harass small business as much as they protect it.

Not only is the political economy of Putinism part and parcel of Putinism writ large but also it came into being at roughly the same time, in 2003–2004. In his first term as president, from 2000 to 2004, Putin's economic course arguably was trending in the direction of stronger formal market institutions, with the state assuming its role as the neutral arbitrator of the economic rules of the game. The October 2003 arrest of the billionaire Mikhail Khodorkovsky, the head of the private oil company Yukos (the so-called Yukos Affair), symbolized and cemented a different direction, with a more aggressive and arbitrary state staking its claim to dominate the economy, including on behalf of regime loyalists, a more centralized form of Russian "crony capitalism."[4] It was probably not a coincidence that 2003 was also the year in which world oil prices started their steep ascent from around $25 per barrel to over $100 per barrel, first for a brief period in 2008, and then consistently in the years 2011–2014. Both Putin's own inclinations and Russia's status as a major hydrocarbons exporter pushed Russia toward its current system in which state control, informal networks, and special deals dominate.

After nine years of rapid growth from 1999 to 2008, from 2009 to 2017 Russia experienced eight years of stagnation. The economy remains too dependent on oil, and the lawyers and guns have become too predatory. There is a tension between one of the core ideas of the code of Putinism, developing Russia into a strong and respected great power, and the habits of control and loyalty, which undermines economic performance. Putinomics as an economic system is under considerable strain, but dismantling it would be even harder, because it would require a change in the core mentality of Russia's rulers.

Russia after Communism

The failure of communism as an economic system meant that capitalism was the only game in town in post-Soviet Russia. But capitalism comes in many forms, and no one really knew how to get from communism to capitalism.[5] At the most basic level, private property had to be restored and prices had to be set by the market (supply and demand) and not by the state. Equally basic, Russia had to rejoin the world economy, both because cutting the Soviet Union off from international trade and competition (autarky) had failed and because the pressure of international competition would make the new Russian economy more efficient. But this basic trajectory left many unanswered questions about timing, sequencing, and speed.

The policy and academic debate in the 1990s tended to focus on the divide between "shock therapy" and "gradualism." So-called shock therapists emphasized the importance of rapid implementation of a trio of policies—liberalization (of trade and prices), stabilization (reducing budget deficits and controlling the money supply), and privatization. Gradualists argued that the most important task was the creation of the institutional framework of capitalism—regulatory, legal, and so on—and that, absent such institutions, shock therapy would fail. Adherents of both positions believed that policy choices mattered a lot for outcomes. In the end, this belief in the consistent implementation of the correct policies gave way to more nuanced arguments about the importance of a range of factors largely beyond the short-run control of economic policymakers, including geography, resource endowments, state capacity, political polarization, and the legacies of a Soviet economic model based on heavy industry and military production.[6]

As it happened, the government of Russian President Boris Yeltsin embraced the language of shock therapy but largely failed at consistently implementing these policies. Prices and trade were liberalized, but not entirely, with special export deals for some products and limits on domestic energy prices. Macroeconomic stabilization was pursued fitfully, with the initial period of hyperinflation (2,500 percent in 1992, 840 percent in 1993) eventually giving way to merely high levels of inflation (by 1996 inflation was down to 22 percent).[7]

The biggest scandal was associated with privatization, in particular the infamous "loans for shares" deal in which some of the crown jewels of the Russian economy were sold off at seemingly favorable prices to a small group of well-connected oligarchs. Although the deal ultimately affected only twelve firms, most of these transactions involved major raw material assets that became the basis of some of Russia's largest corporations. This is how some of Russia's most prominent "oligarchs" were made: Mikhail Khodorkovsky gained control over the Yukos oil company, Boris Berezovsky acquired ownership of the Sibneft oil company, and Vladimir Potanin took over the nickel and palladium giant Norilsk Nickel. In hindsight, some have argued that although the method of privatization was corrupt, once in private hands these firms did quite well and contributed to subsequent economic growth. Much less attention has gone to the over fifteen thousand firms privatized through other means, such as the distribution of vouchers to private citizens. Overall, privatization was less of a boon in increasing productivity than in other postcommunist countries, although over time those privatized firms geographically closer to the West and Moscow began to show promising gains.[8]

The perception that a small group of insiders and political loyalists had unfairly grabbed Russia's most valuable assets further undermined the legitimacy of Russian economic reform in the 1990s. Although Russia did not successfully implement a pure version of shock therapy, and was too politically weak to do so anyway, in the popular Russian imagination it was Yeltsin and his team's policy failures that caused the depression and the collapse of people's living standards. As the Princeton historian Stephen Kotkin observed, "In a great irony, it was not the Soviet past but 'reform' that was compelled to stand trial."[9]

Why was the Soviet past to blame? Most generally, the Soviet economic model of forced collectivization of agriculture, rapid industrialization, militarization, central planning, and state ownership of all factories, land, and stores was wasteful and inefficient. It was also a dead end, and when communism collapsed in the Soviet Union and the wider Soviet bloc, the revolutionary upheaval caused a regionwide depression. As the Bolshevik theorist Nikolay Bukharin put it after the 1917 revolution, "the temporary collapse of productive forces is a law inherent to revolution." More specifically, the liberalization of prices, to allow supply and demand to operate in the medium and long term, in the short term created much uncertainty and disrupted existing links between producers. Thus the whole region witnessed a depression in the early 1990s; the main difference was how long and severe the collapse was, but no country avoided it entirely.[10] Figure 4-1 shows the general pattern across the region; within this context, Russia's collapse was not a unique calamity, as it is sometimes depicted, but part of a larger trend. Russia's economic performance in the 1990s was worse than in eastern Europe, but average for the former Soviet Union as a whole (note that the reform process in eastern Europe started in 1989–1990, so those countries had a two-year head start on the former Soviet countries).[11]

The Soviet legacy had more specific and negative consequences in Russia. The combination of the geographic facts of Russia's cold and size with the Soviet planners' decisions to create a heavily industrialized and militarized economy, and then place many of these factories in remote and cold locations, meant that post-Soviet Russia inherited what Kotkin labeled "the world's largest ever assemblage of obsolete equipment." Because of its climate and size, Russia has always had what one scholar calls "high costs of production." The economist Clifford Gaddy and his colleagues Fiona Hill and Barry Ickes

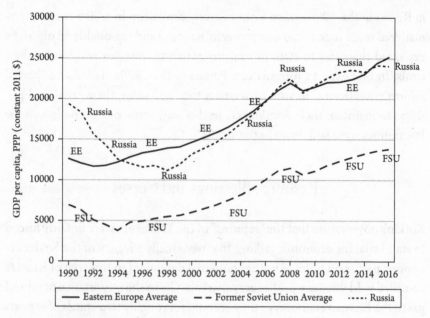

Figure 4-1 GDP per Capita, 1990–2016

have demonstrated how Soviet policies made this problem worse, by locating "factories, machines, and people in the wrong places." Thus, Russia has a large number of big industrial cities in Siberia, the Urals, and the Far East that are far from world markets and unusually cold (which increases production costs), and thus noncompetitive by international standards. Add to this the fact that hundreds of Russian towns and cities are dependent on one key plant—so-called monocities—that may not be viable under capitalism and the spatial allocation problem looks even more daunting.[12]

In short, an economic depression in Russia in the 1990s was inevitable. The real question is whether the country moved in the right direction, despite its massive economic (and political) problems. Here there are reasonable half-full and half-empty positions. On the half-full side, in the 1990s Russia replaced a failed communist economic system with at least rudimentary market capitalist institutions, no small feat in itself. The economic slide was halted, and inflation was brought under control. Many average Russians acquired cost-free the most important piece of property individuals can have, a place to live, as more than 17 million housing units (apartments and houses) were privatized in the 1990s. Arguably, the foundations for economic growth in the 2000s were established in the 1990s; certainly, this is the view of pro-Yeltsin observers. On the half-empty side, the capitalism established in Russia in the 1990s was a form of crony capitalism in which connections mattered more than talent and powerful national and regional-level oligarchs exploited their ties to state officials to enrich themselves and hinder their rivals. In one expert's formulation, Russia in the 1990s stalled at a "partial reform equilibrium" in which "winners take all," using their privileged position to maintain their dominance. In this way, some of the conditions for Putinomics were laid down in the 1990s.[13]

Resource Blessings and Curses

Kotkin's observation that the "reforms" of the Yeltsin era were unfairly forced to stand trial for economic failings that were really a legacy of the Soviet economic past is on point. Another potential defendant in this trial of Russia's so-called wild 90s are world energy markets. Given the importance of oil and gas to the Russian economy—they account for roughly two-thirds of exports and half of state budget revenue—much can be learned about Russian economic performance over the last four decades by looking at the simple factor of world energy prices. The oil shocks of the 1970s helped sustain Leonid Brezhnev's USSR at a time of growing social and economic problems. When oil prices dropped in the 1980s, they helped pull down Mikhail Gorbachev and the entire Soviet Union. Oil prices continued at a persistently low rate in the 1990s during the Yeltsin era, giving him little slack to deal with the shift from communism to capitalism.

Vladimir Putin's experience has been quite different. Indeed, one observer has suggested that we should think of Putin as "Vladimir the Lucky," given his great fortune in coming to power as world energy prices climbed to historically high levels. Figure 4-2 shows the trend in world energy prices over the last twenty-five years. The price of a barrel of oil during Yeltsin's presidency was about $18. Under Putin from 2000 to 2016 the average price was more than 3.5 times that, at over $65 per barrel. If we look at profit from oil and gas sales over time under Putin, their steady increase correlates almost exactly with similarly relentless increases in the Russian stock market, the profits of leading *nonenergy* Russian companies, retail sales, imports, and so forth.[14]

Putin was also lucky in that he came to power when the economic recovery after the 1998 economic crash had already started. A favorable exchange rate that made Russia more internationally competitive and gave a boost to domestic producers, as well as a general regional economic takeoff

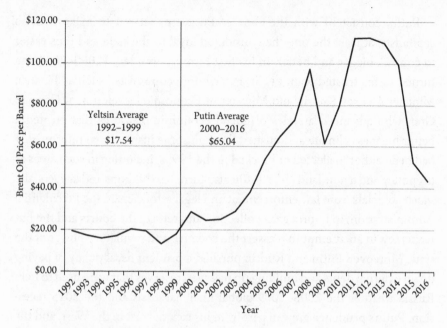

Figure 4-2 Brent Oil Price, 1992–2016

after the postcommunist depression, meant that Russia returned to growth in 1999–2000 (see Figure 4-1). The 1998 economic crisis also had weakened the political power of several key oligarchs and wiped out a bunch of ineffectual banks. Newly privatized oil and mineral companies were able to greatly expand their production in the early 2000s, as the oligarchs sought to grow their companies and fatten their wallets even more.[15]

It is important to note, however, that Putin was not just lucky but also smart. He understood that capitalism had outperformed communism, and he had no interest in overturning the fundamentals of the new system. As his former adviser Gleb Pavlovskiy put it:

> His thinking was that in the Soviet Union we were idiots; we had tried to build a fair society, when we should have been making money. . . . It was a game and we lost, because we didn't do several simple things: we didn't create our own class of capitalists, we didn't give the capitalist predators on our side a chance to develop and devour the capitalist predators on theirs. . . . Putin's idea is that we should be bigger and better capitalists than the capitalists, and should be more consolidated as a state: there should be maximum oneness of state and business.[16]

Putin, consistent with the code of Putinism, set out to make Russia's capitalists, at least the ones he considered loyal to the state and thus easier to control, bigger and better. In his first term as president (2000–2004) he turned to his trusted team of "St. Petersburg economists," such as Finance Minister Aleksey Kudrin and Minister of Economic Development German Gref, who advanced a series of liberal economic measures that created a better business climate and pushed through some institutional reforms that had been either neglected or blocked in the 1990s, including in such areas as tax policy and a new land code. Putin also turned to his guns and lawyers, the *siloviki* officials from law enforcement and legal reformers in the Presidential Administration, to improve tax collection and reform the courts and the bureaucracy, in an attempt to reassert the coercive and regulatory power of the state. Moreover, Putin and Kudrin pursued a prudent fiscal policy of paying down external debts and building up reserves, reserves that were used to help Russia weather the 2008–2009 global financial crisis and the 2015 recession. Putin's prudence grew in part from his lack of trust in the West, and the perceived need to be less dependent on foreign lenders and more in control of Russia's finances.[17]

Still, soaring oil and gas prices were the most important factor in driving Russian economic growth in the 2000s. Overall, from 1999 to 2007 Russia grew at around 7 percent a year, which nearly doubled the size of the economy and led to growing personal incomes, balanced government budgets, and lower unemployment and poverty. The rising tide of oil and gas lifted many boats, so other sectors of the economy, such as construction and services, grew rapidly as well. Russians lived better than they ever had before, and Putin was rewarded with stratospheric approval ratings of around 80 percent at the time he moved from the presidency to the prime minister post in 2008.[18] Internationally, Russia was lumped together with other large, fast growers like China, India, and Brazil and labeled a BRIC, the core group of emerging market economies. Investment dollars flowed in.

By any normal standard, Russia's oil and gas bounty is a huge blessing. So what's all this talk about Russia suffering from a "resource curse?" There are two conventional uses of this term, one economic and one political. The economic one refers to the way in which the influx of dollar receipts drives up the local currency, thereby rendering other sectors of the economy, particularly industry, internationally noncompetitive. The political one contends, as discussed in chapter 2, that resource rich countries are more likely to be authoritarian. At least for Russia, the resource curse has aspects of both of those difficulties, but should really be thought of as a combined political-economic problem. Oil and gas revenues serve both as a way of avoiding necessary but painful steps to lessen and ultimately do away with the legacies of Soviet planning and industrialization and as a method of elite control and enrichment, at the expense of better governance and a more equitable polity and economy.

Because of the crucial role hydrocarbon earnings play in the system, Putin has prioritized controlling this sector above all others. In the mid-1990s he had even written, or had someone write for him, a graduate thesis on the use of Russia's natural resource wealth to rebuild the country.[19] Shortly after becoming president Putin maneuvered Dmitriy Medvedev into the position of chair of the board of Gazprom, the largest natural gas company in the world, and another St. Petersburg loyalist, Aleksey Miller, into the CEO position. Gazprom had been partially privatized in the 1990s (the state retained a 38 percent share), but was returned to state control (50.002 percent) under Putin.

The oil industry also was substantially privatized in the 1990s, and Putin significantly reversed this trend as well. As noted, some of the largest companies, such as Yukos and Sibneft, were transferred to major oligarchs in the "loans-for-shares" process under Yeltsin. Letting this vital asset remain under the control of oligarchs of uncertain loyalty must have seemed foolish to Putin and his associates, given their worldview, and he set about reversing Yeltsin's policies.[20] When Putin came to power in 2000, the state owned only 10 percent of the industry or, more precisely, held majority-shares in companies that produced that percentage of annual oil output. The Yukos affair was the key move in an effort to reassert state control over the oil industry, with its major assets taken over by the state-owned Rosneft (meaning "Russian Oil"—*neft* in Russian means oil). Sibneft, which had been controlled by Berezovsky and his erstwhile partner, the oligarch Roman Abramovich, was bought out by Gazprom in 2005. By 2008 state control had risen to 42 percent. In 2013 Rosneft bought TNK-BP, an oil company jointly controlled by British Petroleum and four Russian oligarchs. Rosneft became the largest oil-producing company in the world, and increased state control of the industry to more than 50 percent. The next year the state took over another major private oil company, Bashneft, in the process temporarily jailing its billionaire owner, who was released after the takeover was completed; two years later, in 2016, Bashneft was sold to Rosneft.[21]

The blessing of all of this oil and gas wealth is that when world energy prices are high, money flows into Russia, spreads throughout the economy,

and enriches ordinary citizens. The curse is that it enriches the rich and powerful most of all, and serves as a disincentive to either share power or reform
the state or economy. Instead, the ruling elite can simply be "a toad sitting
on an oil pipeline," in the memorable phrase of the Russian oppositionist
Aleksey Navalny. Both Putin and Medvedev have repeatedly called for
Russia to reduce its economic dependence on natural resource exports and
to build a more broadly international competitive economy, including in
production, services, agriculture, and high technology. This is supposed
to take place by reforming economic and legal institutions to create the
conditions for modernization and innovation. In reality, Russia has become
even more dependent on natural resource exports under Putin, with their
share in overall exports increasing from around 80 percent in 2000 to about
83 percent today. The oft-stated intentions to diversify the economy have
come to naught.[22]

Russia's increasing dependence on oil and gas exports was driven home
dramatically in 2015, when the economy fell into recession as the international price of oil plunged from about $100 per barrel in 2014 to around $50–
$60 per barrel in 2015. The economy shrunk by over 3.5 percent, and the
ruble plunged, meaning that in dollar terms the Russian economy was now
smaller than Canada's or South Korea's. Although international sanctions
due to the war in Ukraine played some role, the main source of the recession
was declining energy prices. By this point Putin had seemed to give up his
earlier stated intentions of diversifying the economy, instead telling Russians
that the price of oil would recover in a year or two and the economy along
with it. The alternative path of reform, which would require a more impartial
legal system and a more open political system, looked riskier and more difficult than waiting and hoping for a turnaround.

Lawyers and Guns, Upstairs

If oil and gas are the basic source of money for the Russian economy, where
do the lawyers and guns come in? At the pinnacle of the Russian economy,
the Kremlin can manipulate lawyers (courts and prosecutors) and guns (regular and secret police) to maintain control, either formally or informally, of
Russia's leading companies. This is the "upstairs" of the Russian economy,
what others have referred to as a form of "state capitalism."[23] The next two
sections describe the anatomy of this economic system in more detail, first

for the top firms upstairs and then for the small and medium-sized businesses downstairs, outside the sphere of direct state control or domination.

When Putin came to power, he faced the task of figuring out how to manage relations with the oligarchs who dominated the Russian economy and played an important role in politics as well. His service in the Kremlin and the FSB under Yeltsin gave him considerable insider information on their activities, and his St. Petersburg career before that influenced his views of the government–business relationship, one based on informal deals. In his first six months in power, he took two key steps that set the initial tone. First, he drove from the country two prominent oligarchs, Boris Berezovsky and Vladimir Gusinsky, who controlled two of the leading TV channels. In 2001, while already abroad, Berezovsky and Gusinsky had to yield ownership of their TV holdings; Putin was determined to control television himself. Second, Putin met with a small group of leading oligarchs and informed them that they could keep their businesses if they stayed out of politics. According to Moscow legend, this agreement took the form of a "picnic pact" concluded at Putin's dacha in May 2000, although there is no firm evidence that the meeting actually took place. What is known for certain is that Putin did meet with twenty-one top oligarchs at the Kremlin in July 2000 and discussed the terms of the state–business relationship. The oligarchs, Putin had declared in February 2000, would be "equidistant from power," the implication being that the state would deal with them all based on the law, not on special deals. Further, big business would have to pay their taxes in full and support Russian national interests. In exchange, they could keep their property and develop their businesses.[24]

The logic of the alleged deal was clear. Upon coming to power, Putin faced a dilemma: if he punished the oligarchs for their past legal violations, he might hurt the economy, but if he forgave their crimes, he would undermine the rule of law that is essential for modern capitalism. The way out of the dilemma was to set a new "zero-point," letting bygones be bygones but punishing any future violations.[25]

In practice, things were not so easy. First, neither Putin nor the oligarchs could credibly commit to the deal, not only because the exact parameters of the deal were unclear but also because all parties had strong incentives to renege and seek to increase their power, and no credible way of committing to honor the pact in the future. Second, Putin himself had no interest in creating a rule-of-law state in which all parties were equal before the law, including the state itself. Putin controlled the most important lawyers (the court system and prosecutors) and the biggest guns (the police and security services), so he saw no need to stand on a level playing field with the tycoons. As one Russian analyst put it, "the Russian system did not need fixed rules of the game; it needed fixers." And Putin's earliest experiences with capitalism in 1990s St. Petersburg were precisely as a "fixer," a specialist not in developing business but controlling it.[26]

In order to control the oligarchs, Putin not only talked to them but also signaled his superior power. If Russia's leading tycoons believed they had captured the state under Yeltsin, they needed to be disabused of this notion. Gusinsky and Berezovsky were the most important examples in the summer of 2000, but not the only ones. Other prominent Yeltsin-era oligarchs, such as the heads of large private oil and mineral companies, also had problems with prosecutors or tax authorities, although they were able to solve them without being arrested or expropriated.[27]

The 2003 Yukos affair was the most critical moment in Putin's campaign to subordinate big business, and the moment at which Putinomics as a system was fully consolidated. By this time, Khodorkovsky was the richest man in Russia at the age of forty, with a fortune of roughly $15 billion, and with growing economic and political ambitions. His business plans for Yukos included a possible merger with another Russian oil company, Sibneft, selling some segment of this larger merged company to an American oil major like ExxonMobil, and the development of a separate pipeline network independent of the state pipeline monopoly Transneft. Khodorkovsky also was very active politically, criticizing state corruption, financing multiple political parties, and allegedly holding discussions about future constitutional reform options for Russia.[28]

The arrest and imprisonment of Khodorkovsky and other top Yukos officials was meant to destroy the ability of oligarchs to pursue independent policies and affirm their subordinate position to the state. Khodorkovsky's plans arguably would have undermined the ability of the state to control a key piece of the energy sector, a development Putin would not tolerate. Khodorkovsky's moves were particularly troubling from the point of view of Putin's core team because, if they were realized, a major Russian oil company, one believed to have considerable influence with key political parties represented in the Duma, would be controlled partially by American money.[29] These steps, then, were seen as disloyal not only to Putin but also to Russia. Given the mentality of Putin and others in his circle, which includes statist and anti-American beliefs, habits of control and loyalty, and feelings of vulnerability, the Yukos affair is understandable, even if the lawyers and guns needed to bend the law to arrest Khodorkovsky and take over his company.

Putinomics is a form of "state capitalism," in which the "commanding heights" of the economy are controlled either directly or indirectly by the state. Putin's state capitalism differs from market capitalism because the property rights of private business, especially with respect to the largest firms in the most important sectors, are not protected but provisional, subject to state direction and, in extreme cases, expropriation. As the Russian joke goes, there are no billionaires in Russia, only people working as billionaires. How else to understand the comment of some of Russia's richest men that they are willing to give their companies and riches to the state if necessary? Oleg Deripaska, an aluminum tycoon and one of Russia's richest men, said, "if the state says we must give up our companies, we will give them up. I do not separate myself from the state." Similarly, Putin's billionaire friend Gennadiy Timchenko remarked in 2014, "I'll turn in everything to the state any time if this is needed." The CEO of Rosneft and one of Putin's closest allies, Igor Sechin, captured well the logic of Putinomics when he remarked, "What difference does it make whether something is state property or private property?"[30]

Further, major Russian businesses in oil and gas and metals, as well as the top banks, understand that they have to invest in a variety of political and economic projects at the direction of the Kremlin, such as the Sochi Olympics (for more on Sochi, see chapter 5). A St. Petersburg journalist who has followed Putin's career since the 1990s referred to the system as "Orthodox Capitalism," one in which Putin can approach the oligarchs and say, "You're rich, I understand how you got this money—you have to help."[31] Most important, Russia's top companies from the natural resources sector need to help sustain the parts of Russian industry that otherwise could not compete and stay alive, even if they have to lose money doing so.

A particularly striking example of this occurred during the 2009 economic crisis. The billionaire oligarch Oleg Deripaska, who has significant holdings in aluminum, transportation, energy, and manufacturing, was pinched for cash because of the global financial meltdown. Deripaska's company withheld wages from a cement, potash, and alumina factory in the "mono-town" of Pikalevo (population 22,000) near St. Petersburg for three months. City residents grew increasingly desperate for money, and blocked a major highway. This got Putin's attention, and he helicoptered into the city and dressed down a servile Deripaska, accusing him of incompetence and greed, while the cameras rolled. Putin forced Deripaska to pay the wages and get the factory working again, although he also arranged for a state bank to provide funding. Putin didn't care if it made economic sense to keep the factory open—it made political sense. And since, in Putin's view, Deripaska had grown exceedingly rich with Putin's tacit approval, Deripaska had to do as Putin said when political stability was threatened.[32]

For the crucial oil and gas sector, Putin seems most comfortable with state ownership of the most important players—Gazprom (gas), Rosneft (oil), and Transneft (pipelines). Private companies like Lukoil and the shadowy Surgutneftegaz, which does not disclose its ownership structure, can remain private but must coordinate major actions with Putin. For example, Surgutneftegaz trades through Gunvor, the oil trading company owned until 2014 by Timchenko, the close friend of Putin; Timchenko was hit by US sanctions in 2014 and allegedly sold his shares in Gunvor to his Swedish partner the day before the sanctions were announced.[33]

Thus, not only is Putinomics a form of state capitalism in the upstairs section of the economy but also it is a form of "centralized crony capitalism," in which cronies of the president personally both run and profit from the system.[34] This system ensures control by the state and loyalty to Putin. Thus, the political economy of Putinism is consistent with the dominance of informal clan networks. For example, if we look at the ten largest publicly traded companies in Russia in 2013 (according to Forbes), at least six of the ten had current or recent top officials or shareholders with personal links to Putin going back to the 1980s or 1990s, and two others had indirect links. Gazprom and Rosneft are the two most important companies, and have been particularly critical to Putin. Gazprom's CEO, as well as the chair of the board of directors, have throughout most of Putin's rule been close associates from St. Petersburg. Rosneft, Russia's largest oil company, is controlled by one of Putin's closest colleagues for more than two decades, Igor Sechin. The CEO of the largest bank is another Putin associate from St. Petersburg. The head of the pipeline monopoly Transneft served with Putin in the KGB in East Germany.[35]

A similar pattern is seen with some of Russia's state-controlled corporations that are not publicly listed. Perhaps most important is Russian Railways, one of the largest transportation companies in the world, responsible for shipping people and goods (including oil products) across Russia's vast space. Its head until 2015 was Vladimir Yakunin, a former KGB officer from Leningrad who was one of the founders of the Ozero dacha cooperative with Vladimir Putin in 1996 (see chapter 3). Yakunin's replacement attended university in St. Petersburg and is linked to Putin's childhood friends, the Rotenberg brothers. Considering Gazprom (which owns its own pipelines), Transneft, Russian Railways, and the oil-trading company Gunvor together, all of the major conduits for shipping oil and gas within Russia and beyond have been controlled for long periods by Putin's long-standing acquaintances. Another key state company is Rostec, a giant conglomeration of hundreds of defense and high-tech entities. Its head is Viktor Chemezov, a KGB colleague of Putin's from their service together in East Germany in the 1980s.[36]

Other close Putin friends have done very well in business since he came to power, becoming billionaires in the process.[37] For example, Yuriy Kovalchuk, Putin's partner in the Ozero dacha cooperative who was labeled by the US government as "Putin's personal banker," got rich in the Putin years as the largest shareholder in and head of the Bank of Russia, a St. Petersburg bank founded in the 1990s. In the 2000s the bank was able to gain control of a series of small financial companies previously part of Gazprom and play a key role in the creation of the National Media Group, which controls multiple Russian TV stations and newspapers. Television is another commercial sphere that Putin thinks it is important to dominate—it is (or should be) more of a state asset than a private one.

Another prominent example of Putin's friends getting rich is that of the Rotenberg brothers. Arkadiy and Boris Rotenberg practiced judo with Putin as early as the 1960s. Today they are both billionaires, who made their fortunes in a variety of enterprises, including banking, construction, and alcohol factories. Key Rotenberg construction contracts have included pipelines for Gazprom, a new Moscow–St. Petersburg highway, multiple facilities for the Sochi Olympics, and a massive bridge linking Russia to recently annexed Crimea (which is separated from Russia by two miles). Arkadiy Rotenberg was the top recipient of government contracts in Russia in 2016—others in the top five include Rotenberg's son, Putin's then son-in-law, and another one of Putin's close friends.[38]

These examples of Putin's wealthy friends show the extent to which the state capitalism of Putinomics is also a crony capitalism. Big business and the state are not completely separate and neutral interlocutors in any country. But the business–state relationship, and especially the personalistic nature of this relationship, seems much closer and more incestuous in Russia than in your typical developed capitalist country, although probably not that atypical for many developing countries. Relying on old friends in this way makes sense, given Putin's mentality. As one Russian expert put it, "These are trusted people, who will stick with Putin until the end." Putin can count on them to deliver, and this loyalty and personal control is vital to big business deals. From the point of view of Putin and his rich cronies like Rotenberg, this is not corruption, because Rotenberg's billions are compensation for a job well done.[39]

Putin sits at the center of what two American economists call the "rent management system."[40] In economics, "rents" are basically excess returns beyond normal costs and profits that someone receives because of a nonmarket advantage. Putin is the arbiter and enforcer who ensures that the interests of key players (at least, those who play by his rules) are protected; that the state gets its fair share of the windfall from oil, gas, and metals rents; and that the remaining rents are fairly distributed among leading clans. Vital to this system is that oil and gas rents are distributed to the rest of the economy, so, for example, Siberian industrial plants can keep operating and employing their workers. Putinomics runs on special deals, with Putin as the chief fixer; not so different, really, from his role as vice-mayor in St. Petersburg in the 1990s. Indeed, for Putin, cutting special deals is the essence of capitalism; certainly that is how he interacts with the heads of major foreign companies who come calling at his residence outside Moscow. Liberal ideas about market competition and the rule of law are not just an ideal that is impossible to reach in the real world but also, in Putin's view, are yet one more example of Western hypocrisy, whose representatives talk one way in public but behave differently in private.

At the same time, we should not forget that Putin is not all-powerful and there is not one coherent team. Different clans and networks vie for influence in big business and battle over property. For example, when Yukos was busted up many people thought Gazprom would be the main beneficiary. Putin publicly endorsed a plan to merge Rosneft into Gazprom. But Sechin, the head of the Rosneft board at the time, apparently had other ideas. Not only was "his" company not merged with Gazprom, but it ended up grabbing the best pieces of Yukos and becoming over time a major rival to Gazprom. In recent years Sechin and Rosneft seem to have bested Gazprom on several occasions, with Sechin becoming the "de facto informal overseer" of the energy sector and "the main headache" of Gazprom.[41]

Upstairs, Putinomics shares some similarities with the Yeltsin years and its strutting oligarchs, but also has several striking differences—most importantly, the much more powerful position of the Kremlin. A distorted form of capitalism continues, with a high premium on personalistic, informal relations with state officials being necessary for holding on to one's assets. Oil and gas and metals are still the dominant sectors, a fact of life for Russia that will not change. The state plays a larger role in the economy than before— 60–70 percent, according to Russia's Federal Antimonopoly Service. Despite Putin's promise in 2000, he has not done away with the "fusion of state power and capital" that inspired the use of the term "oligarchs" to refer to top businessmen. To the contrary, he seems to have facilitated an even closer merger of state power and capital than existed under Yeltsin.[42]

Furthermore, there are a lot more billionaires in Russia now than there were in the 1990s, largely of course because the country became much richer. But it is still striking to note that in the year 2000 there were *zero* Russians on Forbes's list of dollar billionaires (four had made the list prior to the 1998 economic crisis). In May 2014 there were 107 Russians on the list, including Putin's cronies Timchenko, Kovalchuk, and the Rotenberg brothers. According to Credit Suisse, the number of billionaires as a share of the overall population, and the concentration of wealth in their hands, makes Russia one of the most unequal countries in the world, "apart from [some] small Caribbean nations." Credit Suisse maintains that Russia's 110 billionaires (at the time of the report) hold 35 percent of Russia's entire wealth. Anthony Shorrocks, one of the report's authors, maintained, "the situation in Russia has no parallel. If you look at how Russians have made their money and the sort of political ties that seem to be necessary to maintain it, there are just very few places where the situation is similar."[43]

The upstairs portion of the Russian economy under Putin, then, has done quite well precisely through close connections to the Kremlin. The state either directly owns, or has close informal ties with, many of Russia's leading businesses in such crucial sections as oil and gas, banking, metals, defense industries, and the media. How do things look downstairs, for those businesses too small to be a matter of Putin's concern?

Lawyers and Guns, Downstairs

Any frequent visitor to Russia's major cities, and of course the inhabitants of these cities themselves, can't help but be struck by the transformation of Russia over the last twenty-five years. Most striking of all perhaps is the rapid proliferation of malls and mega-malls. In 2014 Russia passed the United

Kingdom to move into second place in Europe in terms of mall space, behind only France. This is extraordinary, given that Russia's very first mall
opened only in 2000, Putin's first year as president. As of 2013 Moscow
alone had eighty-two malls, including some of the largest in the world. With
IKEA stores, bowling alleys, and lively food courts, this is not your parents'
Moscow.[44]

Against this backdrop of thriving retail trade and construction in the big
cities, small and medium-sized businesses seem to be booming in Russia,
and indeed many are. Obviously, oil and gas wealth are a large part of this,
as money flows into Russia and down through the rest of the economy.
More generally, it reflects Russia's transition to a form of market capitalism
after seventy-five years of communism; Brezhnev did not do malls. But the
picture is more complicated than that of a surging middle class with a fast-
growing consumer infrastructure. First, of course, there are the areas outside
the leading cities, which, although better off than in the 1990s, still lag far
behind the capital cities of Moscow and St. Petersburg.[45] Second, comparative data suggest that Russian small and medium-sized businesses are not
doing as well as the consumer boom in Russian cities would lead us to believe. And third, and most important for our purposes, is that all too often
Russian entrepreneurs find themselves caught in a web spun by state lawyers
and guns preying on the small capitalists that are essential for developing
contemporary market capitalism.

Russia has hundreds of thousands of small and medium-sized businesses,
roughly 250,000 as of 2011. On a per capita basis, this is a relatively typical
number, fewer than in Italy but more than in Germany or Japan. The share
of bank lending to small business in Russia is also roughly in line with that of
other relatively wealthy countries, slightly over 20 percent. So far, so good.
Where Russia lags considerably is in the share of the population working in
small and medium-sized enterprises (SMEs) and how much these businesses
contribute to the economy as a whole. Roughly 19 million Russians work for
SMEs, which amounts to 27 percent of all employees. In contrast, in the world's
34 leading capitalist countries in the Organization for Economic Cooperation
and Development (OECD), 60 to 80 percent of the workforce are employed
by SMEs; in China it is 55 percent. Similarly, Russian small and medium-sized
businesses create about 23 percent of GDP, compared to around 50 to 70 percent in OECD countries. Although Russia has lots of small and medium-sized
businesses, they employ far fewer people, and contribute considerably less to
the economy, than in developed capitalist countries.[46]

Why does the Russian small business sector seem to lag? The main reason is usually described somewhat euphemistically as "institutional factors." In common language, this means corruption, a poor legal system, and in general a "weak" or "bad" state. Political economists increasingly argue that the quality of institutions is a key, if not the key, explanation for economic performance.[47] As one review of academic studies on Russian small business concluded, "institutions and the business environment in Russia seem to be the most important inhibitors for entrepreneurship and small business." The study also noted that little has changed in this respect over the last twenty years.[48]

The most infamous, and one of the most tragic cases, of what these "institutional factors" mean in practice is that of Sergey Magnitsky. Magnitsky was an attorney working for an investment fund called Hermitage Capital. In 2007 corrupt police officers engaged in a search of Hermitage's office, with the goal of acquiring internal corporate documents. Using these documents, they then illegally reregistered three companies in the Hermitage fund under different owners and used their positions to return to the companies 180 million dollars in taxes paid to the Russian state. Magnitsky uncovered the crime and, when he tried to expose it, some of the very same officers turned around and arrested Magnitsky for tax evasion. He was held in detention for a year and died in custody when he was, at best, not given proper medical care and, at worst, tortured.[49] The case became an international cause célèbre, and inspired a US law directed at corrupt Russian officials, due to the ceaseless campaigning of the CEO of Hermitage Capital, Bill Browder, an American-British businessman who was heavily invested in Russia and a one-time booster of Putin who fell out with the Russian government and was expelled from the country.

The Magnitsky case was just one example of the practice of Russian-style corporate "raiding," in which corrupt courts, prosecutors, and police (lawyers and guns) instigate or are drawn into attacks on business by business rivals. "Raiding" can take many forms, but the gist of the practice is that law enforcement instigates a trumped-up criminal case against a businessperson in order to deprive her of all or part of her business (in reality, it is much more likely to be a him than a her). The biggest example was arguably the Yukos case. But thousands of such cases have happened in Russia, and indeed they increased considerably after the Yukos case, which acted as a kind of green light to lower-level lawyers and guns in the state apparatus. Putin noted in December 2015 that in the previous year around 200,000 cases had been opened for various economic crimes, but that only 15 percent of them led to convictions; that mattered little to the owners, however, who in 83 percent of cases lost all or part of their business as a consequence of this "raid." A thorough study by Russian academics concluded that a huge number of criminal cases pertaining to economic crimes are instigated by corrupt law enforcement officials for their own economic benefit. Small business owners see corrupt state officials as a bigger threat than the mafia, which has lost considerable power since the mid-1990s. As a leading Russian sociologist observed, "Criminal repression is used against private entrepreneurs in Russia in a systemic way by the state powers." More colloquially, a St. Petersburg journalist observed wryly, "There are no arguments against a crowbar."[50]

Of course, it cannot be the case that all small businesses come under attack, although most of them are forced to either hire a private security firm or contract with a state law enforcement agency to ensure that potential "problems" with the authorities are resolved. And some evidence suggests that over time the commercial courts have become a more effective way for businesses to resolve disputes both with each other and the state.[51] But problems like state "raiding" offer one important explanation for the relative weakness of small business in Russia.

Both Putin and Medvedev have spoken out frequently about the problem of developing small business; in 2002 Putin denounced "unjustified administrative pressure" on entrepreneurs, and in 2008 Medvedev complained about how the authorities "cause nightmares" for business. Medvedev succeeded in enacting several reforms, including one that changed authority over criminal tax cases against businesses, requiring that only material from the tax office could be used to initiate charges. However, since Putin returned to the presidency in 2012, the Investigative Committee fought successfully to reverse that rule and once again acquired the power to launch tax investigations on its own. Although the Investigative Committee claimed that it needs this power to fight business fraud, most observers believe that the real point was to gain back the ability to use the threat of criminal charges to extort bribes from businesses.[52]

Publicly, both Putin and Medvedev contend that Russia needs to improve substantially its business climate. Indeed, in 2012, on his return to the Kremlin, Putin officially proclaimed the goal of moving Russia up in the World Bank's "Doing Business" ranking from 120th place in 2011 to 50th in 2015 and 20th in 2018. The rankings measure regulations that influence the ease of doing business, such as the ease of opening a business, getting electricity, and registering a business; they do not look at broader issues related to the economy, polity, or legal system. The *Financial Times* pointed out that the "Doing Business" rankings tend to favor the ability to quickly change laws and regulations, rather than delving into how well they are enforced or larger systemic problems such as corruption, which may explain how Russia has been able to improve its scores so quickly. Russia has been more or less on track to reach Putin's ambitious goals, hitting 51st place in 2015 and 40th place in 2016. Russia is ahead of the other large emerging-market economies that make up the BRICS (Brazil, India, China, and South Africa).[53]

Whether this regulatory improvement will lead to a better overall situation in the downstairs part of the Russian economy, especially during a domestic recession, remains to be seen.[54] The evidence so far suggests that changes in the formal regulations don't necessarily mean that small businesses are any better placed to fend off state predation or protect themselves in court. Indeed, a large share of the Russian economy remains "underground," beyond the reach of state inspectors and the tax authorities. In the underground economy, people work in a variety of trades—builders, doctors, mechanics, even small-scale production—and strictly for cash. Although it's hard to measure the size of something that is trying to hide, various experts have estimated that the underground or "shadow" economy is anywhere between 10 and 40 percent of the overall economy. One recent estimate from an official Russian institute maintained that about 40 percent of the working-age population is part of the unofficial economy at some point during the year. The size of the shadow economy has by most estimates declined since the 1990s, especially because of tax reforms enacted in Putin's first term, but it is still the largest unofficial economy among countries at similar or higher levels of wealth. In a 2016 meeting, Putin blamed cops and prosecutors and tax officials for driving people underground—the very same lawyers and guns that Putinomics has empowered.[55]

Overall, Putinomics appears to work against the development of strong small businesses, primarily because of poor institutions. The state's lawyers and guns, which should protect the property rights of business and uphold the law, too often undermine the law and "cause nightmares" for business. The formal rules do not function as they should, forcing entrepreneurs to seek other, often informal means, of protecting their businesses, and discouraging others from starting their own business.

The Future of Putinomics

Putin now finds himself in the situation of the ne'er-do-well young man from the Warren Zevon song, who by the end of the song was "down on his luck," declaring "I'm a desperate man . . . the shit has hit the fan." Since the global economic recession of 2009 Russia has been unable to return to high levels of growth, and in 2015 Russia fell once again into recession. This economic slowdown has been particularly troubling because world oil prices from 2011 to 2014 were at historically high rates of over $100 per barrel (see Figure 4-2); the previous link between high energy prices and fast growth has been severed. Furthermore, the Russian state became addicted to these high world energy prices; in the early 2010s oil and gas revenues accounted for over half of Russian budget receipts, and the state became dependent on world oil prices of around $110–115 per barrel to balance the budget, compared to $20 per barrel in 2005. After several years of budget cuts and belt tightening, Russia still needed world oil prices of $82 per barrel in 2016 to balance the budget, at a time when the price was around $50 per barrel. Prime Minister Medvedev, when confronted by an angry citizen in May 2016 about the government's failure to adjust pensions to keep up with inflation, was reduced to lamely responding, "There is no money. . . . You hang in there!" Putin, in contrast, is not showing any outward signs of desperation, but the current economic strategy seems to depend largely on hoping that world energy prices will rebound and sustained growth will return. World Bank forecasts projected anemic growth for 2017 and 2018 after two years of recession: less than 1.5 percent per year, about half of the world average.[56]

Putinomics can certainly survive, but the system's instability means that the three shaky pillars of lawyers, guns, and oil need some reconstruction. Easy oil money meant that in the period 2004–2014 there was no real political impetus to change a system in which state lawyers and guns play such a large role in the "upstairs" part of the economy and such a malign role in the "downstairs" section. Crony capitalism, in which politically connected billionaires dominate "rent-heavy industries" such as banks, oil and gas, metals, utilities, and infrastructure, has become firmly entrenched; in 2015 Russia was at the very top of The Economist's "crony-capitalism index." Productivity and investment remain low. Russia is economically uncompetitive both with developed economies with innovative and productive work forces and poorer countries with lower wages and competitive manufacturing industries, and thus more dependent than ever on oil and gas exports. Under the circumstances, both foreign and domestic investors prefer to put their money elsewhere. Indeed, according to one Russian investment bank, foreign investors find Russian companies only about half as attractive as Brazilian ones, even though Brazil is also beset by economic and political problems. The longtime Putin associate German Gref, the head of Russia's largest bank, declared in January 2016, "We must honestly admit that we have lost to competitors. . . . We have found ourselves in the ranks of countries that are losing, downshifter countries."[57]

The consensus view among most Russian economists, and a view endorsed both by Putin and Medvedev, is that Russia needs institutional reforms to encourage investment, reduce capital flight, and modernize and diversify the economy. But "institutional reforms" is simply code for a stronger rule of law, less corruption, and more robust protection of private property rights. All of these changes are unlikely absent broader political reforms that increase accountability, transparency, and competition, which would amount to a total reversal of the dominant tendency of Russian politics since Putin came to power. Although leading Russian economic officials have been talking about the need for institutional reform for years, nothing of much importance has happened.[58]

The problem of institutional reform would make Russia's economic challenges daunting enough, but focusing solely on "modernization" and human capital improvements understates the problem, because of the inherited structural misallocations of the Soviet period. Given the noncompetitiveness of much of the Russian economy, especially its industrial sector, Russia's comparative advantage is likely to remain raw material exports for decades to come.[59] Historically the most important market for Russian oil and gas was Europe, but in 2014 Russia signed a major gas deal with China in an attempt to diversify its export markets; the new pipeline is supposed to be operational by the end of 2019. If the survival of Putinism depends on *not* reforming its political and economic institutions, perhaps it can be a "raw material appendage" not only of the West but also of the East. And the political economy of Putinism will thus be dominated by the "toad sitting on the oil pipeline."

Russia is hardly unique among developing market economies in having a state that is more "predatory" than "developmental." The state can sometimes be a fundamental motor of economic development in late-developing economies. The challenge is that state officials often have strong incentives and few barriers to enriching themselves, rather than working for the public good. Russia's resource wealth—and in this sense its curse—makes it even more likely that predation takes priority over development. Further, saying that "everybody does it," while a useful reminder that Russia is not some uniquely flawed economy, both overlooks the fact that not quite everybody does it, and that few countries at Russia's level of wealth do it on the scale that Russia does. As two of Russia's leading economists put it, "Russia's institutions are much worse than they should be given the country's relatively high income."[60]

Putinomics are not unique in that the state plays a large role in the economy, or that the state's role is more predatory and dysfunctional than developmental and helpful, or that informal connections matter more than formal rules, or that regime insiders and their friends benefit disproportionally from this system. These things are sadly true in many places. However, Russia is somewhat unique in that Russia has this type of economy despite being quite "modern" (urbanized, well educated) and rich, that it is the world's largest exporter of oil and gas, that it suffers from both geographic (large, distant, cold) and Soviet structural legacies, that it is a historic great power and is fighting mightily to maintain this status, and that it is run to a large extent by a small group of officials from one city who all know each other, many of whom began their careers in the KGB and other security and intelligence agencies. Many of these latter factors make liberalizing and democratizing institutional reforms unlikely, and also act as a subconscious brake on global economic integration, which is logically understood to be necessary and desirable but is psychologically difficult, given that this same elite largely distrusts the West and believes it is out to get them. There is a contradiction in the code of Putinism between its great power aspirations, which requires economic modernization, and the emphasis on control, which blocks the necessary economic and political reforms.

Ultimately, the question is broader than that of the future of Putinomics—it is a question about the nature of the state that Putin has built. The code of Putinism helps us understand why Russia has a hyperpresidential political system, powerful informal clan networks, and a form of state capitalism highly dependent on lawyers, guns, and oil. It also explains why Putin has built a certain kind of state, one that does some things reasonably well and other things quite poorly and that may not be up to the challenges Russia faces in the twenty-first century.

5

How Russia Is Misruled

Kremlinologists will immediately recognize the hubris in the title of this chapter, so it's only fair to let everyone else in on the joke. In 1953, the year of Stalin's death, the Harvard political scientist Merle Fainsod published *How Russia Is Ruled*, a book one expert described as "the book that defined the field of Soviet studies." Fainsod's goal, as I noted in the introduction, was to describe the "anatomy and physiology" of the Soviet system. His former student Jerry Hough brought out a revised version after Fainsod's death titled *How the Soviet Union Is Governed*. With that title Hough was making two claims: that the Soviet Union and Russia were not the same thing, and that the Soviet Union was governed in a more institutionalized and even pluralistic fashion than the term "ruled" implied. In the early years of Putin's leadership, Allen Lynch published *How Russia Is Not Ruled*, a superb overview of the challenges facing post-Soviet Russia, especially because of its geographic position and historical legacies.[1]

With the title "How Russia Is Misruled," I also am making two claims. First, by talking about ruling rather than governing, I am contending that Putin's role as boss of the informal clan networks is more important than his formal role as president. In reality, of course, both roles are important, but it is in this sense that Putin "rules" more than he "governs." Second, by asserting that Russia is misruled, I am arguing that the Russian state is *relatively* weak and ineffective. A different Russian state would better be able to govern its territory and deliver services to its citizens. This would be a state in which formal institutions matter more, in which the forms of feedback and accountability established by law but crippled in practice—parliament, courts, elections, media, civil society—are allowed to operate, and in which effectiveness is more important than loyalty.

The relative weakness of the Russian state becomes apparent when it is compared to similar states—not advanced democracies like Germany or the United States, but countries that are at similar levels of development, or share a communist past, or with which it closely associates, like the BRICS countries of China, India, Brazil, and South Africa. The quality of the Russian state—the weakness of the rule of law, the amount of corruption, the failure to protect political and economic rights—is lower than it should be, given Russia's level of economic development and the comparatively modern nature—educated and urban—of its society.[2]

In saying that Russia is misruled, I am not saying that the Russian state does not do anything well, or that nothing has improved under Putin. Indeed, there are definite areas in which the Russian state has improved under Putin, and there is little question that in many respects Russians live better than they ever have. It is a claim about what one might reasonably expect, just as one might expect that the United States, given its level of wealth and the amount that it spends on healthcare, would have better health outcomes, in terms of measures like life expectancy or infant mortality. In the case of Russia, high world oil prices from 2004 to 2008, and record-high world oil prices from 2010 to 2014 (see Figure 4-2), brought in 4 trillion dollars in export revenues during those years alone. What did those 4 trillion dollars buy in terms of improvements in government services and state administration? This chapter shows that the outputs provided by the state from this oil windfall were surprisingly meager.[3]

The relative weakness of how Russia is ruled and governed is a direct consequence of the code of Putinism. Elements of the code that emphasize control, order, loyalty, and the primacy of the state, and a corresponding distrust in institutions and a reliance on what Putin called "manual steering," often led to a set of priorities and an approach to administration that is inefficient. This chapter shows how Russia is misruled under Putinism in four steps: by looking at the decision-making process under Putin, considering how the quality of governance should be evaluated, providing some examples of rule and misrule from different spheres, and finally with comparative data on how Russia measures up to its peers. Ultimately, this is a story of disappointing outcomes and missed opportunities.

The President and the Boss

Constitutionally, the president of the Russian Federation "shall determine the guidelines of the internal and foreign policies of the State." Just as in the United States, the president is the most important player in the policy process, from setting the agenda nationally to overseeing executive branch implementation of laws. So far, so good. What is different in Russia, and other electoral authoritarian systems with a powerful president, is that the role of other branches of power, in particular the legislature, is significantly smaller than in true democracies, and also less in reality than the constitution prescribes. The Presidential Administration is the driving force behind most policy change, although the various executive-branch ministries also maintain considerable power.[4]

If we think about political decision-making in terms of checks and balances, in Russia the key actors are not the ones described in the constitution but the informal clan networks. Russia's leading scholarly expert on the elite, Olga Kryshtanovskaya, observed that in the United States the system of weights and counterbalances is based on institutions; in Russia, it is more of a "hybrid state" of both institutions and clans, with clans being de facto more important. Maintaining the "power of the tsar," she argued, is of great consequence. The decision-making process is more autocratic, "like in the army." She believes that the process is intellectually weak, because there are not serious discussions, but only "consultations" conducted by Putin with various key players. Kryshtanovskaya, who has consulted for the Kremlin in the past, noted that there is no systematic attempt to develop scenarios and think through multiple possible courses of action, a process rejected by the Russian system as too unpredictable. A well-connected editor, similarly, contended that Putin's assistants provide information and opinions, but ultimately have little influence on him, and that Putin's tendency to make decisions on his own often leads to mistakes and negative consequences. The system's "biggest minus," according to another journalist, is that everything turns around one person, with all key decisions taken by Putin. Even top figures like the minister of defense, the minister of foreign affairs, and the secretary of the security council are, according to one Russian scholar, "decision-takers, not decision-makers."[5]

The inability to take any decision without Putin is a "big problem," according to one expert, especially because Putin is reluctant to delegate. This can drag out the decision-making process, because people at lower levels in the state are hesitant to act or take initiative. Ivan Rodin, the politics editor at a leading Moscow newspaper, elaborated on this issue. With the political system built as a vertical, all key decisions belong to Putin. But obviously it is not physically possible for Putin to do everything, so various proposals have to be prepared for him. Rodin claims that Putin is careful to get alternative sources of information, especially after 2005, when the Kremlin was caught by surprise by protests in response to changes in social benefits for pensioners and veterans. Further, Rodin notes that people who have known Putin for a long time say that he often drags his feet on making decisions, because he worries about making a mistake. By delaying a decision to the last possible moment, however, Putin narrows the possible options, which often leads to suboptimal results.[6]

A wonderful example of the nature of political decision-making under Putinism comes to us from, of all places, a meeting of the executive committee of the Russian Football (Soccer) Union; a tape of the proceedings was leaked to an opposition newspaper.[7] In July 2014 they were asked to consider an application from football clubs in recently annexed Crimea to join the Football Union. Vitaliy Mutko, minister of sport at the time, recommended that they be accepted into the Union. By this point you will not be surprised to learn that Mutko grew up in Leningrad, and worked in the mayor's office in St. Petersburg with Putin. Attending the meeting were the owners of some of Russia's top football clubs, including several billionaires, as well as Vladimir Yakunin, Putin's close ally and then head of Russian Railways, and Sergey Stepashin, another Petersburger entrusted with multiple top positions by both Yeltsin and Putin.

The proposal to accept the Crimean clubs into the Russian league immediately ran into trouble. One of the billionaires spoke up to note that the members of the executive committee might be placed under international sanctions. Another member wondered aloud who would compensate him for his financial losses, and another mused that Russia might have the 2018 World Cup taken away from it. At this point Yakunin had heard enough. He rounded on the group, accusing them of "crawling on their bellies before them [the West]," declared that Putin was "standing on the parapet alone," and suggested that those who did not support Putin should either get out of the country or behave like proper citizens.

The club owners then adopted a different tack. Of course, they proclaimed, they would do what their country demanded of them, even if it meant big losses. One of them proclaimed he would support the decision "if there is a direct order, no question!" But perhaps, he suggested, maybe Putin doesn't want this—shouldn't we consult with him? After all, a different owner observed, Russia's biggest state-controlled corporations—Gazprom, Rosneft, Russian Railways, Sberbank—aren't going into Crimea, and this isn't by accident. Yakunin proclaimed that it would be "unethical" to contact the president, and Stepashin imagined what he would say to Putin, speculating that Putin would tell him to "buzz off!"—or perhaps something stronger— and that Putin would be right to do so. Why do we need an order, Stepashin insisted, when Crimea is already legally part of Russian territory? One of the owners countered that if Russia was deprived of the 2018 World Cup, then Yakunin and Stepashin would be the ones who would take responsibility for it. A wealthy oligarch noted that he had spent twenty-five years building a company worth 30 billion—incidentally, this is in dollars, not rubles—and that he had 250,000 employees. He was, he insisted, prepared to go fight for his country if necessary, but he was only "prepared to discard everything he had done for twenty-five years" if they consulted with "the first person" in advance. Another owner complained that it was unfair to question their patriotism; after all, with the kind of money they had, they could be sitting abroad relaxing if they weren't true patriots. In the end, the group agreed to wait a few days and check to see if they would be doing the right thing by bringing the Crimean clubs into their league. One of the owners summarized their position, agreeing to do what "the boss"—meaning Putin—wanted. A week after the initial meeting they formally accepted the three Crimean football clubs into their league.

The whole episode is quite enlightening about the nature of decision-making. First, even professional sports associations feel the need to clear important decisions with the president. Imagine this incident multiplied by 100 around the country every day and we can see how decision-making could become ineffective or even paralyzed. Second, Yakunin's status as a member of the Putin clan is more important than any formal title as head of Russian Railways, and he is able to trade on his closeness to Putin to essentially browbeat the other members. Stepashin is also given considerable deference as a longtime associate of Putin from St. Petersburg, even though he is not in the inner circle. Third, although the club owners understood that they had to display their fealty to Putin—pledging their willingness even to fight for their country or ruin their business if necessary—they did fight back within the available limits to try to preserve their interests.

Another flaw in the decision-making process is the attempt to build a top-down "vertical of power" centered in the Kremlin and emanating downward through the multiple levels of power in Russia's ostensibly federal system. But in a country as large and sprawling and heterogeneous as Russia, it is impossible to control everything from Moscow. One year into Putin's first term, in 2001, I met with Russian political geographer Leonid Smirnyagin, who had been an adviser to Boris Yeltsin on regional issues. At the time he noted that the old traditional situation in Russia was one in which there was strong central control in principle, but in practice local interests were very powerful, even though not considered fully legitimate. "Moscow is awesome, but far away" was how Smirnyagin summarized the situation. Fourteen years later, in 2015, Smirnyagin suggested little had changed under Putin, and in some ways things were worse. "Vertical of power" was more a myth than a reality, with Moscow in some ways weaker. Back when Yeltsin was president, regional governors could be dealt with as the representative of local power and interests. Under Putin, with governors de facto appointed by him after 2004, governors were now separate from local clans and interests, more interested in pleasing the president than the voters or local elite groups. Ultimately, Smirnyagin said, loyalty matters more than effectiveness. Another expert on Russia's regions made a similar point, noting that governors merely had to deliver good election results in national elections, keep their regions quiet, and fulfill presidential decrees. With governors only looking to the center, they know their own regions poorly and make mistakes in dealing with local elites. A pro-Putin analyst suggested the same thing, observing that the "vertical of power" was considerably overstated, with regional and local leaders frequently pursuing their own interests, and that having the trust of the president didn't necessarily mean they were effective locally.[8]

It is important to stress that, although the decision-making process is often flawed, with too many decisions pushed up to the top, poor interagency coordination, and behind-the-scenes clan battles as the most meaningful factor in policy struggles, decisions clearly sometimes are motivated by the desire to make real improvements in the lives of average Russians. The fact that the Soviet Union was a welfare state, albeit of a very specific type, means that people expect the government to deliver certain services—badly, perhaps, but they still expect some welfare state provisions. Free healthcare and education, for example, are still considered basic rights, even if in reality hospitals and schools, and doctors and teachers, often employ a variety of schemes to extort "donations" from patients and parents. Basic utilities like electricity and heating, and public transportation on trains, buses, and subways, are very much part of the Russian landscape. For example, when a price dispute between the state Russian Railroads company and regional governments led to the shutdown of commuter train service in multiple regions at the beginning of 2015 (that is, in the middle of winter), Putin acted quickly to get service restored.[9]

This expectation among both the population and elites that the state must continue to provide certain services of a welfare state distinguishes Russian misrule from more authentic versions of kleptocracy—the rule of thieves. Karen Dawisha in *Putin's Kleptocracy* gathers an impressive amount of evidence for systematic corruption among Putin's close confidants; even if she can't provide ironclad proof for all of the accusations, something is clearly rotten in Russia. What Dawisha doesn't discuss is what the Russian state does when it is not stealing. Even if the Russian state often underperforms and underinvests in human and physical capital—education, healthcare, infrastructure—it has not abandoned these responsibilities, and sometimes makes real improvements. In other words, Russia has kleptocratic behavior but it is not a full-blown kleptocracy like the Philippines under Ferdinand Marcos (1965–1986), or Equatorial Guinea for the last four decades. Equatorial Guinea, on paper Africa's richest country with per capita GDP of around $25,000 due to the combination of massive oil wealth and a small population of less than one million, has been described as "an almost perfect kleptocracy" because the president and his cronies keep almost all of the oil wealth for themselves and share very little of it with the population. Putin's Russia, despite its flaws, is very different from this model.[10]

Putin and his team have a series of goals that go beyond mere stealing. Some of these, such as the provision of the basic services of a modern welfare state to the masses, are a product of shared expectations among elites and masses. Failures of government services can affect his mass popularity and the perception among the elite that he is the guarantor of stability—and thus his hold on power. Failures also can be a potential source of protests, such as those that broke out in 2005 over the change in social benefits delivery, when the government tried to replace services like free public transportation for veterans and pensioners with cash payments. More generally, much of Putin's popularity up through 2008 depended on his ability to deliver economic growth and rising incomes, and the perception that he was rebuilding Russian state power and providing order and stability. Today, after the annexation of Crimea, war in Ukraine and Syria, and several years of economic recession and falling living standards, the justification for Putin's rule has changed. As one expert put it, "Putinism is no longer underpinned by the promise of economic growth but by the vision of a resurgent Russian empire."[11]

Thus, consistent with the code of Putinism, over time there has been a clear shift toward a wager on the allure of great power assertion. In the face of economic stagnation, Russians have been asked to sacrifice prosperity for national greatness. This is the model of Russia as a besieged fortress. Russian commentators referred to the battle between "the television and the refrigerator"—the television broadcasting stories about external threats and national resurgence, and the refrigerator becoming barer due to inflationary food prices and bans on the import of a variety of Western foodstuffs.[12] In this battle, an obvious question arises—what should be the standards by which we evaluate how Russia is ruled? Does international standing matter more than popular living standards? Should we measure government performance against its own claims, against popular expectations, or against certain objective criteria?

What Do Russians Want, and What Do They Think They Get?

Economists have an agreed measure of the size of a country's economy, gross domestic product (GDP), which measures the total value of goods and services produced in a country. With GDP, economists can also calculate change from year to year to measure growth (or decline) in the size of an economy, and the relative wealth of a country by measuring GDP per capita. Political scientists, in contrast, do not have an agreed measure of how well a country is governed. Francis Fukuyama, in a recent attempt to make sense of this important issue, defines governance as "a government's ability to make and enforce rules and to deliver services." Fukuyama discusses four different ways of conceiving of good governance—procedural, capacity, output, and autonomy. Procedural approaches emphasize merit in hiring and promotion, technical expertise, and compliance with rules and laws. Capacity measures focus on the extent to which a government can perform basic core functions, such as collecting taxes. Output indicators are designed to look at government performance by measuring basic outcomes in such areas as education (test scores), health (life expectancy), and public safety (murder rates). The notion of bureaucratic autonomy proposes that good governance comes from the ability of agencies to pursue publicly mandated goals without undue micromanaging from politicians or "capture" by nonstate actors such as big business. All of these approaches have their pros and cons, and tell us something about how a country is governed. There is no consensus, however, about which approach is best, and although there has been considerable progress in devising measures to compare countries to each other and to themselves over time, there is not now, and may not ever be, a simple number comparable to GDP to assess how well a country is governed.[13]

Absent that simple measure of governance quality, a more complicated but perhaps more interesting task awaits us. Already, by indicating that Putinism prioritizes ruling over governing, I have suggested that Russia has problems in the realms of procedure and autonomy. The starkest example of how trust and loyalty dominate over technical expertise in hiring starts at the very top in Russia where, as demonstrated in chapters 3 and 4, many of the top positions in the state and the state-controlled sectors of the economy are occupied by Putin loyalists whom he has known for decades. This problem exists at all levels of government; one study found that 85 percent of those in state service in Russia got their job through either direct personal connections or a recommendation from a friend or relative. Russian bureaucracy, although not without technical and educational standards, has historically depended more on "who you know" than "what you know."[14]

The rest of this chapter examines Russian rule and governance from multiple angles, focusing especially on what Fukuyama calls "capacity" and "output." We delve into specific issues, such as the quality of roads and healthcare. We look at key episodes, such as the Sochi Olympics and corruption allegations against the police. And we look at some of the cross-national measures of the quality of governance and see how Russia compares to its peers. Overall, Putinism as a form of rule doesn't look that great.

Perhaps I am looking at the wrong thing, however. In June 2015 I had a long conversation with the Russian journalist Olga Vlasova, who works for the pro-Kremlin journal *Expert*. Vlasova argued that it is a mistake to evaluate the Russian state by the criteria set out by Fukuyama, in which the most important thing is whether the state adheres to the rule of law or is effective in providing services to the population. Thinking about the quality of the state in terms of a set of tasks to carry out, and how effectively it does so, is the wrong approach for Russia. What matters to Russians, Vlasova maintained, is whether its rulers maintain the state's independence and geopolitical position. Given Russia's geographic situation and cultural diversity, there are justified fears of separatism and the disintegration of the state. Not being weak and not breaking up are the core tasks, very different from the United States and Europe. Putin is evaluated by average Russians, she said, based on geopolitics, not whether they are treated fairly by the traffic police.[15]

This is an intriguing idea—is Vlasova right? Well, yes and no. She is right that many Russians highly value Russia's international position and make it a top priority. When asked what they expect out of their president on the eve of every election from 1996 to 2012, one of the most popular answers (between 43 and 58 percent) from average Russians has been "returning to Russia the status of a respected great power." This was the most popular answer in 2004, 2008, and 2012. The only other answer consistently in the same range (between 45 and 58 percent) over the same sixteen-year period was "strengthen law and order."[16]

Several qualifications, however, are in order. When asked a somewhat similar but more specific question, what problems should Putin focus on solving, the most popular response between 2006 and 2014 was "economic growth, growing the economy" (53–73 percent). Foreign policy and security issues, such as "strengthening Russia's position in the international arena" and "strengthening the country's defense capability," were much lower priorities, getting support from 14–26 percent of respondents. Strengthening the economy, improving the lives of ordinary people, and fighting corruption all received more support than strengthening Russia internationally.[17]

The second qualification concerns what it means to be a "respected great power." On the one hand, the demand for international respect is a core component of the code of Putinism, and one that resonates with average Russians. On the other hand, when asked what the features of a great power are, in a 2016 poll the most popular answer was a "high standard of living" (38 percent), closely followed by a "developed modern economy" (37 percent). Having "powerful armed forces," in contrast, drew the support of 26 percent of respondents. Going back to 2003, previous polls show that the most important feature of a great power is a "developed modern economy" (50–55 percent). In general, Russians seem to believe a strong economy and high standards of living are the key to being a great power, and not just a strong military—although they support that also.[18]

In recent years, particularly since the annexation of Crimea in 2014, Putin gets particularly high marks for his defense and foreign policy performance. Two of his top three achievements, according to polls, were raising the defense capability of the country and strengthening Russia's international position. Putin also was rated highly for bringing order to the country, solving the Chechen problem, raising hope and optimism, improving living standards, and developing the economy. Earlier polls rated Putin most highly for raising living standards (consistently in first or second place prior to 2014), strengthening

Russia's international position, raising hope and optimism, and developing the economy. Areas in which Putin performed poorly include the fight against corruption (usually his worst rating), restraining the influence of the oligarchs, and fighting crime. In 2015 Putin's biggest failures also included raising living standards and developing the economy, an obvious reflection of the recession and a topic on which public opinion was split. To the extent that Russians associate being a "respected great power" with economic development and well-being, as the polls just mentioned suggest, Russia's current economic problems could become a problem for Putin if they persist—a big reversal from earlier, when economic performance was seen as his strong suit.[19]

One other set of questions from public opinion polls also bears on what Russians want from their government. Surveys show that Russians don't think that ordinary people have much say in government or that officials care much about what average people think, and they don't think government policies represent the majority's wishes. Rather, Russians tend to say that Putin's activities reflect the interests of the *siloviki* (security, military, and law enforcement agencies and personnel), oligarchs and big business, and bureaucrats. Blue- and white-collar workers and peasants are considered a low priority, with Putin's activities seen as reflecting their interests by less than a quarter of Russians; middle- and upper-middle class interests are considered slightly more important (generally around 25 percent of those polled).[20]

Overall, polls suggest that it is not true that Russians don't care about the sorts of things that social scientists like Fukuyama have in mind when they talk about "governance." Yes, Russians want Russia to be a "respected great power." But they also want a strong economy and better living standards for average people. For most of his time in power Putin has received strong support in those areas, even though Russians don't think Putin is particularly responsive to average working- and middle-class citizens. With the economy in recession and living standards in decline in recent years, Putin's strongest support is no longer for the state of the economy but for his international activities—the "television over the refrigerator." Now it is time for a more concrete examination of what the Russian state does and how well it does it.

The Russian State in Action

The legendary American football coach Vince Lombardi stated, "The measure of who we are is what we do with what we have." This statement is usually used as a source of inspiration, plastered across posters with uplifting backgrounds of training athletes or beautiful vistas. But it is also a pretty good way of thinking about how to evaluate government performance. Given a certain set of resources, what priorities does a state have, and how well does it do at realizing those priorities? To delve deeper into the nature of Russian rule and misrule under Putin, this section discusses some central government tasks. First, we consider the broad-brush question of how Russia spends its money. Then we delve into four specific policy areas. Three of them—building and maintaining roads, healthcare, and law enforcement—are core tasks of any modern government. The fourth, the 2014 Sochi Winter Olympics, was arguably the signature megaproject of Putin's presidency to date (in 2018 Russia will host the World Cup, another Putin megaproject). The Russian state had considerable resources at its disposal over the last eighteen years— how well did it spend its money, and what did it deliver with that spending?

The Master of Coin: How Does the State Spend Its Money?

"The Master of Coin" is the person responsible for state finances in the fictional Game of Thrones. This is a position of great power and responsibility, which also invites considerable intrigue, because money makes the world go round (as well as fighting and sex, if we are to believe the Game of Thrones). At the most general level, a state is what a state spends money on. Although not telling us anything about what it does well, looking at spending does give us a decent sense of what it values. Figure 5-1 shows the trend in Russian spending on four major categories: defense, internal security (police, secret police, prosecutors), healthcare, and education.[21]

Several things stand out about the Russian budget. First, the amount spent on defense and internal security dwarfs spending on healthcare and education. Second, spending on defense as a percentage of the budget actually fell in Putin's first decade, while spending on healthcare increased, albeit from a very low level. This seeming fall in defense spending is misleading, though; in absolute terms military spending also increased considerably. But the rapidly growing economy from 1999 to 2007 meant that the overall size of the budget increased faster than the increase in defense spending. In fact, defense spending from 2000 to 2007 more than doubled, and spending on internal security more than tripled. Third, both internal and external security were designated key priorities between 2010 and 2015. Defense went from less than 13 percent of the budget to over 20 percent in five years, much

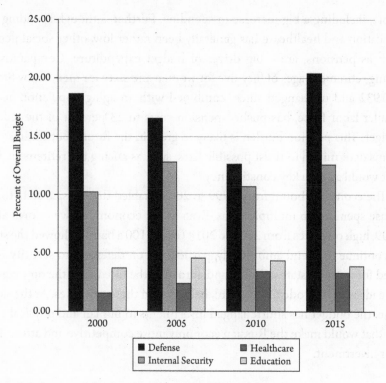

Figure 5-1 Russian Federal Budget Expenditures by Category

of which went to a massive ten-year arms buildup, while internal security increased from 11 to 13 percent. Education and healthcare declined some- what as a priority in this period. With the economy slowing down, forcing Putin and Medvedev to choose between guns and butter, they opted for guns. A Russian deputy prime minister confirmed this choice in 2017, stating that the government intended to continue its rearmament program until 2020; only after that point could more spending be devoted to healthcare, educa- tion, and infrastructure.[22]

Defense and security spending increased considerably as a share of the budget from 2010 to 2015, but prior to that defense spending in particular was not high at all compared to the United States, although it was higher as a share of the economy compared to European Union countries, the other BRICS (Brazil, India, China, and South Africa), and most other post-Soviet countries. Thus, it would be a mistake to see Putin pursuing a sustained policy of militarization from the beginning. Defense rearmament became a priority after the Russian-Georgian War of 2008. Although Russia prevailed easily, the war exposed multiple weaknesses that led to a concerted military reform effort, including a big increase in spending. Further, although spending on education and healthcare has generally been rather low, other social needs, such as pensions, are a big driver of budget expenditure. Comparatively young retirement ages of fifty-five for women and sixty for men, set by Stalin in 1932 and unchanged since, combined with an aging population and a smaller labor force, has pushed pension costs to 23 percent of the federal budget. This pension burden is likely to grow in the future, but Putin so far seems determined to resist possible fixes, such as raising the retirement age, that would anger a key constituency.[23]

The economic boom from 1999 to 2008 enabled the Russian state to increase spending in multiple areas. Even as the economy slowed down after 2009, high oil prices from 2000 to 2014 (over $100 a barrel) allowed the state to continue to spend ambitiously, particularly on defense and security. The need for a strong state at home and abroad in the face of hostile opponents, core ideas of the code of Putinism, help explain these priorities. At the same time, the budget has shortchanged investments in human and physical capital that would make the Russian economy more competitive and attract further investment.

Idiots and Roads

"Idiots and roads (*duraki i dorogi*)" are Russia's two misfortunes, according to a common saying. Given Russia's vast size and harsh climate, an effective transportation network is both necessary and a considerable challenge. Russian roads in some way typify all the diversity of Russia. In Moscow or St. Petersburg, one can be stuck in one's car without moving, enveloped in a traffic jam that will take hours to clear. Indeed, Russia's two largest cities lead Europe in traffic jams, and are in the top ten worldwide in terms of gridlock. In rural Russia, one can also be stuck in one's car without moving, because the rainy season has turned dirt-track roads to impassable mud pits. Even in the highways between major cities, one can sit in traffic for hours or even days without moving. In November–December 2012 a big snowstorm stranded ten thousand vehicles on the Moscow–St. Petersburg highway for days in a standstill that stretched for 70–125 miles. An American journalist drove the Moscow–St. Petersburg highway in 2013 and reported that "the surface of the highway, while paved, varies from corduroy to jaw-rattling patchwork. Sometimes it has four lanes, sometimes two, with few medians and frequently no lane markings at all. . . . It is the most heavily traveled cargo route in Russia, and yet for truck drivers complying with safety regulations, it takes twenty-four hours to travel between the two cities."[24]

The situation on Russian roads, including highways, is considerably worse further from Moscow. A Russian professor specializing in transportation issues notes that the Russian road configuration looks more like a star than a grid, because all roads lead to Moscow. Two-thirds of spending on roads takes place within thirty miles of Moscow. The Lena Highway in the Russian Far East gained particular notoriety; even though it was a designated federal highway, until 2014 sections of it were not paved, frequently making the highway impassible when it is not frozen. It is nicknamed the "highway from hell," and multiple websites have featured the Lena Highway in their lists of worst roads in the world, with photos of cars and trucks stuck in deep mud.[25]

The poor state of Russian road infrastructure frequently generates absurdist tales worthy of the nineteenth century Russian-Ukrainian author Nikolay Gogol. My good friend Irina, from St. Petersburg, has a dacha (country house) several hours south of the city, a place I have visited many times. When the Soviet Union still existed, it was possible to get to the dacha by taking a train to the nearest town and then a bus to a nearby recreational facility, from which one could walk to the village. The state-sponsored recreational facility closed down after the Soviet collapse, so a car became necessary to get to the dacha, especially if one had to bring supplies. The small village of dachas was on a river, and there was a rickety wooden bridge across a connecting stream to get to the village. Crossing that bridge in a car was a terrifying experience, especially after Gazprom workers accidentally rammed the bridge and knocked it askew. Eventually the bridge collapsed, and Gazprom was in no hurry to fix it. Villagers appealed to the local authorities, who said that only three people in the village were actually registered there (Russians have to register at a primary place of residence, and most of the dacha owners were registered in the city). Therefore, it would be cheaper for the district authorities to simply move those three people to town than to build a new bridge. In the meantime, several dacha owners who were quite wealthy came up with their own private solutions. One person had a helicopter that he would call when he needed to get stuff across the stream to his house. Another person had a seaplane that would take off from a nearby lake and land on the river. And a third person bought an old armored personnel carrier and could cross the stream that way. Everyone else had to leave their cars on the other side of the stream, wade across, and carry their belongings and supplies to their dachas. Eventually, the local authorities relented and replaced the bridge.

Poor-quality roads are considered a key reason for the deadly nature of Russian roads. On a per capita basis, Russia has about twenty traffic fatalities per 100,000 population per year. This is roughly twice the rate in the United States and four times the rate in Germany. If we compare Russia to some of its European peers at similar levels of economic development, such as Croatia, Latvia, and Lithuania, we find a similar discrepancy. The annual traffic fatality rate in all three countries is about half that in Russia, despite being much more densely populated and having a lot more cars per capita. Russia does somewhat better compared to the other BRICS. In terms of traffic fatalities per capita, Russia does slightly better than South Africa, about the same as Brazil, and considerably worse than India and China. If we compare the BRICS in terms of fatalities per number of cars, however, Russia actually does the best, with China, South Africa, and India having two or three times the number of deaths per vehicle.[26]

Putin has been very critical of the state of Russia's road network, and the effectiveness to date of efforts to improve it. In 2014 he noted that Russian roads are often of poor quality and that a lot of money is wasted on efforts to improve it; he referred to "black holes" in the budget through which money disappears, with some sections of road fixed year after year, using outdated methods from the Soviet period. In 2011 he announced an ambitious plan of building new roads over the next decade, but the 2015 recession meant that spending was cut back considerably. For this plan to be realized the pace of road construction would have to be four times what it was during Putin's first two terms as president from 2000 to 2008, when the economy was growing rapidly. National road construction in that period was actually barely half of that achieved under Boris Yeltsin, despite the economic boom of the 2000s.[27]

Obviously, the size and climate of Russia are a major factor in the poor state of Russian roads. However, many experts contend that corruption and waste in road construction are also important contributors to Russia's problematic roads. A graphic prepared by the state news agency RIA Novosti in 2010 put the average cost of road construction for one kilometer of road as 17.6 million dollars in Russia, compared to 6.9 million in the European Union, 5.9 million in the United States, and 2.2 million dollars per kilometer in China. Russian state television claimed that the cost per kilometer of a four-lane highway was three to four times higher in Russia than in China or Brazil. The state agency responsible for Russia's road system claims that these comparisons are not valid, basically because the critics are comparing apples and oranges, using estimates with different inputs for different countries, for different road types, and so on. In some respects, this response seems to be well grounded, although they should probably tell their president and prime minister, who also have cited similar figures. For example, Medvedev stated he considered road construction a luxury given how much money is wasted, maintaining that costs could be reduced by at least 30 percent by introducing modern technology and eliminating corruption. Similarly, the head of the State Audit Chamber unfavorably compared the costs of road construction in Russia to those in Europe, the United States, and China, blaming poor control and management as well as "kickbacks," a form of corruption in which a percentage of the costs of a contract are paid to the bureaucrat ("kicked back") who signs off on the deal.[28]

One of the most prominent highway projects under Putin is the construction of a badly needed new toll highway connecting Moscow and St. Petersburg. The route of the new highway passes through a forest in the Moscow suburbs, and local and national environmentalists rallied to protect the forest. A local journalist who had campaigned against the highway was violently attacked and later died from his injuries. Investigations showed that one of the key players in the project is Arkadiy Rotenberg, Putin's childhood judo friend. Rotenberg was first on the list of "kings of state orders" compiled by the Russian version of *Forbes* three years straight, from 2014 to 2016 (see chapter 4). In 2015 Rotenberg's construction company was awarded the multi-billion-dollar contract to build a bridge connecting the Russian mainland with Crimea, which currently can only be accessed by ferry or through Ukraine. This 3-billion-dollar project, several sources claim, is causing huge cuts in other road and bridge projects.[29]

In 2015, well into Putin's rule, the World Economic Forum's Global Competitiveness report ranked Russia 124th out of 139 countries on the quality of its roads.[30] Overall, the failure to significantly improve Russia's road infrastructure in terms of quantity or quality, the relatively high rates of traffic fatalities, the high construction costs (arguably caused by corruption), and crony dealing for major road construction projects, is a good example of how Russia is misruled.

To Live and Die in Russia

Are Russians dying at uncommonly high rates, and, if so, is the government to blame? Critics think so, with one Russian-American journalist contending, "Russians [are] dying in numbers, and at ages, and of causes never seen in any other country" not at war.[31] Although there is some truth in these claims, it is also true that Russians are living longer under Putin than they were in the 1990s, and the government deserves some credit for recent improvements. Russia is not doing as well as it should—partially a product of misrule—but it has started doing better.

In many respects, Russian health and mortality statistics are shocking. Russian population declined by more than 5 million people between 1990 and 2010, the second biggest drop in the world, although quite a few other east European countries had a proportional drop that was even larger. Russian life expectancy in 2010 was no higher than it was in 1990—indeed, it was barely higher than it was in 1960. Male life expectancy was particularly low, registering below sixty for more than a decade from 1993 to 2005, although climbing after that. Survival curves for Russian men—the probability that adult men will live to a certain age—matched those of African men. Male life expectancy is low because of high rates of cardiovascular disease and high rates of deaths from "external causes"—accidents, suicides, murders, and so on.[32]

Thinking about Russian health, and what it might tell us about how Russia is ruled, three basic issues arise: How does Russia compare to its peer countries? What is the trajectory for health outcomes under Putin? And to what extent is the government responsible? In terms of comparison to its peer countries, by most measures Russia does not do very well. Life expectancy is perhaps the most widely used indicator of health for cross-national comparison. According to World Health Organization statistics, Russian life expectancy in 2015 was seventy, placing it in 110th place, just below North Korea and Bolivia, countries much poorer than Russia. Life expectancy for men, according to the WHO, was sixty-five, putting it in 127th place along with Gabon and Mongolia. Russia does poorly compared to other countries at similar levels of economic development in not only life expectancy but also in such health and wellness indicators as the obesity rate, deaths due to air pollution, premature deaths from noncommunicable diseases, water and sanitation quality, and the suicide rate.[33]

If Russian health indicators are quite poor comparatively, the good news is that the trajectory has been upward for over a decade. The fertility rate has gone up, the death rate has gone down, the number of deaths from external causes has declined considerably, and life expectancy increased markedly from 2003 to 2013, rising from around 65 to around 70 in the space of a decade. Although Russia's demographic picture in the long run is still not great, with the population inevitably declining in coming decades as the number of women of child-bearing age drops markedly and the population as a whole gets older, the demographic picture improved considerably as the economy and living standards grew.[34]

Do Putin and the Russian government deserve credit for this turnaround? On the one hand, as Russian experts have noted, the recent improvement is to a certain extent "compensatory—demographics have only just reached the point they were at when the Soviet Union collapsed."[35] Russia still lags far behind most countries at a similar level of development. On the other hand, to the extent that Putin deserves some credit for the economic growth of the 2000s—and, as discussed in chapter 4, he deserves some but far from all—then the improvement in health indicators can in part be attributed to Putin and the Russian government. What we really need to consider with our third hand, however, is specific initiatives undertaken by the government to improve the healthcare system and Russian health.

Here the picture is mixed, but with definite positive steps for which the government should take credit. In 2005 healthcare became a "national priority project," and funding increased considerably over the next five years, both in absolute terms and as a share of the budget, as shown above. However, also as noted, this relative priority to healthcare lessened after 2010. Healthcare spending both in terms of its share of the economy and on a per capita basis lags well behind that of the world's thirty-four leading capitalist countries in the Organization for Economic Cooperation and Development (OECD), and indeed was lower than that of all OECD countries except Mexico. Public spending on healthcare as a percentage of GDP in Russia has been around 3.5 percent of GDP, compared to around 6–7 percent for the wealthier OECD countries.[36]

The more important issue is not so much the amount of public funding for healthcare, although that is obviously important, but the efficiency with which that money is spent. As a 2012 OECD report remarked dryly, "There are doubts as to whether the Russian health system is getting good value for the resources it spends." For example, Russian expenditures on healthcare per capita were roughly similar to the amount spent in countries at similar levels of development, such as Mexico, Turkey, Chile, and Poland, but life expectancy in Russia lags well behind these countries. According to the OECD, Russia's "health outcomes are similar to those achieved by some countries which spend 30 to 40% less."[37]

Judy Twigg, an expert on Russian healthcare, observes that despite the boost in healthcare spending, the quality of Russian hospitals and clinics is often "woefully backward." She notes that 40 percent of facilities, according to official reports, require major repairs or rebuilding, nearly a third don't have hot running water, 10 percent lack central heating, and a similar percentage lack sewage. The OECD report also called attention to the poor state of hospitals and clinics and the frequent lack of relevant supplies.[38] That has certainly been my, thankfully limited, experience with Russian medical facilities. The first encounter was in the 2000s, when I went to visit a friend at a Moscow hospital. Despite being located in the wealthy capital, the hospital was dark, drab, and depressing, and seemed strangely deserted. The second experience was thousands of miles from Moscow, in the remote and relatively poor Altay Republic, on the southern border of Russia next to Kazakhstan and Mongolia. My son cut his leg and needed stitches (I was teaching in St. Petersburg for a semester, and we were visiting friends in a small village in Altay). Both the village doctor and the clinic in a nearby town, inexplicably, had no equipment to do stitches, so we had to drive to the children's hospital in the republic capital to get care. To this day, one of the few sentences in Russian that my son remembers is "I have two stitches (*u menya dva shva*)."

One final reason Russia has such poor healthcare ratings is only indirectly related to government policy or effectiveness—the terrible lifestyle decisions made by many Russians. Heart disease, cancer, and deaths from factors such as injury, suicide, poisoning, traffic deaths, and other accidents are all quite high in Russia compared to many countries around the world. Some of the most commonly cited factors causing these high mortality rates of preventable causes include alcohol consumption—especially of vodka, and binge drinking of vodka—smoking, poor diet, and other unhealthy lifestyle choices.[39]

The Russian government has begun to respond appropriately to this challenge, particularly by dealing with excessive alcohol and tobacco use. In the last decade Russia has adopted a series of policies that have proved effective elsewhere in reducing alcohol and tobacco use, including higher taxes, restricted selling hours for alcohol, limitations on advertising, banning smoking in public spaces (including bars and restaurants and public transport), and public health warnings and campaigns. Although, arguably, taxes could be raised further—cigarettes and alcohol are still cheap compared to most of Russia's European neighbors—the policy direction pursued by Putin and Medvedev in this area is clearly appropriate. Tobacco and alcohol consumption are down dramatically over the last decade. Even Putin's own personal example as the abstemious, self-disciplined sports and fitness fanatic may be playing a positive role—although few Russians will be working out in the $3,220 silk and cashmere track suit that Putin donned for a photo-op with Medvedev in 2015.[40]

Overall, Russia's health profile is bad but getting better. An infusion of rubles, especially in the mid to late-2000s, certainly helped this improvement, as did economic growth more generally. Comparative analysis suggests that Russia still gets less bang for the buck than it should from its health-care spending, a symptom of misrule. But the recent focus on public health measures to combat smoking and drinking is just what the doctor ordered, so overall the Putinist state gets decent marks for its efforts in this realm.

Law Enforcement: A Disordered Police State

Upholding law and order is a key state task everywhere in the world. European kings and queens, and Russian tsars and tsarinas, dreamed of creating a "well-ordered police state" to enforce their rule. The masses, on the other hand, dream of a law enforcement system that protects them, not represses them.

Russia's police state under Putin is more dis-ordered than well-ordered. A fitting symbol of this disorder is former police Major Denis Yevsyukov, a Moscow cop who went on a drunken shooting spree in a Moscow supermarket in April 2009, killing two people and wounding seven. It quickly came out that Yevsyukov had a whole series of blemishes on his service record, but that he had been protected through informal clan connections—specifically, his father had served in Kursk with the then-head of the Moscow police. The "Yevsyukov affair," as it came to be called, ignited a firestorm of criticism of the police, including from within the ranks of the police themselves.[41]

Problems in the quality of Russian law enforcement are well known to Putin and other Russian leaders, and have been repeatedly criticized throughout his rule. In 2005, Putin stated, "We need law enforcement organs that honest citizens will be proud of, rather than crossing to the other side of the street when they see a man in uniform." A former police general and the head of the Duma Security Committee remarked that the quality of personnel in the law enforcement organs was so bad that many of those serving "in different circumstances might be sitting in prison." This recognition of persistent problems with Russian police and law enforcement led Medvedev to launch a major reform effort, which culminated with a new "Law on the Police" in 2011 and a purge of many high-ranking police generals.[42]

The performance of law enforcement under Putin is generally indicative of bad governance and misrule. Corruption is rife. Russian cops shake
down average citizens, run protection rackets overseeing private businesses
(called "roofing" in Russian parlance), enter disputes between companies if
paid to do so ("raiding"), and often have links with organized crime. Sergey
Stepashin, the St. Petersburg Putin ally mentioned earlier when discussing
soccer, stated in 2007, "law enforcement employees themselves are going
down the criminal path and committing such serious crimes as kidnapping,
drug trafficking, and 'roofing' commercial structures." A well-known Russian
commentator wrote in 2008, "The most striking thing about everyday life in
the Russia of Vladimir Putin . . . is the incredible corruption of the courts, the
police, the special forces—all the institutions that are supposed to uphold
law and order in a democracy and that in Russia today have been transformed
into a cancer that is devouring the state."[43]

By some indicators, it appears that over time under Putin the state of law
and order has gotten better in Russia. For example, the official murder rate
has been on a consistent downward trajectory for over a decade. In 2002 the
homicide rate was over 30 per 100,000, but it dropped to 20 per 100,000 in
2007 and in 2014 was down to 9 per 100,000. This is a striking decrease in
a twelve-year period, even if on a comparative basis the Russian murder rate
remains the highest in Europe, ten times higher than the rate in Germany and
France. Compared to the BRICS, Russia's murder rate is much higher than
the rate in China and India but considerably lower than that in Brazil and
South Africa. However, recent academic research, including by a Russian government research institute, has called the official statistics into serious doubt.
There are a number of ways these statistics can be manipulated, as was done
in the Soviet period. For example, murders can be categorized as "events of
unidentified intent," a category that can mask the true homicide rate; the use
of this category has grown in recent years in Russia. An international team
of demographers, including one from the Russian State Statistical Service,
reestimated Russia's murder rate and concluded that it actually is around 20
per 100,000 as of 2011, double the official rate. Thus, it is unclear how much
of the decline in Russia's homicide rate is real. Even if the rate is indeed lower
than in the past, the most important reason is probably a higher standard of
living and increasing social stability after the trauma of the Soviet collapse,
factors that are at best only partially due to state performance and the quality
of governance.[44]

International ratings of issues related to personal safety and the rule of law suggest that the Russian state performs badly in this area. The Social Progress Index ranks Russia 107th out of 161 countries in terms of personal safety for citizens, a measure based on traffic deaths, the homicide rate, the level of violent crime, perceived levels of criminality, and political terror. On each of these components, Russia is rated as "relatively weak" compared to countries at similar levels of income. The Rule of Law Index, an initiative of the World Justice Project nongovernmental organization (NGO), ranks countries according to eight different categories, such as the level of corruption, order and security, and criminal and civil justice. The index is based on expert surveys. In 2016 Russia placed 92 out of 113 countries, between the much poorer countries of Ecuador and Uzbekistan. All of the BRICS, even China, scored higher than Russia. Russia was one of the worst performers in both its income category and its region.[45]

One reason that Russia under Putin is a disordered police state is that raising the quality of law enforcement has been a low priority of state rulers. The issue was succinctly captured by one of Russia's best-known authors of detective novels, Boris Akunin, who noted that, in contrast to the Western police motto of "to serve and protect . . . the motto of our state, and especially of the police (which is perceived of as the state in the mass consciousness): 'To squeeze and rob.'" The squeeze can be administered to political opponents brought up on bogus charges, or to NGOs that engage in troublesome activities like election monitoring or publicizing human rights abuses by the state, or to opposition groups who wish to exercise their constitutionally promised rights of the freedom to organize and demonstrate. The state can rob from wealthy oligarchs, using criminal proceedings to take away their companies, and from small business owners, who can be targeted by lower-level law enforcement officials. After the Yukos affair, when the billionaire Mikhail Khodorkovsky was thrown in jail and his oil company was taken over by the state oil company Rosneft, headed by Putin's longtime Petersburg ally Igor Sechin, the number of cases of economic crimes grew by 50–70 percent a year. As the director of the Institute for the Rule of Law in St. Petersburg explained, law enforcement officials work not according to the law, but according to informal understandings of what is and is not permissible, which is signaled by behavior at the top. The problem with Russian law enforcement is not one of resources or personnel—Russia actually has a comparatively high number of law enforcement personnel and pays them relatively well, according to one detailed investigation—but one of official tolerance for squeezing and robbing.[46]

This tolerance of squeezing and robbing, and the informal clan battles that swirl around this activity, means there are periodic eruptions of major scandals involving law enforcement agencies—the police, the secret police, prosecutors, and investigators. The Yevsyukov affair, which focused public attention on a police force that seemed as dangerous to the public as it does to criminals, was one such event. Another was the "Three Whales" case, which lasted from 2000 to 2010 and implicated almost all of the leading law enforcement agencies in corruption. Named after the "Three Whales" Moscow furniture store, the case provided evidence of smuggling, money laundering, illicit trade, "roofing" (state protection rackets) of private companies, clan connections used to avoid the law and target clan enemies, and violent attacks on witnesses and investigative journalists. One journalist dubbed the case "the main scandal of the Putin era," and it ended with a scandalous whimper, when in 2010 several private businessmen were convicted of smuggling, but all of the state officials implicated in the case got off scot-free. Another Russian law and crime journalist observed, in a 2011 article about the struggle between the police and the secret police for control over illegal banking operations, "Russia's so-called law enforcement organs and special services are absolutely useless and even harmful in the struggle with corruption today. No one in these structures understands who among them is fighting corruption and who is participating in it."[47]

The American journalist C. J. Chivers, writing in 2008, maintained that "Putin's signature legacy" was the building "of a more sophisticated and rational police state than the failed USSR."[48] However, Russia's police state does not appear to be particularly sophisticated or rational; it is more a disordered police state than a well-ordered one. Although there are indications of some positive trends in fighting violent crime, Russia still performs poorly at delivering security and the rule of law to its citizens, despite the considerable investment of state resources in this sector. This inefficient return on investment indicates, at a minimum, considerable misrule. The more troubling conclusion, though, is that the ruling authorities have the very law enforcement and security system that they want—one that is an effective club against potential political opponents, but that otherwise is as likely to prey on their own citizens as protect them.

Sochi Olympics: Let the Games Begin

A final example of how Russia is misruled comes not from a specific sector but from Putin's signature megaproject, the Sochi 2014 Winter Olympics. The Sochi Olympics cost a mind-blowing 50 billion dollars. This price tag made them the most expensive Olympics in history, more expensive than all of the previous winter Olympics combined and exceeding the previous record, 40 billion dollars for the Beijing Summer Olympics. Why was Sochi so expensive?[49]

Part of the reason for the high costs followed from the decision to host a "Winter Olympics in the Subtropics," the title of a report on Sochi overspending by the Russian opposition politician Boris Nemtsov, who was born in Sochi and was murdered in 2015. Sochi is on the Black Sea in southern Russia, a place before the Olympics best known for its palm trees and summer beach resorts—seemingly one of the most unlikely places for a Winter Olympics in a country known for its cold and harsh winters. The idea, which Putin managed to sell to the International Olympic Committee, was to transform the western end of the Caucasus Mountains near Sochi into a world-class winter resort area, thereby making Sochi and the surrounding area into a year-round vacation spot.

Crony dealing was central to the Sochi Olympics. Most of the costs, given the way in which the whole region needed to be transformed to host a major winter resort, involved a series of gigantic construction projects. Perhaps the biggest was a thirty-one-mile road and railway link from the beach near Sochi up into the mountains to the ski resort. The cost of this project alone was nearly 9 billion dollars; according to one estimate, "for the sum the government spent on the road, it could have been paved entirely with a centimeter-thick coating of beluga caviar." The project was headed by Russian Railways, which at the time was controlled by Vladimir Yakunin, Putin's friend and dacha neighbor. Putin's childhood friends Arkadiy and Boris Rotenberg also won multiple large contracts to build infrastructure for the Sochi Olympics; according to one estimate, a total of twenty-one contracts worth 7 billion dollars. One expert concluded, "The will to reconstruct Sochi demonstrates a gigantomania that is unusual even by Russian standards. . . . The principal legacy of this gigantomania, however, will be infrastructure that is utterly disproportional and far too expensive for everyday needs."[50]

The Sochi megaproject not only put money in the pockets of Putin's friends but also took money out of the pockets of other oligarchs who are not part of Putin's inner circle. The billionaires Oleg Deripaska and Vladimir Potanin were given an offer that they could not refuse—strong hints that they should invest in Sochi for the good of the country. This is the "Orthodox capitalism" of Putinomics described in the last chapter, by which billionaires are told, "You're rich. . . . I understand how you got this money . . . you have to help." Credits to finance these projects were issued by the state bank VEB (Vnesheconombank), described as a "second budget" by the former deputy chair of the Central Bank. Most reports suggested that Deripaska and Potanin would take a loss on their investments, but that gaining the favor of Putin and the state was worth the price.

A few local environmental activists protested the destruction caused by the various building projects, including damage to a river by the new road and railway and the use of land taken from a national park for the ski runs. The most prominent of them, Yevgeny Vitishko, received a three-year jail sentence for spray-painting a fence that he deemed illegal; before that he had received a fifteen-day sentence for swearing in public, the timing of which coincided with the actual games. Amnesty International labeled Vitishko a "prisoner of conscience."[51]

The Sochi Olympics offer a window into the nature of Putinism. Given the high priority of the project, Putin took to spending more and more time at one of his presidential residences in Sochi, frequently hosting government meetings there. One Russian analyst dubbed Sochi "the de-facto southern capital." This was "manual rule" for a project that was too big to be allowed to fail. Sochi is just the largest example of what one journalist called "the culture of informal mechanisms of control and the battle for influence as a proxy for personal enrichment" that define the system. A Russian construction manager, who immigrated to London after coming under pressure to pay larger kickbacks than he was willing to pay, remarked to a reporter, "Sochi is just what is happening in Russia everywhere."[52]

Sochi was not just a domestic affair, however, but an international event meant to build up Russia's status in the world. In multiple respects the games themselves were a big success: beautiful opening and closing ceremonies showcased the best of Russian history and culture, the threatened terrorist attacks never materialized, and Russia led the medal table. Despite its record price tag, Sochi might have been remembered as a positive international Russian achievement if it had not been eclipsed by the annexation of Crimea less than a month after the games ended. Two years after Sochi was over any residual positive effects of the Olympics were completely undermined by the revelations about a state-sponsored doping program to boost Russian athletes and cover up their cheating; Russia's medal haul was apparently a sham. Putin, predictably, blamed the negative reports about Russian doping on the United States, suggesting it was "turning sport into an instrument of geopolitical pressure," trying to "dictate its will" to the international sporting community, and trying to "form a negative image" of Russia. In Putin's mind, the doping scandal was yet another example of Western hypocrisy and the use of double standards to humiliate Russia.[53] The code of Putinism affected not only how Russia ran the Sochi Olympics—"the culture of informal mechanisms of control"—but how it interpreted criticism of Russia's performance and behavior. Because the West disrespects Russia and is out to get it, according to the code, it unfairly singles out Russia for condemnation—an issue we return to in the next chapter.

Comparing Russia

These vignettes tell us a great deal about how Putin's Russia is ruled and misruled. For critics—the dominant mode of Western writing about Russia—there are plenty of examples of dysfunctional state behavior: the most expensive Olympics in history, cops and spies warring with each other, soccer club owners having to call "the boss" to make important decisions, expensive and poor-quality roads leading to high traffic fatalities, underfunded hospitals and clinics contributing to comparatively low life expectancy, and a state budget oriented increasingly toward defense and security and away from investments in education and healthcare. For boosters of Russia—most Russian media outlets, and a vocal minority of analysts in the West—there are also positive developments to point to: a declining murder rate (at least officially), higher life expectancy, a Sochi Olympics that bolstered Russian national pride, a rebuilt military able to stand up for Russian interests, seemingly successful public health campaigns against smoking and drinking, and so on.[54]

The hard part is moving beyond vignettes, anecdotes, and a detailed focus on this or that sector to a holistic picture of Russian rule. Even more important is to figure out how to answer the central question, "Compared to what?" Indeed, when looking at the state of Russia's roads, healthcare system, or law enforcement and security, we relied in part on comparative data to judge Russia's performance.

One obvious thing to do is to compare Russia to its past, but even that is not as easy as it sounds. For example, we know that the Russian economy grew faster in the 2000s than in the 1990s. But does that mean that Russia is ruled more effectively under Putin than Yeltsin? Perhaps. But it is also worth knowing that all European postcommunist countries experienced economic depression after the transition to capitalism, that oil prices were much lower in the 1990s than in the 2000s, that high demand from China also played an important role in Russian growth in the 2000s, and that Russian performance in both the 1990s and 2000s was roughly average for the post-Soviet region—neither the best nor the worst in either decade. Thus, even a comparison to the past is trickier than it may appear.

Besides comparing a country to its past, the most frequent comparison is to other countries. For example, I just noted that comparing Russia to other postcommunist and post-Soviet countries can be instructive. Frequently Russia is compared to the United States, its former superpower rival, or other large countries in Europe, such as Germany, which is another traditional European great power. Certainly many Russians compare themselves to citizens in the advanced capitalist countries. This comparison is arguably unfair, however, because these countries are wealthier than Russia and are established democracies, and have been for decades or centuries.

Russia frequently touts its relationship with the other BRICS—Brazil, India, China, and South Africa. The notion of the BRICs—small s, without South Africa at the time—was advanced by a British economist, who noted in 2001 the growing importance of the four largest "emerging market" economies of China, India, Russia, and Brazil. The term stuck, so much so that the BRIC countries created a formal organization in 2009 and expanded in 2010 with the addition of South Africa. Comparing Russia to the other BRICS—what I will label the BICS—seems fairer than comparing it to the United States or Germany, even if many Russians see themselves as in a different category than Brazil, India, and South Africa.

At the same time, on a per capita basis Russia is by far the wealthiest of the BRICS. Since we know that many positive political outcomes, including the degree of democracy and the effectiveness of the state bureaucracy, are to a significant degree correlated with economic wealth, comparing Russia only to the "BICS" (BRICS minus Russia) in theory should lead to flattering comparisons for Russia. Therefore, we will also compare Russia to its income category, using World Bank categories. This is a bit tricky for Russia, since it was classified as an "upper-middle-income" country in 2004–2011 and

2015–2016, but "high income non-OECD" in 2012–2014; thus, we compare Russia to both sets of countries.

In addition to figuring out to whom we should compare Russia, we also need to know how we should compare it. As noted already, there is no single agreed measure of the quality or effectiveness of governance. However, over the last several decades a series of international and nongovernmental organizations have tried to devise measures of governance and institutional performance that allow the comparison of countries around the world. Some of these measures use subjective indicators based on expert surveys, some try to use objective indicators such as life expectancy or the murder rate, and some combine the two approaches. We will use three different internationally prominent efforts to evaluate governance around the world: The Worldwide Governance Indicators (WGI) prepared by the World Bank; the Global Competitiveness Index (GCI) of the World Economic Forum; and the Social Progress Index (SPI) of the nonprofit Social Progress Imperative. Taken together, they provide some numerical rankings that allow us to compare the quality of Russian rule to some of its peers.

The Worldwide Governance Indicators (WGI) of the World Bank have been ranking most countries in the world on six dimensions since 1996: Political Stability/No Violence, Rule of Law, Control of Corruption, Regulatory Quality, Government Effectiveness, and Voice and Accountability. Each country then receives a score for each indicator on a scale of 2.5 to -2.5, with zero being the average and higher scores being better and lower scores worse. The WGI also generates percentage rankings, so one can quickly observe how a country compares to every other country in the world. For example, in 2015 Russia's best score was for Government Effectiveness at 48 percent, putting it almost exactly in the middle of the more than 200 countries and territories included in the study, whereas its worst score was for Political Stability and Absence of Violence/Terrorism at 13 percent, meaning more than 85 percent of countries do better than Russia in this area.[55]

How does Russia compare to the BICS and countries at its income level on the WGI? Figure 5-2 shows Russia's composite WGI score, combining the six different indicators into a single measure of "governance," compared to that of the BICS average and the average for upper-middle-income and high-income non-OECD countries.[56] The results are from 1996 to 2015, so they show change over time from the middle of the Yeltsin era through the first sixteen years of Putin's rule. As you can see, Russia significantly underperforms compared both to the small club of large emerging market

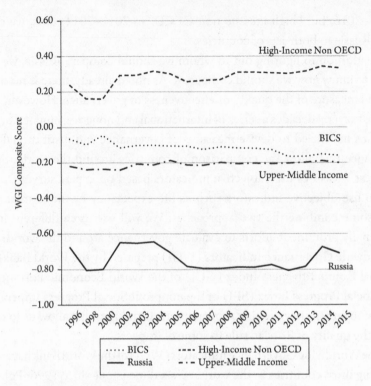

Figure 5-2 World Governance Indicator Score

economies and to countries at similar levels of economic development. In fact, Russia is the wealthiest of the BRICS, but the worst performer in the WGI ratings, even though as a general rule wealth and good governance tend to go together. This is even more clear when we look at income groupings; as recently as 2014 Russia was a "high-income" country, but it is far behind not only high-income countries but also upper-middle-income ones. Further, according to the WGI, there has been little change overall during the Putin era; after a noticeable jump in 2002, Russia's trajectory since that time is even somewhat downward. To put it differently, as Russia grew significantly richer throughout the 2000s, and at a time when many people, especially in Russia, gave Putin credit for restoring stability and order, the quality of governance was low and stagnant.

The second comparative measure of Russian governance used here comes from the World Economic Forum's Global Competitiveness Index (GCI). The GCI provides a snapshot of the competitiveness of different national economies. A survey of business executives plays an important role in constructing the GCI. Components of the GCI include twelve different pillars, including infrastructure, education, and market size, scored on a scale from one to seven. For our purposes, the most important pillar is the "institutions" pillar, which includes such issues as protection of property rights, judicial independence, government transparency, and protections for investors.[57]

How does Russia stack up on the GCI Institutions score? In 2015 Russia came in at exactly 100 out of 140 ranked countries, sandwiched between Algeria and Uganda. Needless to say, this is a pretty low showing for Russia. This was well below its overall GCI rank of forty-five. Russia does well in terms of market size, education, and macroeconomic fundamentals (budget balance, debt, inflation, and so on), but poor in terms of institutions, innovation, and financial market development. Figure 5-3 shows Russia's GCI Institutions score compared to the BICS average and the average for the Former Soviet Union. Here again, Russia underperforms compared to these peers. Russia has been on a positive trajectory for the past decade, although in 2015 its score was roughly the same as it had been in 2004. After fifteen years of Putinism, Russia still lagged far behind its chosen peer group of the BICS and its post-Soviet neighbors, most of whom are considerably poorer than Russia.

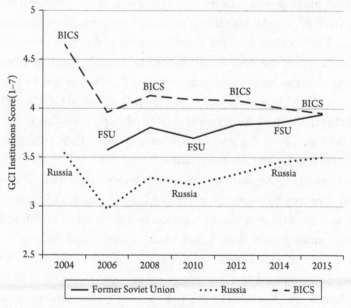

Figure 5-3 Global Competitiveness Institutions Score
Note: Former Soviet Union category does not include scores for Belarus, Turkmenistan, or Uzbekistan, due to insufficient data

The third comparative measure of Russian government performance is the Social Progress Index.[58] This is a relatively new measure, designed to separate social progress from economic performance; it is what Fukuyama would call an "output" indicator. That is, how are countries doing at providing socially desirable outcomes like well-being, meeting human needs, and individual opportunity? It includes direct measures of things like healthcare, personal safety, environmental conditions, education, personal rights, and inclusion. These different sectors are evaluated separately and then combined to create a composite SPI score, which ranges from zero to one hundred. In 2017 Russia was ranked sixty-seventh overall, between South Africa and Philippines. Russia was ahead of China and India but behind Brazil and South Africa. The SPI reports also compare countries to the closest fifteen countries in terms of GDP per capita; Russia's comparison set included countries such as Chile, Greece, and Malaysia. Education was a relative area of strength for Russia, whereas it lagged in areas such as health and wellness, personal safety, water and sanitation, and personal freedoms and rights.

Since the SPI is a relatively new index and thus doesn't show much change over time, I use a different method to show how Russia is doing in delivering services to its population compared to other countries. Figure 5-4 provides a scatterplot, plotting each country based on two factors—its overall SPI score and its GDP per capita. Intuitively, we would expect richer countries to do better, and in fact they do—the trendline in the graph goes up as countries get richer. Further, the steep ascent of the line in the beginning, followed by a leveling out, also makes intuitive sense—a $5,000 increase in per capita GDP has a much bigger effect for a country with an initial GDP per capita of $5,000 than it does for a country with a GDP per capita of $40,000. Countries whose dots are above the line are performing better than anticipated, and countries below the line are doing worse.

Russia, as the figure shows, is an underperformer for its level of wealth, and thus appears well below the trend line. Indeed, Russia's SPI score is comparable to that of countries with less than half the level of wealth of Russia. Countries much poorer than Russia, such as Jordan and Bolivia, do about the same as Russia, and some much poorer countries, like Costa Rica, do a lot better. Compared to other countries at roughly the same level of income, Russia and Kazakhstan are the two big underperformers. Russia's other peers—countries like Chile, Greece, Latvia, and Malaysia—do noticeably better.

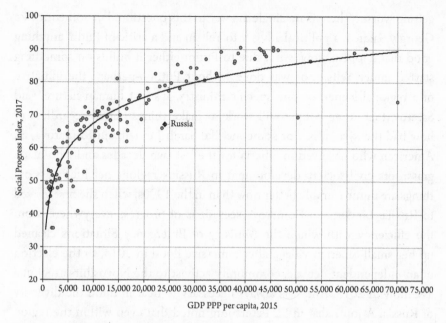

Figure 5-4 Social Progress Index and GDP per Capita

Thus, all three of these different ways of measuring good governance conclude that Russia does badly compared to its most relevant peers—its neighbors, countries at similar levels of wealth, and countries from the club of large emerging markets (BICS). Of course, if we were to compare Russia to the countries that historically it has seen as its main competitors and peer group—countries like France, Great Britain, Germany, and the United States—Russia would look even worse. The poor quality of governance experienced by Russian citizens is striking for a relatively wealthy country that is considered one of the world's great powers. Of course, Vladimir Putin is not responsible for Russia's poor governance when he came to power. He is responsible, however, for presiding over a system of rule in which Russia made only marginal improvements in some areas of governance and none in others, despite eighteen years in power and considerable economic resources.

Getting Better All the Time?

In the classic Beatles song "Getting Better," Paul McCartney proclaims, "It's getting better all the time!" only to be answered by the more cynical John Lennon, "Can't get no worse!" Is Russian rule good or bad, getting better or getting worse? There is no single answer to this question. For someone like Georgiy Satarov, a political adviser to Yeltsin and a critic of Putin, anything good that happens now is not due to Putin; either it builds on something started under Yeltsin, or was done without Putin—perhaps the initiative of a regional leader, or one specific ministry. It's just human nature, said Satarov, that some people will work to make things better, regardless of how bad the system is. For someone like Sarah Lindemann-Komarova, an American who has lived in Siberia for the last two decades and who made grassroots civil-society development in Russia's regions her life's passion, things are immeasurably better now than in the 1990s, when she first moved to Russia. Lindemann-Komarova sees signs of progress everywhere, from the efficiency with which the Ministry of Emergency Situations cleaned up her small Siberian village after a massive flood in 2014, to the election of an independent, female, community activist to the Novosibirsk regional assembly in 2015. And it is always necessary to bear in mind the diversity of Russia. A journalist in St. Petersburg noted that even within the region around St. Petersburg one could experience the extremes between "Poland and Afghanistan," going from a modern European city to dying villages in which the majority of people are addicted to heroin.[59]

Overall, the Russian state under Putin governs worse than it should, given Russia's relative wealth and the huge influx of oil and gas riches in the 2000s. Misrule is a direct consequence of the Putinist system, one that depends more on ruling than governing, a system in which personalities, centralized control, and loyalty matter more than institutional development and checks and balances. A Russian journalist in 2015 summarized the problem with the Kremlin narrative that Putin has "restored order":

> You can talk as much as you like about how Putin has imposed order. But I have to say, order is not when any cop can take any businessman's business away from him, and it is not when any bureaucrat can run down a pregnant woman on the street [referring to a notorious hit-and-run accident in 2009 when a speeding off-duty cop ran over and killed a pregnant woman]. Order is the opposite, it's when they can't do that. And the problem is that our cops and our bureaucrats, I'm afraid, really don't understand that.[60]

Under Putin, a strong state is pursued not to introduce the rule of law for everyone, nor to counter both grand and petty corruption, nor to create broad-based development, but to return Russia to the ranks of great powers, especially in the military realm. It is perhaps not surprising that military reform is an area of relative success, although there is also an element of good fortune here. In 2007, after seven years of stalled reforms and wasted spending, Putin took a chance on a loyal, well-connected defense minister with no experience who had the good sense to listen to some very smart experts about what needed to be done.[61]

Perhaps, as Olga Vlasova argued, this is what Russians really want—geopolitical status and a state ready to fend off its enemies, and not the efficient delivery of social services, or even public order and safety. One Russian expert told the *New York Times* in 2015, "Russia is a country that is ready to tolerate pain for the sake of national greatness." Historically that may have been true. Polls cited earlier, however, suggest that Russians also value economic development, higher living standards, and fighting corruption, so perhaps the national tolerance for pain is not as high as it once was? Will national greatness be an adequate substitute for good governance? Perhaps. But there are costs of misrule, including—and perhaps especially—for Russian citizens. Many of those were discussed earlier—poor life expectancy, bad roads, high murder rates, the world's most expensive Olympics. Misrule, which is in part a consequence of the code of Putinism and the approach to governing that follows from it, ultimately will make it harder for Russia to sustain its great power ambitions.

Punching above Its Weight

Economic stagnation and political misrule would seem to be a weak foundation for Putin's quest to restore Russia's rightful place as a respected great power. Yet commentators the world over, including in Russia and the United States, have declared that Putin is winning, or perhaps I should say #WINNING! The year 2016, in particular, was "the year Putin won," as one commentator argued, and who would disagree? The Syrian city of Aleppo finally fell to Russia's aerial assaults, seemingly cementing the victory of the Syrian strongman Bashar al-Assad in a brutal civil war. Europe was buffeted by crisis after crisis, from refugee flows to terrorist attacks to the rise of right-wing populist leaders who challenged the fundamental values and institutions of liberal democracy; the victory of the Brexit referendum on British membership in the European Union (EU) was the most astonishing manifestation of Europe's time of troubles. To top it all off, Donald Trump stunned the world by being elected president of the United States—with Putin's secret backing, according to US intelligence officials. Given that Trump had extolled Putin's leadership qualities during the campaign, called into question US security guarantees around the world, and appointed top people with favorable attitudes toward Putin, it seemed the post–Cold War international order, and arguably even the post–World War II order, was crumbling, with Putin's Russia as the main beneficiary.[1]

This was an outcome Putin fervently desired. The code of Putinism has at its core the notion that Russia must be a strong state and a great power, and it is highly suspicious of the United States and the global system it promotes and upholds. Feelings of humiliation and resentment in the aftermath of the Soviet collapse further fuel this drive to restore Russian power. Putin's Russia is not seeking global hegemony, but it does want to upend the Western-dominated order that promotes democracy and human rights and insists on the right of Russia's neighbors to choose their own foreign policy course independent from Russian tutelage. It wants to be treated as an equal great power deciding the key issues in global security, respected and deferred to by the other great powers, especially the United States. Putin wants, to borrow a phrase, to make Russia great again.

Is Putin winning, and in the process making Russia great again? Given what we learned in the previous two chapters about the weakness of the Russian economy and the ways in which Russia is misruled, increasing Russia's international power and influence at the same time would be quite the feat. Understanding the code of Putinism and how it shapes Russian foreign policy helps us understand this apparent paradox. Based on the size of its population and economy, Russia is a declining power, weaker than it has been in over 300 years. It has no genuine allies among the world's other great powers. Yet under Putin it is "punching above its weight," in the words of a top Russian analyst, putting itself at the center of many major global issues.[2] The code of Putinism, with its conviction that Russia must be a great power, its suspicion of US intentions, and its feelings of resentment, lost status, and vulnerability, drive a foreign policy that many in the West see as confrontational and aggressive but that Russia's rulers view as prudent, defensive, and a necessary response to perceived Western pressure and hostility.

The chapter begins by setting out Russia's power position in the international system. In terms of economic and demographic power and potential, Russia is weaker than the Soviet Union, or imperial Russia in the eighteenth and nineteenth centuries. Unlike the Soviet Union, it is not the leader of a powerful military alliance, nor the foremost champion of an ideology that inspires millions around the world. Thus, it is misleading to talk about a new Cold War, which involved global military and ideological competition between relatively equal superpowers.

Current bad relations between Russia and the West are due to a fundamental mismatch between liberal internationalism based on political and economic freedom (democracy, market capitalism, and the rule of law), and the code of Putinism, with its great power statism, illiberalism, habits of personal control, and feelings of resentment and humiliation. Putin and the Russian political elite believe that the post–Cold War settlement was unfairly imposed on Russia during a period of weakness in the 1990s. Putinist foreign policy seeks to right this perceived wrong and give Russia its due as a great power, with recognition of its legitimate interests, particularly in the post-Soviet space. The problem is that the West sees the current international order as broadly legitimate and interprets Russian assertions of its perceived interests as a challenge to peace and stability. Russia wants great power diplomacy as practiced in Europe in the nineteenth and twentieth centuries, something the West sees as no longer viable in the twenty-first century. According to the code of Putinism, American justifications of this liberal order, and support for human rights and democracy in Eurasia and elsewhere, are mere hypocrisy and a cover for American pursuit of hegemony.

The rest of the chapter charts Putin's effort to reestablish Russia as a leading great power. The goal is to explain Russian foreign policy based on the premises of the code of Putinism, not to give a comprehensive history of Russian foreign policy under Putin.[3] The rational pursuit of national interest offers a partial window into Russian foreign policy, but an analysis based on the code of Putinism, and the ideas, habits, and emotions that inform the code, offers a more comprehensive and persuasive account. This interpretation is laid out through a consideration of key episodes throughout the Putin era, with a particular focus on Russia's relations with the West. Despite Russia's engagement with countries like China and India, its foreign policy identity is still defined primarily vis-à-vis Europe and the United States.[4]

A Great Geopolitical Tragedy

The collapse of the Soviet Union in 1991 was one of the pivotal turning points in the twentieth century. Putin famously referred to the Soviet collapse as "one of the greatest geopolitical catastrophes of the century."[5] To some observers this was an outrageous statement, in light of major events such as World War I, World War II, the Holocaust, and various other wars and genocides. Indeed, in the West, the Soviet collapse was a highly positive event, bringing about the relatively peaceful end of the Cold War, the seeming triumph of democracy in Russia and elsewhere in eastern Europe and Eurasia, and the lessening of the threat of nuclear Armageddon. Some even interpreted his statement as implying that he intends to recreate the Soviet Union. From Putin's point of view, however, the real point was that the collapse of the Soviet Union meant the breakdown of the great Russian state and a dramatic loss of power and status. That is why he defined the catastrophe as "geopolitical."

If we look at basic indicators of geopolitical power, it's hard to disagree with Putin about the effects of the Soviet collapse. Russia lost control of more than two million square miles of territory—more than the entire area of the EU. Russia's population and the size of its economy, compared to that of the Soviet Union, were virtually cut in half overnight—and this was before the economic and demographic implosion of the 1990s. Figure 6-1 shows just how dramatic the collapse was.[6]

This is a stunning graph. When people say that Russia is weaker now than it has been in over 300 years, this is what they are talking about.[7] In 1700, under Tsar Peter the Great, Russia was twice as big as Putin's Russia in terms of population and the economy, relative to the world total. Peter established Russia as an empire and European great power with his defeat of Sweden in 1721, and it continued to expand territorially, demographically, and economically throughout the eighteenth and nineteenth centuries. Russia probably peaked as a great power during the Cold War (between 1946–1989), when the Soviet Union was around 8–10 percent of the global economy and 6–7 percent of world population. It was a nuclear superpower that had the world's largest military and led one of the two main power blocs. The Soviet collapse dealt a blow to Russia's great power status that is almost certainly irreversible.

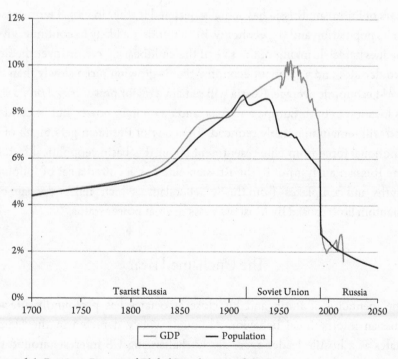

Figure 6-1 Russia as Percent of Global Population and GDP

Russia's decline is one of the two big geopolitical stories of the last fifty years. The other one is China's rise from about 5 percent of the global economy fifty years ago to now making up around 15–17 percent of the world economy. In contrast, in the same time period, Russia fell from around 8–10 percent of global output to about 2 percent. Russia is currently on good terms with China, but in the 1950s it was the big brother in the relationship, and adjusting to the role of weaker partner is not an easy process. The Chinese themselves, according to one Russian expert, don't think Russia has the "all-around" attributes to be a great power anymore, particularly "real economic strength."[8]

Of course, in many respects Russia remains a great power, despite its problems and its substantial loss of geopolitical power. It is one of the two leading nuclear powers, one of the five permanent members of the Security Council, the largest country in the world, remains in the top ten by population, and possesses among the world's largest reserves of oil and gas. Economic growth in the 2000s, and military reform after 2008, certainly helped repair two of Russia's main deficiencies in the 1990s. But the fundamental geographic, demographic, and economic consequences of the Soviet collapse for Russian national power are not going to change. After eighteen years of Putinism, Russia has actually declined further in global terms based on its population and the economy. Both trends are likely to continue, given the inevitable shrinking of the size of the childbearing cohort over the next two decades and a stagnant economy that is growing more slowly than the world economic average. Russia will remain a major power based on its size, its location in both Europe and Asia, and its military power, but its status is and will remain inevitably reduced. The code of Putinism gets much of its emotional force from elite resentment about this basic geopolitical fact. As one Russian analyst put it, the Russian elite has acquired a set of "phobias, myths, and complexes" from the Soviet collapse, which "reflect the pain of a phantom limb caused by Moscow's loss of great power status."[9]

The Unchained Bear

The mentality of Putin and his close associates has profoundly affected Russian international behavior. Although widely depicted in the United States as a hostile leader aggressively challenging US interests around the world, Putin, not surprisingly, sees things quite differently. Joss Whedon, the

American director of the first two *Avengers* movies and creator of the cult classic TV show *Buffy the Vampire Slayer*, once told an actor playing a villain to bear in mind that "bad guys don't think that they're bad guys, bad guys think that they're heroes."[10] Putin, similarly, obviously doesn't think he's the bad guy, he thinks he's the hero. More specifically, from Putin's point of view Russia is not playing offense—Russia is playing defense.

Putin memorably stated his position in a December 2014 press conference, when he was asked about whether Russia's economic problems—the ruble was in seeming free fall that month, having lost half of its value relative to the dollar in a little over three weeks—were "payback" for the annexation of Crimea. No, Putin said, this was not payback for Crimea—rather, it was the price of "our natural desire to preserve ourselves as a nation, a civilization, a state." Then he got colorful:

> Sometimes I think to myself: perhaps our bear should just sit quietly, stop chasing piglets around the taiga and feed upon berries and honey. Maybe they would leave him alone? No, they won't, because they will always try to put him in chains. And as soon as they chain him, they will rip out his teeth and claws. In today's understanding that would mean our nuclear deterrent forces.

Putin then repeated the myth that top Western officials believe that it is unjust for Russia to control Siberia and that its "immeasurable wealth" should be divided up, something his close ally and Security Council secretary Nikolay Patrushev has also stated on multiple occasions.[11] He continued:

> And then, after they've ripped out its claws and teeth, the bear won't be needed at all. They'll turn it into a scarecrow, and that will be it. Therefore it has nothing to do with Crimea. It has to do with the fact that we are defending our independence, our sovereignty, and our right to exist. . . . We want to survive and to fight, changing for the better . . . the structure of our economy, to be more independent, to get through this—or we want our skin to hang on a wall. That is the choice we face. Crimea has nothing to do with it.[12]

In this vivid metaphor, Putin neatly captured how he sees Russia's place in the contemporary world order. Russia is quiet and peaceful, and would like to be left alone. But "they"—meaning the West in general and the United

States in particular—have aggressive intentions toward Russia, up to and including depriving it of its very right to exist. Elsewhere in his statement he accused the United States of supporting terrorism inside Russia and of "unprecedented attempts, obviously coordinated" to discredit the 2014 Sochi Olympics. Russia's economic problems in 2014 were just one more manifestation of this American effort to chain the Russian bear.

One American journalist described this quote as "insane-sounding," "absolutely crazy," "bizarre," and "bananas crazy," before going on to say that it was "essential" for understanding Russia today.[13] Describing Putin's statement as "bananas crazy" doesn't help us figure out Russia's foreign policy, though, and particularly how the world looks *and feels* to Russia's leadership. Rather, the code of Putinism helps us make sense of it. First of all, the Russian bear has to be strong to protect itself—meaning a strong state internally and a great power externally. Suspicion of the West in general, and the United States in particular, is another core idea expressed by Putin's tale of the bear. On the emotional level, we see feelings of resentment and vulnerability, and a plea for respect. And Putin's colorful story of the peaceful bear that needs its claws and teeth to defend itself also came with some habitual macho posturing, and the implication that those who disagree with his economic approach were siding with those who want to hang the bear's pelt on a wall. Order and unity are necessary to keep the bear safe and alive.

This mentality of the Russian elite, captured by the image of Russia as a threatened bear or besieged fortress, is directly at odds with the dominant Western narrative of an aggressive, nationalist Russia trying to subvert an international order that has brought peace and prosperity to Europe after centuries of conflict. This fundamental mismatch in outlook has led many to contend that we have entered a "new Cold War." The term obscures more than it clarifies, because of the massive gap in power today and the lack of a full-blown ideological conflict like the one between capitalism and communism. But one distinguished American expert has observed that the current cooling of relations is like the Cold War in one key respect—both sides almost completely blame the other.[14] In the West, we had narratives of the triumph of freedom and "the end of history," especially in the 1990s when Russia was down and out after the Soviet collapse. The enlargement of the North Atlantic Treaty Organization (NATO) and the EU to include former Soviet satellite countries was the most significant institutional manifestation of this Western perspective. In contrast, the main Russian storyline emphasized humiliation and mistreatment by the West, and an unjust effort to impose the West's rules on Russia, with no regard for legitimate Russian interests. These contrasting narratives serve as competing mental frames that help explain the deterioration of relations between Russia and the West.

Don't Get No Respect

Readers of a certain age will recall comedian Rodney Dangerfield's tagline, "I don't get no respect!" Vladimir Putin can sympathize. The story of the evolution of Putin's foreign policy from 2000 to the present is largely one about Putin's growing disillusionment and anger about the failure of the West to give Russia, and him, the respect that he believes they deserve as one of the world's leading great powers. Although Putin initially seemed open to working with the West and the United States in international relations, within the space of a few years he had concluded that the West was not ready to deal with him on terms he considered appropriate—indeed, it was out to get him. As in the domestic realm, it took Putin a few years to consolidate his control over foreign policy, but the mentality of his team helped push his policies in a more confrontational direction vis-à-vis the West as time went on, particularly after 2004.

Early on in his presidency, before Putinism as a code was fully solidified, Putin moved cautiously in the international arena, and domestic priorities were paramount. He initially left Yeltsin's foreign and defense ministers in place, although he put old associates from the Leningrad KGB in charge of the Security Council and the Federal Security Service (FSB). He sent positive signals to the West, even saying on several occasions that Russia might someday join NATO. He didn't seem to think this would happen anytime soon, and his principle concern was what NATO would look like, proposing "a serious transformation of that bloc into a predominantly political organization" in which Russia had "full-fledged participation in decision-making." Some second-tier officials in the George W. Bush administration argued for a NATO invitation to Russia for future membership, but pursuing such a major change didn't gain much traction for a variety of reasons, including the difficulty of bringing such a large country—one that shared a lengthy border with a rising China—into the core political-military alliance of the West. Putin's authoritarian direction at home was another potential obstacle to future NATO membership. It also was assumed that Russia's interpretation of "full-fledged participation in decision-making" would mean some kind of special status that NATO was unwilling to give. Indeed, reportedly Putin thought Russia shouldn't have to apply to join and then wait for NATO's approval, like other states, but should be asked to unite as an equal partner.[15]

Regardless, grand plans to remake the international security architecture would have to wait. First, Putin had to consolidate power at home and begin the process of rebuilding Russia's economic and military power. Symbolic of the deterioration of the armed forces in the 1990s was the sinking of the Kursk submarine in August 2000 due to a faulty torpedo onboard, killing all 118 members of the crew. In an emotional meeting with family members of the dead, Putin said he would answer for his 100 days as president, but he would "sit with you on the same bench" to question those who had been in charge during the previous fifteen years. He specifically lashed out at those on television who "lie" and who over the previous ten years had "destroyed the army and navy" and who wished to continue to "rob the country, the army and the navy." Putin clearly had in mind the oligarchs Boris Berezovsky and Vladimir Gusinsky, with whom he was engaged in a battle for control over national television (see chapter 2).[16]

During his first two terms as president, from 2000 to 2008, the Russian government devoted considerable resources to rebuilding what Putin called the "half-decayed" armed forces. Equally important for Putin was a concerted effort to pay off Russia's foreign debt and reduce dependence on foreign finance. The Russian state began to repay this debt, which was over 130 billion dollars when Putin took power, ahead of schedule. By 2005 Russia had paid off its obligations to the International Monetary Fund, more than three years ahead of schedule. Russia also began to stockpile hard currency, so by the end of 2004 Russia's foreign exchange holdings outstripped its foreign debt. Both the increase in military and security spending and the determined effort to pay down Russia's debts reflected a desire on the part of Putin and his team to lessen outside influence over Russia, increase their own control and independence, and boost Russia's international standing.[17]

The 9/11 terrorist attacks represented a profound shock to the global political order, and created the possibility of fundamental changes to the international state system. Vladimir Putin was determined that Russia, as one of the world's great powers, play a fundamental role in shaping this new global order. He was famously the first world leader to reach President Bush on the telephone after the attacks, offering his condolences and support. He made good on these commitments in significant respects, in particular by not objecting to US military bases in Central Asia, by sharing intelligence information about Afghanistan, and by permitting the United States to re-supply its military forces in Afghanistan through Russian airspace. In return, Putin hoped to secure the end of a hostile Taliban regime in Afghanistan, greater understanding from the West for Russia's war in Chechnya and its own terrorist problems, and, more generally, Western respect for his inter-pretation of Russia's legitimate interests in the post-Soviet region and in the world.[18]

The brief US-Russian cooperation after 9/11, however, was short-lived. Over the next few years, as Putin consolidated power at home and grew more confident in his foreign policy judgments, he grew increasingly disillusioned with the United States. A trio of American decisions in 2001–2003 was par-ticularly exasperating. First, in December 2001 the United States announced its withdrawal from the 1972 ABM (antiballistic missile) Treaty, a corner-stone of superpower arms control agreements. Given that nuclear weapons were one of the main symbols of Russia's great power status, US efforts to develop missile defense technology were seen as a potential threat to Russia's nuclear deterrent capability. Second, a NATO summit in November 2002 set in motion the further expansion of the alliance to incorporate more postcommunist countries, including the three Baltic states of Estonia, Latvia, and Lithuania. Russians found the inclusion of the Baltic states particularly problematic, given that the three countries had been part of the Soviet Union from 1940 (they were forcibly annexed by Stalin) to the 1991 Soviet collapse and that they directly bordered on Russia. Third, and perhaps most impor-tant, was the US-led war in Iraq. Russia strongly opposed the 2003 Iraq War, and Putin joined forces with French President Jacques Chirac and German Chancellor Gerhard Schroeder to argue against it. When the United States and its coalition partners went ahead anyway, Putin was further disillu-sioned. One Russian journalist describes Iraq as the "most important turning point" in US-Russian relations, maintaining that Putin's relations with the United States never recovered after that point. By 2003, then, the Russian po-litical leadership was convinced that Russia was not going to be appropriately respected or given its appropriate status by the United States, even when it sought to cooperate.[19]

The year 2004 marked the consolidation of Putinism in its mature form. It also was a crucial milestone for the foreign policy vision within the code of Putinism. First, as discussed in chapter 1, Putin's address to the nation after the September 2004 Beslan terrorist attack—"They want to cut from us a tasty piece of pie, others are helping them"—articulated a darker vision of US policy toward Russia, one in which the United States was not simply ignoring Russia's legitimate interests but actively hostile to them. Putin would later claim that the Russian security services detected direct US support for North Caucasus rebel fighters, and that the United States did nothing to stop it when he complained about it.[20]

The second key foreign policy event of 2004 for Russia's rulers was the "Orange Revolution" in Ukraine. During Ukraine's presidential elections in late 2004, credible allegations emerged of electoral fraud in favor of Viktor Yanukovych—the prime minister and candidate of sitting president Leonid Kuchma—leading to protests in the center of Kyiv, the Ukrainian capital. After several weeks of uncertainly and massive protests, the Ukrainian Supreme Court ruled that the election needed a do-over, given the fraud. The run-off election was won by the opposition candidate Viktor Yushchenko. The Kremlin, which had heavily supported Yanukovych, was stunned by the result. Russia's rulers explained Yanukovych's failure with the notion that the West and the United States had conspired to install Yushchenko. It is true that the United States and the EU had provided financial support to a variety of civil society and opposition groups, and had denounced the fraudulent elections, although most scholarly experts point to splits among the Ukrainian elite as the key driving force of the Orange Revolution.[21]

The close temporal coincidence of the Beslan attack and the Orange Revolution helped cement the idea among Putin and his team that the United States, along with its Western allies, was truly out to get them, and was willing to go quite far to achieve its goal of weakening Russia. Putin after Beslan, writes one Russian journalist, "instinctively accused enemies of wanting to deliver surreptitiously a blow against Russia. The defeat in Ukraine left him no doubt at all."[22] The notion that Putin's anti-Americanism was "instinctive" captures the habitual and emotional elements of the code of Putinism. Although the state of US-Russian relations waxed and waned after 2004, by the beginning of Putin's second term, the image of Russia as a besieged fortress was an important influence on domestic and foreign policy.

Once the code of Putinism achieved its mature form around 2004, Russia sought to reassert more vigorously its rightful claims to great power respect, especially in the post-Soviet space. Putin complained frequently about US behavior in the world, and domestically sought to limit the influence of nongovernmental organizations (NGOs) that were funded by Western interests. For example, in 2007 at the Munich Security Conference he told a room full of leading Western politicians and security experts that the United States "has overstepped its national borders in every sphere: economic, political, humanitarian. It imposes itself on other states. Who likes this?" Later that year, he complained that, although Russia wanted to be not only a "partner, but a friend" to the United States, the United States seemingly "doesn't need friends. We have the impression that the USA needs vassals that it can command." It treats Russia, he said, as "not completely civilized, still a bit wild," so the United States must take on the "civilizing role" of cleaning up Russia, "because they can't do it themselves."[23]

Putin's feelings of resentment about disrespect by the United States continued to the very end of his second term as president. In February 2008, the United States and multiple European states recognized Kosovo as an independent state, against the wishes of Russia and Serbia (in 1999, Russia and NATO disagreed sharply about NATO's decision to bomb Serbia over the conflict in the territory of Kosovo, especially without UN Security Council approval). Then in April 2008, NATO officially welcomed the "aspirations" of the former Soviet republics Ukraine and Georgia to join, stating, "We agreed today that these countries will become members of NATO." Although this sounds pretty definitive, it was actually a compromise between countries, like the United States, that wanted to sign these countries up for a clear plan toward membership and other states, like Germany, that didn't think these countries were ready and knew that such a step would further inflame Russia. Putin lobbied hard against the further expansion of NATO into the post-Soviet space, allegedly telling Bush, "You understand, George, that Ukraine—it's not even a state! What is Ukraine? Part of its territory is Eastern Europe, and a significant part was given by us!"[24]

By the time Putin handed over power to Dmitriy Medvedev in May 2008, he had decided that American lack of respect for Russian interests camouflaged a more sinister agenda directed toward keeping Russia weak and subordinate. And it must be clearly acknowledged that many of Putin's criticisms of US foreign policy were warranted and widely shared. Indeed, one of America's leading political scientists observed back in 1999 that, in the eyes of many around the world, the United States is a "rogue superpower." This characterization of American behavior was written *before* the Kosovo war, US withdrawal from the ABM treaty, the 2004 round of NATO expansion that added another seven east European countries to the alliance, the deployment of missile defense systems in eastern Europe, and the Iraq war. Russia clearly had grounds for concern and complaint. One former Bush

administration official later stated, "We neglected the Aretha Franklin principle with Russia—we did not give them enough respect."[25]

Not everyone, however, buys this story about too little respect. Another
former US official and Russia expert who worked in both Republican and
Democratic administrations, Stephen Sestanovich, observes that previously "a more common complaint was that Washington was obsessively
attentive to Moscow's wounded self-regard." Successive US presidents—
from George H. W. Bush through Barack Obama—courted Soviet and
Russian leaders to try to "lift the psychological burden" of losing the Cold
War and the Soviet collapse. Russia was invited to join the world's leading
industrial democracies when the G-7 became the G-8, was brought into
the World Trade Organization, was given an institutionalized voice within
NATO with the creation of the NATO-Russia Council and a Russian ambassador permanently at NATO headquarters, participated in peacekeeping
operations in Bosnia and Kosovo, and was granted tens of billions of dollars
in economic assistance. Perhaps this was not enough for a former superpower, "mere window-dressing in an unequal relationship." Maybe so. But
Sestanovich reminds us of another thing that Russian officials never mention
when they talk about the US and NATO threat—the United States has radically cut its military forces in Europe, and most NATO countries have also
cut their forces substantially. At the end of the Cold War, the United States
had 350,000 troops in Europe. Now it has 62,000, and the majority of those
are naval and air force personnel, not army troops, more oriented toward
the Middle East than Europe and Russia. The number of bases has been cut
back by 75 percent, as have the number of aircraft, there are no permanent
US armor units in Europe, and there is no longer a US aircraft carrier group
in the Mediterranean. The United States and NATO, in short, do not have
the deployed capability to present a military threat to Russia, other than the
US nuclear deterrent. The heightened Russian concern with the American
threat, Sestanovich argues, is a product of "the personal outlook of Vladimir
Putin. . . . Gorbachev and Yeltsin . . . did not blame the West for all their
misfortunes. Putin does."[26]

The United States definitely did things that would be a cause of concern
for any Russian president, and made plenty of mistakes in world politics
in general and with respect to Russia in particular. The code of Putinism,
however, led Russia's rulers to magnify these anxieties even further. This is
most obvious when we look at Putinist attitudes about US democracy promotion. What gives the Russia as a "besieged fortress" metaphor its edge is

that the threats are seen on *both* sides of the wall: not only are there external actors like the United States who are trying to batter down its walls but also there are internal enemies working with the invader to overthrow the regime from within. In this metaphor, civil society assistance is like a Trojan horse, something disguised as a gift that is really a weapon of war. A Putinist mentality that is illiberal, anti-American, fearful of appearing weak, and habitually disposed toward unity and order at home lends itself to somewhat of an obsession with threats and enemies. What the United States calls democracy promotion, Russia regards as externally sponsored attempts at regime change. The interaction of the code of Putinism with American tendencies toward sanctimoniousness about the universality of its liberal and democratic values and its perceived benign role in the world produces a particularly combustible mix.

Counterpunch

Russia in 2008 seemed at the top of its game. Its economy had nearly doubled in size since 1999, and, with world oil prices briefly hitting $140 per barrel that summer, it was being hailed as an "energy superpower." Putin had deftly managed "the 2008 problem" by steering his loyal associate Medvedev into the Kremlin, while keeping watch over him and the broader economic and political system from his perch as prime minister and leader of the ruling party United Russia. Life was good, or so it seemed.

Although Russia and Russians were feeling rather confident, at least compared to a decade earlier, not all was well. On the international stage, in particular, Russia was frustrated at what it viewed as its unfairly limited role in the world and the lack of respect exhibited by the United States for legitimate Russian interests. The recognition of Kosovo's independence and the pledge to bring Georgia and Ukraine into NATO in the future were just the latest examples of this mistreatment. Two events later in 2008—the war in Georgia and the international economic recession set off by the American financial collapse—brought home how uncertain the world could be, and how much further Russia still had to go. It would not be until 2014 that Putin felt Russia had the wherewithal, and the urgent necessity, of counterpunching against the threat from the West.

The small country of Georgia, of course, may see things differently. It got punched pretty hard in August 2008. But from the geopolitical point of view, the Georgia war was more of a warning jab from Russia than a full round-house. Since 1992, Georgia had to contend with two main rebellious regions that were legally part of Georgia but de facto largely autonomous—Abkhazia and South Ossetia. Ethnic differences, Russian covert and overt support, the weakness of the Georgian central government, and political mistakes all contributed to brief internal wars followed by a much longer period of cold peace, or "frozen conflicts." Georgian President Mikhail Saakashvili, who came to power in 2003 in a "colored revolution"—another fall of a post-Soviet regime that Russia blamed on the United States—promised to restore Georgia's territorial integrity and take back control of Abkhazia and South Ossetia.

The frozen conflict became a hot one for five days in August 2008. The escalation came first in South Ossetia, but Russia responded to Georgian military moves against the capital of South Ossetia in response to rebel shelling with an invasion of both South Ossetia and Abkhazia. Indeed, Russian troops pushed beyond the two separatist regions into central Georgia, and its air force bombed several Georgian cities. Russia and Georgia both blamed the other side for the escalation to outright war. Even if we accept the Russian position that it sent in troops to protect its peacekeepers in South Ossetia, the decision to occupy both Abkhazia and South Ossetia and recognize them as independent states clearly, as the EU fact-finding report put it dryly, "went far beyond the reasonable limits of defense."[27] Only four countries—Russia, Nicaragua, Venezuela, and Naura (a Pacific island country of ten thousand people)—have recognized Abkhazia and South Ossetia as independent states.

The Russia-Georgia War made several things clear. First, Putin, although now prime minister and no longer president, was still the central decision-maker, even on issues outside his formal mandate. It was Putin, not Medvedev, who flew from the Beijing Olympics to the Russian region of North Ossetia across the border from the fighting to spearhead the campaign. Second, despite Russia's easy victory in the conflict, the war also showed multiple deficiencies with the armed forces, which helped pave the way for a major reform and rearmament campaign. The positive effects of these efforts would later become evident in Ukraine and Syria. Finally, the invasion of Georgia, just a few months after NATO had declared that Georgia would one day become a member of the alliance, was a firm signal of Russia's strong objections to the further expansion of NATO into the post-Soviet space. This signal was about both Russian interests and elite emotions—"fury as much as grand strategy," in the words of one American expert—and brought home to Western leaders the transformation of Russia under Putin into "a reassertive, resentful power."[28]

Russia tried after the war with Georgia to articulate a new approach to European security that would give Russia the status it deserved. Medvedev argued that Russia had regions of "privileged interests"; to Western elites, this sounded like a call for spheres of influence, to be negotiated by the great powers over the heads of smaller states. In 2009 Medvedev proposed a new European Security Treaty. The core idea of his proposal was that European states and multinational organizations (including alliances) could not take actions that "significantly" affected the security of other European states without their approval. Although many Western officials and experts agreed that something needed to be done to repair relations with Russia and figure out a way to cooperate in European security affairs, in general Medvedev's proposals were treated rather skeptically. The meaning of "significantly affecting security" was obviously vague, but the intent was clear—no longer could other countries take security steps in Europe without Russia's consent. Even those who sympathized with Russian complaints about Western policies were unlikely to give Russia—or any other state for that matter—a blanket veto over another state's security policies. The Western reaction, according to one Russian expert, was a "cold shower" for a disappointed Medvedev and Putin.[29]

Although this effort to redefine European security relations went nowhere, US-Russian relations did get marginally better for much of the Medvedev presidency. Medvedev and Obama sought to improve US-Russia relations, an effort dubbed "the reset." A New START (Strategic Arms Reduction Treaty) agreement that cut the two states' nuclear arsenals was signed in 2010 and ratified in 2011. Russia joined the World Trade Organization (WTO) with US support in 2011 after an eighteen-year negotiation process. Russia and the United States also were able to work together on issues such as Afghanistan and nonproliferation (particularly North Korea and Iran).

The Obama-Medvedev reset, like previous efforts to build a more positive US-Russian relationship after the Cold War, faltered over a host of issues. The 2011 Arab Spring, with uprisings in multiple authoritarian Middle Eastern states, became one source of disagreement, first within the Putin-Medvedev tandem and then between the United States and Russia. Medvedev decided to abstain from a UN Security Council vote on a "no-fly zone" for Libya, where the government of Muammar Gaddafi was battling insurgents inspired by the revolutions in neighboring Tunisia and Egypt, rather than vetoing it. According to some accounts, Putin was not consulted about the decision and was enraged. He publicly labeled the UN resolution a "medieval call for a Crusade." Medvedev, having had his presidential authority openly challenged, said it was "unacceptable" to use terms like "Crusade" in this case, which would bring about a "clash of civilizations." Gaddafi's subsequent overthrow and murder—he was caught hiding in a drain pipe, and his half-naked body was abused by rebels—made a big impression on Putin, who emotionally denounced the "horrific, disgusting scenes" of the killing. Some of Putin's associates saw the hand of Washington in the Arab Spring uprisings, believing they were an American plot to bring down regimes on good terms with Russia, such as in Libya and Syria—just like the "colored revolutions" in countries like Ukraine and Georgia. The Arab Spring reinforced Putin's hatred of revolutions and political disorder.[30]

With Putin's decision to return to the presidency, announced to the Russian public in September 2011, the stage was set for a further deterioration of US-Russian relations. But it wasn't NATO expansion or Iraq or any other traditional irritant that was the primary cause of renewed tensions. Indeed, the Obama administration was trying to wind down the US presence in Iraq and had shown no interest in extending NATO to Ukraine or Georgia. Rather, it was Russian domestic politics that became the next major source of tension. Putin believed that the United States was behind public protests in Moscow against the falsified December 2011 parliamentary elections, publicly stating that the protests were in response to a "signal" from Secretary of State Hillary Clinton. The idea of Russia as a besieged fortress, which had been somewhat dormant during the Medvedev presidency, came back stronger than ever. Upon his election to a third presidential term in March 2012, Putin began to tighten the screws at home. Those NGOs receiving foreign funding were branded as "foreign agents," and a public campaign was launched to link the Russian opposition to "alien" Western values, including with the Pussy Riot case and the so-called gay propaganda law. The elite was ordered to "renationalize" its assets and bring them home; government officials with bank accounts and property abroad might prove disloyal to Russia. Obama's ambassador to Moscow, Michael McFaul, was attacked in the state media as an exporter of "colored revolution" to Russia and constantly harassed. Putin also continued his attacks on American hypocrisy, double standards, and unfair treatment of Russia, remarking in 2012 to a reporter who challenged Russia's decision to stop the adoption of Russian orphans by Americans, "Is it normal if they humiliate you? Do you like it? Are you a sado-masochist? They shouldn't humiliate our country."[31]

The real Russian counterpunch, however, came after the Ukrainian revolution of February 2014. The precipitating event for the protests that eventually brought down the government was the decision of Ukrainian President Viktor Yanukovych to not sign a proposed association agreement between Ukraine and the EU in November 2013, one he had previously said he would sign. Yanukovych, you'll recall, had been on the losing side of the 2004 Orange revolution, but was elected to the presidency in a fair election in 2010. Putin, who was promoting his concept of a Eurasian Economic Union in the former Soviet space as an alternative to the EU, provided a series of incentives to Yanukovych to align more closely with Russia, including 15 billion dollars in credit and cheaper natural gas prices. Yanukovych's ham-handed efforts to crack down on those protesting against his decision simply fueled further larger rallies, which gripped the center of Kyiv for several months in the dead of winter. Putin actively followed the developments in Ukraine. He had made clear since the beginning of his presidency that Ukraine was a top priority for him, reportedly telling his associates, "if we don't do something, we will lose it." During the protests in Kyiv, Putin was in frequent contact with Yanukovych.[32]

Equally on Putin's mind at the time were the final preparations for the February 2014 Winter Olympics in Sochi. Sochi was a major prestige project for Russia and for Putin personally, so he was rankled by foreign criticism of Russia's domestic political order, of corruption in the construction process for the games (see chapter 5), and of some of the problems getting Sochi ready for the big opening (Western reporters and social media users gleefully tweeted photos of bathrooms with two toilets in one stall, brown tap water in the hotels, and other deficiencies under the hashtag #SochiProblems). An annoyed Putin, according to his press secretary, said that outsiders would stop criticizing Russia only "when we dissolve our army, when we concede all our natural resources to them . . . , and when we sell all of our land to Western investors."[33]

In the end, the Sochi Olympics were a considerable success, but the party was utterly spoiled for Putin by the collapse of Yanukovych's government in the aftermath of several days of violent confrontation in central Kyiv, which left over one hundred people dead.[34] Putin later revealed that he personally helped coordinate Yanukovych's overland flight to Russia. More consequently, Putin ordered the infiltration of Russian special forces into the

Ukrainian region of Crimea, with the goal of "returning Crimea into Russia" (prior to 1954, Crimea had been part of the Russian republic inside the Soviet Union, before being transferred to the Ukrainian republic). This was clearly Putin's personal initiative. He later recounted how there were only four people with him the night when he made the decision. The names of these four people have not been confirmed, but one well-informed account suggests that it was Minister of Defense Sergey Shoygu, head of the FSB Aleksandr Bortnikov, presidential chief of staff Sergey Ivanov, and Secretary of the Security Council Nikolay Patrushev. If correct, three of the four participants were, like Putin, Leningraders who began their careers in the KGB in the 1970s, and ones who have quite similar worldviews. The fourth man present, Shoygu, had known Putin since the 1990s and had worked for him since 2000, having demonstrated his loyalty in multiple ways.[35]

Within a month of this monumental decision, Crimea had indeed "returned to Russia," although from the point of view of international law, including several agreements to which Russia was a direct signatory, Crimea was rightfully part of an independent Ukraine. The military takeover of Crimea was the first such forcible annexation by one European state of part of its neighbor's territory since the end of World War II.[36] Russia's grab of Crimea, condemned by most of the world as an illegal violation of Ukraine's sovereignty and territorial integrity, was viewed by Putin as a necessary and defensive response to yet another American-instigated "colored revolution." The events in Kyiv, Putin said, were not a popular uprising but "an anticonstitutional coup and armed seizure of power." He accused the West of interference in Ukraine, drawing a comparison to "American employees of some laboratory . . . conducting experiments like on rats, not understanding the consequences of what they are doing."[37]

Putin and his team apparently believed that there was a strong possibility that the new pro-European Ukrainian government would kick Russia's Black Sea Fleet out of Crimea, despite a basing agreement between the two countries that lasted until 2042, and be put on a fast track to NATO membership. In his March 2014 speech justifying the annexation of Crimea, Putin said that there was a real possibility that NATO would have created a naval base there, which "would have created a threat for all of southern Russia." As far back as 2008, Putin allegedly said in private that if Ukraine were to join NATO it would have to do so without Crimea and eastern Ukraine.[38]

Contra Putin's assertions, there doesn't seem to be any good evidence that the 2014 revolution in Ukraine was planned in Washington, or that there was an American plan to bring Ukraine into NATO, push the Russians out of Crimea, and establish American bases there. But Putin and his team were convinced that the Americans were out to get them and, more specifically, that Washington was sponsoring revolutions in the former Soviet space under the guise of promoting democracy. Given this mentality, a defensive overreaction to the sudden collapse of Ukraine's government becomes understandable. The issue went beyond either rational calculations of Russian interests or the specific ideas of Putin and his close allies from the Leningrad KGB. For example, the Ministry of Finance was not asked what the costs of the Crimea decision would be before it was taken. One Russian foreign policy expert told me that the Crimea annexation was a "quite emotional, improvised decision," and that Putin felt betrayed by European leaders, whose last-ditch effort to engineer a peaceful end to the crisis collapsed when Yanukovych's support evaporated and he fled the capital. More generally, remarked another Russian observer, Putin felt that he had "tolerated humiliation from the West for many years," and that the annexation of Crimea was not so much a pragmatic defense of Russian interests but "the redemption of his own humiliation."[39]

The annexation of Crimea, it turned out, was only the beginning. In the spring of 2014 the violent conflict spread to southeast Ukraine on the border with Russia, an area known as the Donbas. Putin, while denying Russian military involvement, suggested that much of southern and eastern Ukraine was legitimately part of Russia historically, since it had been part of the Russian empire in tsarist times and had only become part of Ukraine "for God knows what reason" under the Soviet government in the 1920s. Despite Putin's denials, there is clear evidence that Russian military personnel have participated in the fighting in Ukraine. By supporting armed rebellion in the Donbas, Russia hoped to force a political solution that would decentralize power and give the more pro-Russian regions of Ukraine a de facto veto over Ukrainian political, economic, and military alignment with the West.[40]

When considering Russian strategy in Ukraine, it is important to keep the big picture in mind. From the beginning of his presidency, Putin was determined to prevent the "loss" of Ukraine. In 2013, Putin's goal was to bring all of Ukraine into his Eurasian Economic Union. After the 2014 Ukrainian uprising and the annexation of Crimea, Russia has put itself in the situation where it is propping up a rebellion in a tiny corner of Ukraine, with all of the associated political, economic, and human costs. The current pro-European Ukrainian government may yet collapse, and there are strong cultural, historic, and economic ties between Russia and Ukraine, especially its eastern regions, that in the long run may lead to closer Russian-Ukrainian relations once again. But so far Putin doesn't seem to be "winning" in Ukraine.

Most galling, perhaps, for Russia's leaders, is that most foreign leaders, particularly in the West, don't think and feel about the Ukraine crisis the way they do. Putin and his key associates are, as one Russian journalist put it, "absolutely certain that they were right, that they were not aggressors but victims. That they were not attacking, but defending—they were forced to defend themselves, because they were attacked by America." Instead of understanding and respect for Russian prerogatives in its "sphere of privileged interests," Russia was met with attempted isolation. The EU and the United States, as well as several other countries, levied sanctions both against specific Russian elites and sectors of the Russian economy. Many of Putin's closest associates were personally sanctioned, and their business interests in Europe and the United States came under threat. For example, Putin's billionaire friend Gennadiy Timchenko, who was given a pivotal role in the oil trading business under Putin, lamented that he couldn't visit his family and dog in the south of France, his wife had difficulty paying for medical care in Germany, and his Gulfstream private jet was grounded. This was the price he had to pay for being acquainted with Putin, he said, and he expressed his willingness to turn over everything to the state if necessary. Although few Russians are probably feeling particularly sorry for Timchenko's intense suffering, the more serious issue is that Putin's Crimea decision put in doubt the ability of Russia's elite to legitimate their wealth not just in Russia, but in the West, one of the most important objectives of postcommunist Russia's ruling class. Hundreds of state officials, and many more businesspeople who don't work for the state, own property abroad, and almost exclusively in EU-member countries or the United States. This mismatch between property and principles, in which the West is where officials park their money and families but the West is simultaneously attacked as anti-Russian and hypocritical, is just one of the paradoxes of Putinism.[41]

The high-water mark of Putin's isolation came at the G-20 (the twenty leading world economies) summit in Australia in November 2014. The meeting came just a few months after pro-Russian rebels had accidentally shot down a civilian airliner with a Russian-supplied missile, killing nearly three hundred people. Putin was shunned by Western leaders—one headline called him "Putin the pariah"—and told bluntly by the Canadian prime minister to "get out of Ukraine." He was even stuck on the edge of the traditional group photo. When he sat down for a one-on-one meeting with German Chancellor Angela Merkel, he spent two hours going through "a litany of resentments," including over NATO and EU enlargement, the Iraq war, and the Libya intervention. Putin left the summit early, claiming he needed to get some sleep on the long flight home. Everyone knows that when someone leaves a party early claiming that they are tired, it really means that they are not having a good time. One Russian journalist told me that Putin "endured with difficulty" his treatment in Australia. Putin sees himself "as a big man in a big country" who is not accorded the status and recognition he is deserved.[42]

Putin's next major counterpunch came in Syria in September 2015. Russia's air force unexpectedly intervened in the Syrian civil war on the side of Bashar al-Assad. This was Russia's first major military intervention outside the former Soviet Union since the country's 1991 dissolution. The Syrian regime, which in the summer of 2015 appeared to be on the verge of collapse after more than four years of civil war, was able to shift the momentum in its favor over the next year with the help of the Russian military and Iranian fighters. Russia had both specific and more general aims with its intervention. With respect to Syria, Russia wanted to keep its last true ally in the Middle East in power and maintain its access to a Russian naval facility in the country. Further, as noted above, members of the Russian political elite attributed the uprisings of the Arab Spring to American interference, designed to destabilize Russia-friendly regimes, and they were determined to push back. More generally, though, Putin was determined to break out of Russia's isolation and reestablish Russia as a great power that could not be ignored. As one US journalist put it, Putin's foreign policy is "about avenging the wrongs inflicted on Russia over the past decades, the insults and grievances borne by a generation." Putin chafed at Obama's 2014 description of Russia as a mere "regional power"—Syria was, in part, his response. As one of Russia's leading foreign affairs analysts put it, Russia's intervention in Syria showed that only Moscow and Washington, just like during the Cold War, "are able to take important decisions and put them into practice."[43]

Putin's most audacious counterpunch of all came in 2016, when Russia intervened in the US presidential election. Of course, Putin denies this, although he did suggest at one point that perhaps the cyber component was the work of "patriotic" Russian hackers on their own initiative.[44] The bulk of the publicly available evidence, however, suggests otherwise. This is not the place to review all of the proof, especially since the case for Russian interference is based on lots of pieces put together, rather than one smoking gun. The formal January 2017 report issued by the Director of National Intelligence (DNI) was hampered by fears of revealing secret "sources and methods" and thus was very disappointing, revealing little new information. But it is hard to reject all of the evidence, including definitive statements on the issue from US intelligence and law enforcement agencies and personnel, as well as multiple investigative accounts by experts and journalists laying out the publicly available information, sometimes with sourcing based on secret data. Some of the notable bits of evidence include (these are just examples):

- tell-tale signs and patterns that connected the hackers responsible for the infiltration of the Democratic National Committee (DNC) and the Hillary Clinton campaign to previous Russian cyberattacks;
- a leaked top-secret US intelligence report linking Russia to attacks on local election officials and election software suppliers in the United States;
- an intercepted May 2016 conversation of a Russian military intelligence officer bragging that Russia was going to mess with the American election to get payback against Hillary Clinton for her (presumed) effort to inspire street protests against Putin in December 2011;
- reports by a Kremlin-connected think tank, acquired by US intelligence, laying out Russia's social media and "fake news" campaign to attack Clinton and sow doubt about the legitimacy of US elections.[45]

It is not at all surprising, in fact, that Russian intelligence agencies would try to hack into the DNC, the Republican National Committee, the accounts of government officials and political operatives, and other influential Americans. Information acquired this way could help Russia formulate its policy toward the United States. What was unprecedented was the decision to leak this information in an effort to affect the election. At a minimum, it appears the goal was to, as the DNI report put it, "undermine public faith in the US democratic process, denigrate Secretary Clinton, and harm her electability and potential presidency." The DNI also concluded that eventually Putin and Russia "developed a clear preference" for Trump. Even so, given that Putin seems to believe that American elections are as rigged as Russian ones (see chapter 1), the Russian government may not have thought that Trump could actually win, so questioning the legitimacy of the election and weakening Clinton was an objective on its own. Now that Trump is president, Russia is more inclined to argue that deep-seated "Russophobia" among the American political and media elite is preventing Trump from improving relations with Russia.[46]

Cynics would also point out, quite correctly, that this is hardly the first time major powers have interfered in the election of other countries—something both the United States and the Soviet Union did many times during the Cold War. Russians point out, also correctly, that US President Bill Clinton made his support for Boris Yeltsin in Russia's 1996 presidential election rather obvious—in an April 1996 press conference in Moscow, for example, Clinton compared Yeltsin to Abraham Lincoln. But there is a clear difference between what Russia did in 2016—leaking internal party communications acquired through cyber hacking and running an aggressive fake news campaign on social media to discredit one candidate—and what the United States and the EU have done in Russia and Eurasia in the last couple of decades, which was to very openly fund NGOs promoting human rights, a free press, and fair elections (among many other things). To Putin and almost all of his closest associates, however, all this talk about promoting democracy and human rights is deeply cynical, designed to conceal the true purpose of American policy, which is to overthrow governments it doesn't like—including Russia's. Official Russian military and security documents speak openly about the danger from this threat of external subversion to Russia and its neighbors.[47]

In terms of understanding Russian foreign policy, perhaps the most interesting part of the DNI report is its discussion of Putin's motives for electoral interference. The report notes that Putin blames the United States both for press reports about secret bank accounts held by his close associates—the so-called Panama Papers—and investigations into doping by Russian athletes, which he sees as efforts to smear Russia and him personally. Further, it states that Putin "holds a grudge" against Hillary Clinton because of the 2011–2012 Moscow protests. The *New York Times* observed, "Perhaps most arresting is the assessment [that Putin] sees the election attack as payback—not offense, but defense." They quoted a former CIA officer, who remarked, "From the Russian perspective, this is punching back."[48]

Can't Win for Winning

Vladimir Putin keeps winning—how could he not, being the most powerful man in the world for four years running, according to *Forbes* magazine?—yet he can't seem to catch a break. Even if Russian intervention did play some role in Trump's election—which is not proven, by the way—it might be a case of be careful what you wish for.[49] On the positive side for Russia, Trump's election has brought to power an American president who is more hostile to democracy promotion abroad than any in living memory, has brought chaos to the policy process in Washington, and arguably even called into question the strength and unity of the Western liberal democratic order. On the other hand, Trump has not been able to deliver on his goal of improved relations with Russia, and members of Congress, Republicans and Democrats alike, were so distrustful of Trump's relationship with Putin that they passed a law locking in sanctions against Russia. The sanctions were more a way for Congress to say "we don't like what you're doing" than a useful tool to bring about specific policy changes, and entrenching them in legislation deprives not only Trump but also potentially future presidents of valuable policy flexibility.[50] Russian-American relations under Trump, at least so far, are no better than they were under Obama.

The palpable dislike of Obama among many Russian foreign policy elites was always hard to understand. Putin and his closest allies repeatedly attacked the United States under Obama for pursuing a policy of "total, world domination" that sought to weaken Russia, up to and including bringing about its disintegration. As a former American diplomat observed, Obama was simultaneously "vilified by his American critics for spineless inaction in the face of Russian aggression" and "anathematized by Moscow as the evil genius behind a massive Western conspiracy to undermine Russian interests in every possible way."[51] The true reason for the animosity toward Obama probably had more to do with the growing feeling of being under siege in Moscow, due to the 2011–2012 electoral protests, the Arab Spring, the 2014 Ukraine crisis, and years of economic slowdown and stagnation, than anything done by Obama. Further, especially once the reset petered out and Putin returned to the Kremlin, Obama apparently decided that major breakthroughs with Moscow were unlikely, and he devoted himself to other regions, like East Asia and the Middle East. This relative neglect of Russia's concerns, and the harsh dismissal of Russia as a mere "regional power," rankled Team Putin. As one Russian journalist put it, "It's an emotional story of Russia not being treated like a superpower and, for many of them, it's a personal story."[52]

Thus, if military intervention in Georgia in 2008 and Ukraine in 2014 were efforts to revise a *European* order unjustly imposed on Russia, Syria and the interference in the 2016 US election were designed to revise an *international* order unjustly imposed on Russia.[53] Putin has been pretty clear about how he wants the system to change. In a 2015 speech to the UN General Assembly, he opened with a tribute to the 1945 Yalta summit at the end of World War II, at which The Big Three—Stalin, Churchill, and Roosevelt—made the "key decisions on the principles defining interaction between states." The Yalta system, he continued, "saved the world from large-scale upheavals." An influential Russian analyst extended this point, arguing that a new approach to global governance needs to be created. There is no alternative, he contends, to a "return to the Concert of Nations concept. At first, if these efforts succeed, we will have a Group of Three—Russia, China, and the U.S." Other countries could be added later, such as India, Japan, Brazil, and some from Europe.[54]

Russia as a respected great power, one of a new Big Three, consulted on all major international questions, and deferred to on issues within its sphere of influence—this is the goal of a Putinist foreign policy. This is what "winning" would look like for the code of Putinism, the purpose of strenuous efforts to punch above Russia's weight. Despite all of Putin's alleged foreign policy "wins" in recent years, however, this ultimate victory seems out of reach, for two main reasons—one about ideas, the other about power.

The first reason, about ideas, is that many states in the international system aren't prepared to return to a Concert of Nations concept. Most importantly for Russia, this vision is no longer viable for Europe. Merkel, the leading politician in western Europe, has firmly criticized Russia's actions in Ukraine as a threat to European stability. While in Moscow in 2015 for the seventieth anniversary of the end of World War II, she denounced the annexation of Crimea as "criminal and illegal." Elsewhere she stated that the Crimea takeover called the "entire European peace order into question," reflecting "old thinking about spheres of influence, which runs roughshod over international law." She made clear that Russia had no veto over decisions about who joins the EU.[55]

Not only do the major western European powers resist a return to a spheres-of-influence world but so also do the smaller states whose fates would be decided by the great powers. Experts have observed that the countries in the former Soviet space in which Russia has used military power without a host government invitation since the end of the Cold War—Moldova, Georgia, and Ukraine—are also among the most resistant to Russia's effort to keep them in its orbit. As one former US diplomat put it, "the harder Russia squeezes its neighbors, the more they will turn to Euroatlantic institutions as a refuge."[56]

Accepting that Europe can't return to a spheres-of-influence system dominated by the great powers doesn't mean that Russian security concerns in the region should be ignored. It's not surprising that Russia doesn't like NATO expansion, for example, even though it would be nice if Russian leaders would sometimes acknowledge that NATO greatly reduced its military forces once the Soviet threat disappeared, and that NATO is in no position to launch an invasion of Russia. A major problem with NATO enlargement from the beginning was that there was no clear answer to the reasonable question, "where does it stop?" If it's hard to imagine a NATO with Russia as a member, at least in the short to medium run, it also seems unwise and even unfair to say every other post-Soviet state in Europe *can* join if they apply and meet the membership criteria. Saying that Russia can also apply doesn't really solve the problem, since everyone recognizes that Russia is different, given its size, military power, and long border with China, and that trying to integrate it into NATO is a much larger challenge than any other potential new member. The problem of what to do with countries that Samuel Charap and Timothy Colton call "the In-Betweens"—countries like Georgia and Ukraine, between Russia and an enlarged NATO—has never been satisfactorily solved. No one has, to my knowledge, come up with a solution to this problem that satisfies NATO, Russia, and the In-Betweens, because it's like putting a square peg in a round hole. The concession Putin wants—recognition of a sphere of influence in the former Soviet space—is one the West almost certainly will refuse to give. More dialogue is certainly called for, but after the Ukraine crisis, both sides are more suspicious than ever. And, it is worth emphasizing, NATO expansion arguably is not even the most vexing issue for Putin and his group—colored revolutions in neighboring states increased feelings of vulnerability and encirclement in the Kremlin at least as much as NATO enlargement did. The challenge of a new European security architecture ultimately is more political than military.[57]

Making the problem even more difficult is that it seems that Putin doesn't believe Western leaders when they tell him that the era of great power spheres of influence is in the past. As one Russian expert put it, "He thinks the new globalization is just a fig leaf for what's really going on, which is that Western leaders want to divide up the world without him and leave Russia without a slice."[58] The failure of these Western leaders to give Russia its deserved status, in Putin's view, is just further evidence that they are hypocrites who have it in for Russia.

The contrast between Russia's relations with the West and its relations with China is instructive. The rise of China arguably represents a much bigger challenge to Russia's great power status than any American or European policies. China has greatly expanded its economic and political influence in areas of Russian "privileged interests," such as Central Asia. China, though, is careful to exhibit the outward signs of respect for Russia's status, and it does not criticize Russian domestic affairs—Russia and China are united in opposition to Western hectoring about issues such as democracy and human rights. Because the Russian and Chinese elite are on the same page ideationally—both are statist and illiberal—and because China doesn't push Team Putin's emotional buttons, the longer-term consequences of China's rise for Russian power and status are given less attention than perhaps is warranted.

The second reason that Putin can't win, at least given the ambitions he has set for Russia's place in the world, takes us back to the beginning: that Russia is punching above its weight. Let's look at the hypothetical "Big Three" of the United States, China, and Russia. They are the world's three biggest military spenders, but they are not at all equal in this respect. The United States represents one-third of all world military expenditures, spending almost three times as much as China and nearly nine times as much as Russia. If we look at the world economy, the big three are the United States, China, and the EU (if we treat it as a single economy). Russia doesn't crack the top ten, with an economy fourteen times smaller than the US one, and almost nine times smaller than China. In population, there is really a "Big Two" of China and India, but the United States is in third place. Russia is ninth, less than half the size of the United States and nine times smaller than China. Yes, Russia is a very important country—that's one reason everyone is talking about it—the largest one in the world and one of two nuclear superpowers. Historically, Russia's claim to great power status always depended more on its size, location, and military might, not its level of economic development.[59] But ultimately military power is generated from a state's economic and demographic potential, which makes Russian aspirations for a "Big Three" of Russia, China, and the United States look extremely ambitious, if not downright fanciful.

This mismatch between capabilities and ambition, the desire to punch above its weight, is not likely to get better going forward. China's economic dynamism, as noted, has made it a major force to contend with in areas historically dominated by Russia, such as Central Asia. Europe, similarly, has extended its influence into areas traditionally dominated by Russia. The future of the West, of course, is rather uncertain now, with both the EU and the United States facing major challenges. But the United States and Europe together (meaning either the EU or NATO) still represent almost half of the world economy and more than half of world military spending, and there doesn't seem to be any obvious alternative to the liberal international order built by Europe and North America and joined by many other states around the world—at least not yet. Thomas Graham, one of America's most prominent Russia experts, suggests that one reason Russia seems to be trying so hard to remake the international order right now is because it senses its ability to do so going forward may be compromised by economic stagnation and domestic political weakness. The feeling of vulnerability among the Putinist elite—one British expert thinks the best word to describe them is "scared"—is motivated both by these very real relative disadvantages and a code based on resentment, suspicion of the United States, and a desire to maintain control and unity at home.[60] With Putin on an apparently unstoppable run of nearly twenty-five years in charge—at the time of writing, he seemed destined to win easily a fourth term as president in 2018—Russians clearly believe he is the man to deliver on these ambitions and promises.

Putinism Forever?

When Vladimir Putin became president on December 31, 1999, the *Ottawa Citizen* marked the event with a provocative and rather offensive op-ed titled "Russia under Putin Will Suck, As Always." John Robson began by observing that Putin's rise has "everyone wondering if he's the miracle man who will finally make Russia a normal state." Robson never defined what he meant by a normal state, but his answer, buried underneath a collection of insults, cultural stereotypes, and one-sided history, was obviously no. Russia, Robson declared, was "cursed by nature" and "doomed by history and culture."

I have my undergraduate students at Syracuse University read this op-ed the first week of class. Why? One reason is that in the space of a page and a half it hits many common stereotypes about Russia and Russians, especially that Russia is "doomed by history and culture" and that it can never become a "normal state." A second reason is that it poses the question of whether Putin is a "miracle man" and how much he can change Russia. To some Russians he is indeed a miracle man. For example, the ruler of the Chechen Republic inside Russia, Ramzan Kadyrov, declared in 2007, "Allah appointed him to his position. . . . Putin saved our people, he is a hero. He not only saved us [the Chechens], he saved Russia. . . . Putin is a gift from God, he gave us our freedom."[1]

Kadyrov is not the only one who sees Putin as some kind of savior. This book began with the claim by a top Putin aide, "There is no Putin—There is no Russia." This official, Vyacheslav Volodin, doubled down on his assertion in 2017 while looking ahead to the 2018 presidential election, stating:

> For those who want a future for Russia, the well-being of the country and its citizens, a peaceful sky above, there is only one candidate. . . . Only one man can do the job—Putin. And we are not the only ones who understand that. Our enemies also understand that, and they

have not given up on their goal of dismembering Russia and taking her sovereignty.[2]

A Russian friend of mine agreed, telling me in June 2017 there is no one else who can rule Russia now but Putin, and that Putin will be able to leave when a "new smart guy" shows up. According to one well-connected journalist, Putin also sees himself as indispensable and the savior of Russia, without whom Russia would collapse.[3]

The indispensable nature of Putin to the system is a key reason that everyone assumed that he would be re-elected in March 2018. By the time you are reading this, we will know if these assumptions were correct, and if Putin is beginning his fourth term as president. If so, he can legally serve until 2024, by which point he will have been Russia's top ruler for almost twenty-five years and will be seventy-two years old. After a quarter-century in power, the hyperbolic claim by Volodin of "no Putin, no Russia" will seem quite accurate to many Russian citizens; they will remember no other leader (only a few future Russian pedants would bother to point out that someone named Dmitriy Medvedev was also president for four years in there).

The central claim of this book is that there is not just an indispensable leader named Putin but also something called *Putinism*. The code of Putinism, generally shared by the key members of Putin's team, is what gives Putin's reign its distinct stamp. It is the particular combination of ideas, habits, and emotions that plays an important role in guiding policy and decision-making. Understanding the code helps us make sense of what Putin has done and where Russia is today.

Russia was not "doomed" to move in an authoritarian direction in 2000; rather, Putin and his team made a series of choices that over time closed the political space in Russia further and further. At the end of the Boris Yeltsin era, Russia had a political system with elements of both democracy and authoritarianism, but elections were generally competitive, television was not controlled by the Kremlin, regional governors had real, independent power (arguably too much), and nongovernmental organizations had plenty of room to organize, including in opposition to the state. Putin's form of hyperpresidentialism does allow some political competition, and some space for alternative groups and voices, but it is much more limited than under Yeltsin, and real challenges to the ruling group are effectively choked off.

Russia now has a much more authoritarian political system than is typical for relatively wealthy countries with an educated and urbanized society.

Political scientists have shown that Russia is one of the wealthiest countries in the world to have reverted to authoritarianism after establishing democracy—even if we don't count oil when calculating Russia's wealth. Almost all of the world's richest autocracies are Muslim petro-state monarchies, like Qatar or Saudi Arabia. Russia is not like these other countries, including in the economic realm. Although US Senator John McCain once quipped that Russia is "a gas station masquerading as a country," this is not true; the Russian economy has large industrial and service sectors, making it considerably more diverse than that of other relatively wealthy authoritarian states. In short, Russian authoritarianism is unusual in comparative terms.[4]

To be sure, Russia also has other attributes that point away from a more democratic political system, including its challenging geographic circumstances, its authoritarian traditions, and the abundance of oil and gas (smaller as a percentage of the economy than other petro-states, but still highly important). Complex conditions are not unavoidable curses, however, and political leaders always have choices. The mentality of Putin and his allies—statist, conservative, possessing feelings of vulnerability and disposed toward order and unity—was central to Russia's authoritarian direction since 2000.

More important than Putin's post as president (and prime minister for four years) is his status as boss of the clans. The informal politics of competing clan networks is fundamental to Russian politics and understanding the nature of Putinism. At first, especially before 2004 or so, Putin was first among equals, playing a difficult balancing game between leftover powerbrokers and oligarchs from the Yeltsin era, conservative chekists (ex-KGB people) from St. Petersburg, and a more liberal team of economists and lawyers from his time as vice mayor of St. Petersburg. Lurking in the background, at least initially, were other insiders with growing economic clout; some were childhood friends of Putin, some were acquaintances and partners and dacha neighbors from St. Petersburg, some were connections made in the KGB, including in East Germany. These various cronies were given increasing responsibility for key economic sectors—oil and gas, transportation and communications, construction and banking. Russian analysts often refer to these different groups as clans, a term I have used as well, with the proviso that they are not fixed entities united by blood ties, but adaptable configurations of economic and political elites connected through various networks that cross formal boundaries between the state and business. Elite clans still exist, and the clash of clans is ongoing, but Putin is not just the broker now, he is the Sun of the solar system around which competing groups orbit, all of them subject to the gravitational pull of the boss. They have a voice, but Putin holds the veto. Over time he has become more tsar-like, sidelining some of his previous close associates and promoting a younger generation of colorless bodyguards and aides to top positions. Loyalty is now due to Putin himself, not the Putin team.

The nature of the economy, the policy process, government performance, and foreign policy are all consequences of Putinism as a code and as a political system combining hyperpresidentialism with informal clan networks. Putinomics, rooted in the desire for control and loyalty, is a form of crony capitalism in which many of the most important businesses, whether state or privately owned, are in the hands of Putin's close associates from his hometown or from his earlier service in the KGB or the St. Petersburg mayor's office. Putinomics as an economic system is top-heavy, with small and medium-size businesses contributing less to the overall economy than they might if Russia had better political, economic, and legal institutions. Russia was able to grow rapidly from 1999 to 2008 because of a general regional recovery after the Soviet collapse, increasing energy prices, high world demand, and, to be fair, relatively competent management of fiscal and monetary policy by the state. On the other hand, Russia's inability to return to high growth rates after the 2009 recession, despite historically high world oil prices, showed the limits of Putinomics. The sputtering economy presents a major challenge for Putin going forward. He may be forced to adopt unpopular measures, such as raising taxes and the retirement age, with unpredictable social consequences.[5]

Another major challenge to Putinism is the quality of the state. Corruption and the "unrule of law" are persistent problems in Russia.[6] They certainly precede Putin. Initially there was some hope that the tough KGB guy with the law degree would impose order and fight corruption, and he promised to do so frequently in his speeches. Most evaluations, however, suggest little progress on these fronts. Indeed, Putinism, with its reliance on informal networks over formal institutions, and with the preference for loyalty over competence, means that the Russian state remains highly ineffective, in spite of Putin's pretentions to be the great state-builder. It would be unfair to say that nothing has been done, and some social and economic indicators improved noticeably under Putin. Overall, however, the payoff from the economic boom of the 2000s in terms of better governance has been remarkably slim.

Central to the code of Putinism is maintaining Russia's status as a great power. The Russian people, and many international observers, give Putin high marks for restoring Russian economic and military power after the low point of the Soviet collapse and the subsequent economic depression. Russia's assertive behavior in Georgia, Ukraine, and Syria, and a determined rearmament push, have conveyed the image that the Russian Bear is back. On the other hand, Russia represents less than 2 percent of the world economy and world population, and has no other major powers as an ally—China is a "strategic partner," but hardly a military or political ally. Putin's counterpunch against the West has made the task of making Russia a respected great power in the future more difficult, isolating it politically from important economic partners and increasing its dependence on China going forward. Feelings of resentment and vulnerability, key elements of the code of Putinism, helped motivate a series of decisions that have made the sense of living in a besieged fortress even more palpable to Russia's rulers.

The code of Putinism is critical to understanding Russia's last two decades, and the choices Team Putin made. These choices were the product of certain impulses and feelings and a specific worldview. When faced with a critical juncture, Putin and his closest circle were driven in a particular direction by this code. Further, the essence of this code became increasingly resentful, anti-American, conservative, and obsessed with order and control over time.

The code, of course, is not the only thing that matters. All people, even the most powerful man in the world (Putin, according to *Forbes* magazine), face a series of constraints on their behavior. Further, people typically think about their rational self-interest and how to make themselves better off as they make decisions. The point about the code is not that Putin and his close allies are *less* rational or *more* motivated by habits, emotions, and ideas than anyone else. The point is that they are human and, like the rest of us, they are driven by a complex set of factors. Indeed, deciding what's in your interest in the first place depends on what matters to you, which is driven in part by feelings, values, and habits. Importantly, in the Russian political system, given the prominence of the leader and the weakness of institutional constraints, there is more space for the mentality of the ruling group to play a significant role and drive outcomes.

Often it might be hard to tell which factors—the code, circumstances, or rational self-interest—mattered most, because they all played some role.[7] Take, for example, the Yukos affair, in which Mikhail Khodorkovsky, then Russia's richest man, was arrested and his company taken over by the

state-controlled Rosneft, managed since 2004 by Putin's close ally Igor
Sechin (see chapter 4). The pursuit of power and wealth offers a simple and
plausible reason for the Yukos affair. Elements of the code, however, give us a
fuller picture. For example, statist ideas and habits of control and order put a
premium on state domination of key economic sectors, even if this arguably
harmed Russia's long-term economic development.[8] Anti-American ideas
and feelings of vulnerability made the Kremlin particularly worried about
Khodorkovsky's plans for a deal with a major American oil company—
would American money flow into Russian politics through the Yukos back
door? Better to bring the company under state control and put it in the hands
of a loyal ally than to leave it with a potentially disloyal Khodorkovsky. In this
case, rationality and the code seemed to reinforce each other.

Other steps taken by Putin seem hard to explain solely based on the narrow
self-interest of him and his allies. The major defense buildup over the last
decade is about what Russia's rulers think is good for Russia as a major great
power, not about self-enrichment. Even more to the point, if Putin was just a
power-hungry thief, many of his domestic socioeconomic initiatives—such
as policies designed to cut smoking and alcoholism (see chapter 5)—make
no sense. I also would argue that we can only understand three of Putin's
most consequential foreign policy decisions in recent years—the annexation
of Crimea, the intervention in Syria, and interference in the 2016 US presidential election—with reference to the code (see chapter 6). Great-power
resentments, feelings of vulnerability, and illiberal and anti-American ideas
help explain these policies. For example, the code led Putin to perceive the
chaotic and highly contingent 2014 Euromaidan revolution in Ukraine as a
US conspiracy designed to unnaturally pull Ukraine out of Russia's orbit and
bring it under American domination. The annexation of Crimea and Russian
covert support for a separatist war in southeast Ukraine have hurt Russia's
economy, its international standing with key partners, and, most concretely,
the wealth and business interests of some of Putin's closest associates, given the
sanctions placed on them. Russian actions in Ukraine also have led to greater
support in Ukraine for a trajectory toward the West and away from Russia,
increasing the likelihood that Putin's fear of "losing" Ukraine will come true.
As one Russian writer put it, the "divorce" between Russia and Ukraine "will
not be considered a plus for the head of Russia in future history textbooks."
A more sober response to the 2014 Euromaidan revolution would not have
damaged Russia's standing in Ukraine and the rest of Europe so badly.[9]

The point, to reiterate, is not to say that the code of Putinism explains everything about Russian politics. Rather, the central claim is that understanding the mentality of Putin and his associates is a critical piece of a broader understanding of the road Russia has traveled over the last two decades, more comprehensive and persuasive than versions based either on a narrow rationalist account or on the irresistible pull of historical, geographic, cultural, or economic factors. Understanding Putin's Russia requires understanding the code of Putinism.

Putinism and the Quest for a "Normal State"

To many Russians, Putin has been a savior, a miracle man. Most Western observers, especially among the political elite, see him very differently, "as a kind of Bond villain," in the words of one Russian journalist. Some have speculated that Putin likes all of this attention, even if negative, and that it is better than "feeling ignored," as he did for so many years. But, as noted in the last chapter, the "villain" doesn't think he's the villain, he thinks he's the hero. Putin thinks he's Bond, not Blofeld. Western observers, who don't share Putin's feelings, habits, and ideas, and thus don't understand his mentality, find it easier to see him as a villain. Putin thinks he has rebuilt the Russian state, restored its territorial integrity, and protected Russia's sovereignty— heroic achievements indeed.[10]

So what does a "normal state" mean to Vladimir Putin? At the very beginning of his presidency, when he set the goal of building a strong Russian state, he specified, "strong state power in Russia is a democratic, law-based, capable, federal state."[11] A democratic, effective, rule-of-law state is also what most Russians have in mind when they talk about becoming a "normal country." In this respect, Putin the miracle man has turned water into vinegar rather than wine. Russia is less democratic and federal than in 2000, and the "unrule of law" prevails. The Russian state might be more capable in some respects than it was under Yeltsin, but given the favorable circumstances created by a decade of extremely high world energy prices and rapid economic growth, Russia is misruled compared to its peer countries.

Perhaps, even after eighteen years, it is too early to expect Russia to have achieved the vision of normalcy that Putin articulated at the beginning of his presidency, in which personal rule gives way to strong institutions and the rule of law. Putin, it seems, believes that creating this type of "normal state" can only happen at the appropriate time. He stated in 2007:

> We, emerging from a deep systemic crisis, were forced to do a lot in a so-called "manual regime." When will that time arrive when most things, or the basic things, can function in an automatic regime? After we create the necessary legal conditions and mechanisms, when all elements of a market economy work to the full extent. . . . This demands time. . . . When the legal, and economic, and social base has grown up and become stable, then we will not need manual steering. . . . I think that will be in fifteen–twenty years.[12]

Fifteen or twenty years from 2007 would put us around 2022–2027. Putin, assuming reelection in 2018, is now on track to rule until 2024. Putin stated that such long tenures for leaders is reasonable under certain conditions, noting that Western leaders like De Gaulle and Franklin Delano Roosevelt served for more than a decade: "When a country is in complicated and difficult circumstances, coming out of a crisis, standing on its feet, elements of stability, including in the political sphere, are extremely important." On several occasions, he has invoked the comparison to Roosevelt, who served as US president during the Great Depression and World War II, was elected to four terms, and served twelve years as president before his death.[13]

Both the emphasis on Russia's deep crisis, and the invocation of long-serving foreign democratic leaders, are meant to suggest that what looks to be abnormal—one man as principal ruler of a country for twenty-five years—should be seen as normal. Medvedev's four years as president from 2008 to 2012 allow Putin to claim he wasn't president for twenty-five straight years, but the phenomenon of "tandemocracy" under the Putin-Medvedev system just reinforces how abnormal Putin's long period of rule is compared to "normal" countries, where the person who holds the top constitutional office is also the most important political figure.

For many Russians, becoming a "normal country" was not only about establishing democracy and a capable rule-of-law state—it was at least as much about making Russia into a developed market economy. For Putin as well, economic development was a fundamental goal. In his programmatic statement at the beginning of his presidency, Putin set the goal of growing at 8 percent a year for fifteen years, in order to catch up with countries like Portugal and Spain in terms of GDP per capita. From 2000 to 2016 Russia achieved an average rate of economic growth that was about half of Putin's target—3.9 percent. This is certainly a respectable number, but the overall average obscures a fundamental truth and huge problem. From 2000 to 2008, Russia grew at a rate of almost 7 percent per year. In contrast, from 2009 to 2016 Russian economic growth was basically flat—an average of 0.4 percent a year, an economic "lost decade," in the words of one Russian commentator. Boom has turned to bust, and Russia shows no sign of catching Portugal and Spain, even though both countries were hit hard by the Euro crisis that started in 2009. Russian GDP per capita is roughly 50–80 percent of Portugal, and 35–70 percent of Spain, depending on whether one uses nominal dollar rates or adjusts for differences in purchasing power across the three countries. The averages, of course, also mask considerable internal diversity. Moscow, and to a lesser extent St. Petersburg, are relatively wealthy European cities, with the malls, sushi restaurants, and traffic jams to attest to their status. Other parts of Russia—such as the North Caucasus, several ethnic republics in Siberia, and poor agricultural areas in central Russia—live more at the level of the developing world.[14]

Putin's other key goal—and a marker of normality for Russia—was to return Russia to the ranks of the world's great powers. It still possesses many attributes of a great power; it is the largest country in the world, one of the two leading nuclear powers, one of the five permanent members of the Security Council, and it contains among the world's largest reserves of oil and gas. All of those things have been true for more than fifty years and are unlikely to change. At the same time, it is hard to see a country that makes up less than 2 percent of world population and the world economy as an equal to leading powers such as China and the United States. A commitment to a strong military and an active foreign policy allows Russia to punch above its weight, but this approach may not be sustainable if the economy and the political system can't be made more effective.

What Russia really needs to become a "normal country," according to influential Russian analyst Dmitry Trenin, is for Putin to give up "the comfort of Kremlin control" and instead "to embark on the hard path of modern nation-building." Among the changes Russia needs, according to Trenin, are:

- A meritocratic elite devoted to helping the country and its citizens, rather than defending clan interests;
- Fair rules of the game, rooted in the rule of law, independent courts, and clean law enforcement organs;

- A more competitive economy based not on state enterprises but "responsible private business";
- A modern bureaucracy "accountable to the public."

Without these things, Trenin concluded, "Russia will squander its resources and ultimately lose its cherished independence: to China, if not to America."[15]

Is Putin ready to "embark on the hard path of modern nation-building?" The answer should be clear by now. Putin has had eighteen years in power, and Russia is no closer to a modern bureaucracy, the rule of law, a more diverse economy, and an elite focused on public service and accountability than when he took power. There seems little reason to think Putinism will pursue this orientation toward building a modern—or if you prefer, "normal"—state and economy now. That leaves the alternative path suggested by Trenin, "the comfort of Kremlin control." This is a problem because, in the words of a leading American political scientist, "only rule-based institutions can lead the breakthrough to higher levels of economic development." Without major political and legal reform, Russia seems condemned to economic underperformance, further eroding its place in the world.[16]

Perhaps one of the most worrying aspects of the future of Putinism are signs that Putin's core group of associates is working to install their children in positions of power and influence. Many elite children have found comfortable and potentially lucrative positions in Russian state-controlled companies (such as Gazprom or Rosneft) or companies owned by Putin's cronies.[17] A dramatic example is that of Kirill Shamalov, Putin's alleged former son-in-law. Shamalov's father is one of Putin's friends from the Ozero dacha cooperative created in 1996, someone who has reportedly been connected with Putin himself in business for decades, and who was involved in the construction of an enormous palace on the Black Sea ostensibly intended for Putin. Kirill Shamalov is a member of the Board for the chemicals company Sibur, in which Putin's billionaire friend Gennadiy Timchenko is a major shareholder. In 2014 Timchenko sold 17 percent of the shares of Sibur to Kirill Shamalov, but three years later Shamalov sold these shares back to a different Sibur owner after his marriage to Putin's daughter collapsed.[18]

For Russian opposition figures, this is the nightmare vision of Russia's future—one in which the current ruling group holds on to power as long as possible, and tries to pass their wealth and power on to their kids and other designated successors. The tsarist empire had a ruling class and nobility that held onto power for centuries, but the 1917 Bolshevik revolution eliminated the old order and built a new one around Marxist-Leninist ideology and loy-alty to the Communist Party. Post-Soviet Russia originally committed to a democratic order in which the rule of law would predominate and polit-ical power would alternate between competing political parties. This vision, shaky at best in the Yeltsin years, seems to have been abandoned under Putinism. Is a new nobility on the rise?

Members of the elite who think that the current system is moving toward a new version of the tsarist order in Russia, one that will preserve their family's high status for decades or longer, are probably delusional. As Putin's close associate Vladimir Yakunin observed in 2016, Putin has not formed a secure "ruling class like Russia had during czarist times." Elites who think that their property and privileges are eternal are mistaken, he claimed, because their wealth and position depends on what Putin thinks is good for Russia.[19]

The code of Putinism suggests that Putin will keep fighting to restore his vision of the Russian state and Russian greatness, regardless of how many palaces and yachts he and his cronies acquire in the process. Self-enrichment is not the only goal. Putinism undeniably has elements both of kleptocracy and nepotism, but there is much more to the system's purpose than that—specifically, what a former Putin advisor called "the resurrection of the great state in which we had lived." The problem is that the very same code, with its conservatism, sense of vulnerability and resentment, and insistence on con-trol and order, will prevent Putin from pursuing "the hard path of modern nation-building." Unless Putin can break out of the mentality that has shaped his leadership for the past eighteen years—a highly unlikely development—his attempts to muddle through economic stagnation and state ineffective-ness will amount to a slow muddling down.[20]

The signs of muddling down are unmistakable. Putin's close associate and former finance minister Aleksey Kudrin rings the alarm bell repeatedly, asserting that the current economic stagnation is erasing the earlier gains made under Putin and predicting that economic growth will not exceed 1 percent a year until 2020. Even more alarming was the prediction of the Economic Development Ministry that living standards would not improve before 2035 (!). More and more people talk about a new "era of stagnation," the term Mikhail Gorbachev used to describe the Soviet Union in the 1970s and early 1980s under Leonid Brezhnev. Little wonder, then, that two-thirds of Russians stated in August 2016 that they "rely only on themselves and avoid engaging with the authorities." Russians are pessimistic both about prospects for change and their ability to influence politics. Putin himself remains highly popular, but this is probably because, in the words of one Russian analyst, "he has become . . . a brand synonymous with Russia."[21]

Putinism, then, may be arriving at a "dead end," a judgment I heard multiple times from experts in Moscow.[22] The reason the dead end metaphor seems so apt is because it suggests both that the road ahead is impassable, and that getting back on track and moving forward is harder than just a turn to the right or the left. The uncertainty about the metaphor is that some dead end roads can go on for quite some time. There are too many unknown variables, from the price of oil to Putin's health to unforeseeable shocks, to predict how long the road is, and how difficult it will be to turn around.

Exit from Putinism

Is there an exit from Putinism? There are multiple possible exits, but they are all hard to imagine. A radical change in policy, like the one advocated by Trenin, seems unlikely. What remains? To the Russian analyst Dmitry Oreshkin, all of the other options are equally implausible. There is no serious electoral mechanism for replacing Putin. That leaves irregular changes of power, either a revolution from below or a palace coup at the top. Oreshkin doesn't believe in those options either, although a palace coup seems more likely than a revolution. He is left with the conviction that the current trajectory is unsustainable, and the fear that violence will inevitably play a role in how Putinism ends. In his worst nightmares, the country itself may not survive.[23]

Is Russia, then, doomed by nature or history or culture? By no means. Germany and Japan were said to be doomed to authoritarianism and militarism, but they are now democratic, prosperous, and peaceful societies. Latin America, not long ago dominated by harsh military rule, is now largely democratic. The alleged Russian desire for a strong hand, a powerful tsar, is considerably more complicated than this stereotype; Russians have repeatedly expressed their wish to be able to freely elect their leaders, even if they also think that a strong leader is highly desirable (who wants a weak leader?).[24]

What Putin and his group don't understand, according to one Russian political scientist, is that it is a natural phenomenon for people to become citizens, not subjects, over time. This process has come late in Russia, because under the Soviet system a proper middle class that owned property that it wished to pass on was impossible. But the Soviet Union was an educated and industrialized society, even if it had zero competition in either the political or economic realm. The end of communism meant that economic competition became a reality, as did private property. A middle class has been born that has started to demand dignity, participation, and respect. Even if not all of them conceive of this as democracy, these demands point in that direction.[25]

Saying Russia is not doomed, and that its society contains the seeds of a more open and democratic political system, tells us nothing about how it might get from here to there. Indeed, multiple countries in post-Soviet Eurasia that experienced apparent democratic revolutions later cycled back to a more authoritarian form of government. In systems in which presidents have disproportionate power compared to parliaments and prime ministers, and in which informal clans tend to dominate politics and economics, exiting authoritarianism and a system of clan networks is very difficult. As economic and governance problems mount, pressure for change is likely to increase. Clan wars over a shrinking pie may grow more intense. As Putin ages, and the battle for succession heats up, Russian elites may start to hedge their bets in order to protect their position under a potential new "boss of the clans," weakening Putin's position. Even before Putin stood for his fourth term as president, Russian experts had started to devise formulas to predict his most likely future successor.[26]

One well-known Russian political analyst argued that any Putin successor will face "five circles of hell," regardless of when or how the post-Putin era begins. These five circles are:

1. An inefficient economic system built on crony capitalism and state business;
2. A central political system in which all key institutions outside the presidency—political parties, the parliament, civil society—have been "destroyed";
3. A federal political order in which the regional elite has been "castrated" in favor of weak and talentless leaders installed from the center;
4. A foreign policy in crisis, marked by confrontation with the West and partnership with a China that will want some returns from its investment in the relationship;
5. A weak state, in which the government and bureaucracy are incapable of regularized governance and decision-making because of habituation to "manual rule."[27]

These five circles of hell accurately summarize the results of Putinism to date, and the challenges that any ruler in a post-Putin Russia will face. Any post-Putin ruler, however, will also inherit some less hellish conditions that give some grounds for optimism. The economic system, despite its problems, is fundamentally capitalist, with at least the legal and institutional basics in place, a major achievement of the postcommunist period that no major political force wants to reverse. The constitution, although it gives the president far too much power, also contains the basic institutional structure of liberalism and democracy, enshrining a separation of powers, federalism, judicial review, and civil rights and liberties. No matter how abused in practice, this constitution is something to build on, one that in principle can be amended to redistribute power in a more balanced fashion. Russian society remains highly educated and urbanized, which tends to correlate with more open government. And it is wealthier and more open to the outside world than at any point in its history. Moreover, this outside world is one in which market capitalism and pluralistic democracy are the most prominent and accepted forms of economic and political organization. This is particularly true in Europe, whose culture and lifestyle is the one most sought by average Russians, the vast majority of whom live in continental Europe. Even Putin and his cronies, despite their anti-Westernism and the partnership with China, are more oriented toward Europe than Asia or anywhere else.

Perhaps the biggest wildcard for the future of Putinism isn't even in Russia, but the future of the West as the desired economic and political model. If Russia's future seems uncertain and potentially dismal, recent events in the United States and Europe have suggested that the West's status as the aspirational model for many people throughout the postcommunist world and parts of the developing world is equally uncertain. Indeed, Western liberal democracy may even be losing the support of many citizens in America and Europe.[28] The rise of populist forces in the West, evidenced most dramatically by the UK "Brexit" vote and the US election of Donald Trump, presents a major challenge to the post–World War II liberal order that promoted the relatively open flow of goods, ideas, and people across borders, and later the expansion of rights to women and racial and sexual minorities at home.

The code of Putinism, in contrast, embraces conservative and illiberal values of tradition, hierarchy, and order. On Russia Day in 2017, Putin emphasized the "significance of our own roots and traditions," the need to maintain a "strong, self-sufficient, independent country," and the centrality of "the power of the state in securing political stability, unity of purpose, and the consolidation of society."[29] Putin, skeptical of ever reaching accommodation with the West, increasingly has sought to undermine the image of the West and its liberal values, both at home and abroad, and he seems to have notched some major successes in this effort. Putin apparently thinks that undermining the stability of the West will limit pressure on Russia to live up to its public commitments to democracy and human rights—and he may be right. A weak and divided West might limit not only pressure on Russia, however, but also profits for Russia. An EU in decline could buy less Russian oil and gas, as could a China engaged in a potential trade war with the United States. These potential outcomes are purely hypothetical at this point, of course, but if the rise of populism in the West creates economic problems in Europe and North America it is likely to accelerate Russia's economic muddling down, even if it gives Putinism some political breathing space.

Putin worries about how he will go down in history, how his legacy will be remembered. In Putin's mind, and in the view of his supporters, he will be remembered as a strong leader, rebuilding the Russian state and Russia's status as a great power, pulling it out of the deep crisis into which it had been plunged by Gorbachev and Yeltsin. He did this in traditional autocratic style, by ruling and not governing. What Putin has never understood is that success in the twenty-first century, especially for a relatively advanced country like Russia, involves building a state in which a leader can step aside, having confidence that stable government institutions and the good sense of citizens will keep the country on track to further development and prosperity. In this sense, Putinism is a regressive, not progressive, phenomenon. One supporter remarked, "Putin is higher than institutions, he is stronger than institutions."[30] A successful country, however, is one in which institutions are stronger than rulers. That is a lesson that, in these troubled times, is relevant not only for Russia.

NOTES

Introduction

1. Alena Sivkova, "Yest' Putin—Yest' Rossiya, net Putina—net Rossii," *Izvestiya*, October 22, 2014; Sergey Markov, "Interv'yu," *Ekho Moskvy*, October 23, 2014.
2. See chapter 1 for the full elaboration of the code, including the inspiration for the trinity of ideas, habits, and emotions in the work of Max Weber.
3. In the social sciences, this is called the "structure versus agency" debate. Both obviously matter; this book gives priority to agency. For alternatives stressing Russian history and culture, oil, and communist legacies, see respectively: Steven Rosefielde and Stefan Hedlund, *Russia since 1980* (Cambridge University Press, 2009); M. Steven Fish, *Democracy Derailed in Russia: The Failure of Open Politics* (Cambridge University Press, 2005), 114–138; Grigore Pop-Eleches and Joshua A. Tucker, *Communism's Shadow: Historical Legacies and Contemporary Political Attitudes* (Princeton University Press, 2017). For an economic approach combining oil and gas wealth and communist legacies to explain Putinism, see: Clifford G. Gaddy and Barry Ickes, *Bear Traps on Russia's Path to Modernization* (Routledge, 2013).
4. *Ot pervogo litsa: Razgovory s Vladimirom Putinym* (Vagrius, 2000), 37; Roman Anin, Olesya Shmagun, and Dmitry Velikovsky, "The Secret Caretaker," *The Panama Papers*, April 3, 2016. For rationalist alternatives to the code of Putinism argument, see, for example: Vladimir Gel'man, *Authoritarian Russia: Analyzing Post-Soviet Regime Change* (University of Pittsburgh Press, 2015); Karen Dawisha, *Putin's Kleptocracy: Who Owns Russia?* (Simon & Schuster, 2014).
5. Andrei Shleifer and Daniel Treisman, "A Normal Country," *Foreign Affairs*, 83, 2 (March/April 2004), 20–38; Daniel Treisman, *The Return: Russia's Journey from Gorbachev to Medvedev* (Free Press, 2011). To be crystal clear: I am not saying that Russia is "abnormal" in some pejorative sense, nor are other critics of the Shleifer-Treisman "normal country" thesis. It's simply a way of talking about situations in which Russian outcomes don't seem to fit with general expectations based on existing social science theories.
6. The discussion of the political system and its effects is divided across three chapters: chapter 2 on hyperpresidentialism, chapter 3 on informal clan networks, and chapter 5 on misrule and bad governance. Chapter 4 covers economics, and chapter 6 deals with foreign policy.
7. Christopher Walker and Sylvana Habdank-Kołaczkowska, "Fragile Frontier: Democracy's Growing Vulnerability in Central and Southeastern Europe," *Nations in Transit 2012* (Freedom House, 2012); Hajrudin Somun, "Putinization of Not Only Balkans, but

Europe as Well," *Today's Zaman,* June 15, 2014; Ayse Zarakol, "Turkey and Russia, Erdoğan and Putin," *PONARS Eurasia Policy Memo,* 444 (October 2016).

Chapter 1

1. Author's interview with Vyacheslav Nikonov, July 2014; Dale R. Herspring, "Introduction," in Dale R. Herspring, ed., *Putin's Russia: Past Imperfect, Future Uncertain,* 3rd ed. (Rowman & Littlefield, 2007), 3.
2. Author's interview with Yuriy Nesterov, July 2014.
3. Vladimir Gel'man, *Authoritarian Russia: Analyzing Post-Soviet Regime Change* (University of Pittsburgh Press, 2015), xii; Karen Dawisha, *Putin's Kleptocracy: Who Owns Russia?* (Simon & Schuster, 2014). Prominent examples of this general approach to authoritarian leaders include: Bruce Bueno de Mesquita and Alastair Smith, *The Dictator's Handbook: Why Bad Behavior Is Almost Always Good Politics* (Public Affairs, 2011); Milan W. Svolik, *The Politics of Authoritarian Rule* (Cambridge University Press, 2012). The two most important academic books that offer a general account of the trajectory of post-Soviet regimes, including Russia, share this perspective: Steven Levitsky and Lucan Way, *Competitive Authoritarianism: Hybrid Regimes after the Cold War* (Cambridge University Press, 2010); Henry Hale, *Patronal Politics: Eurasian Regime Dynamics in Comparative Perspective* (Cambridge University Press, 2014).
4. Max Weber, *Economy and Society* (University of California Press, 1978), 24–26.
5. Calvert W. Jones, "Seeing Like an Autocrat: Liberal Social Engineering in an Illiberal State," *Perspective on Politics,* 13, 1 (March 2015), 24–25.
6. I borrow the term "code," although not the method, from Nathan Leites's attempt to catalog the "operational code" of the Soviet elite under Lenin and Stalin: Nathan Leites, *A Study of Bolshevism* (Free Press, 1953).
7. Juan Linz, *Totalitarian and Authoritarian Regimes* (Lynne Rienner, 2000 edition), 162; Stephen E. Hanson, *Post-Imperial Democracies: Ideology and Party Formation in Third Republic France, Weimar Germany, and Post-Soviet Russia* (Cambridge University Press, 2010), 13–22. Hanson notes that psychological research suggests Weber's four-part typology of individual social action is more accurate than one reduced to instrumental rationality, and just as falsifiable. I thank Boris Makarenko for suggesting Linz's distinction between ideology and mentality.
8. On 2003–2004 as a decisive break, see, for example, the interview with former Kremlin insider Gleb Pavlovsky: Tatiana Zhurzhenko and Ivan Krastev, "Gleb Pavlovsky: The Final Act," *openDemocracy,* May 15, 2011.
9. Vladimir Putin, "Rossiya na rubezhe tysyacheletiy," *Nezavisimaya Gazeta,* December 30, 1999; *Ot pervogo litsa: Razgovory s Vladimirom Putinym* (Vagrius, 2000), 167–168.
10. Vladimir Putin, "Stenograficheskiy otchet o vstreche s uchastnikami tret'ego zasedaniya Mezhdunarodnogo diskussionnogo kluba 'Valday'," *Kremlin.ru,* September 9, 2006; Vladimir Putin, "Intervyu zhurnalistam pechatnykh sredstv massovoy informatsii iz stran—chlenov 'Gruppy vos'mi'," *Kremlin.ru,* June 4, 2007; Fiona Hill and Clifford G. Gaddy, *Mr. Putin: Operative in the Kremlin* (Brookings Institution Press, 2013), 35.
11. A useful introduction is: Francis Fukuyama, *State-Building: Governance and World Order in the 21st Century* (Cornell University Press, 2004).
12. Yusif Legan, *KGB-FSB. Vzglyad iznutri* ("Tsentrkniga," 2001), Vol. 2, 297; Author's interview with Maria Lipman, May 2013. On the historical Russian service state, see for example: Stefan Hedlund, "Vladimir the Great, Grand Prince of Muscovy: Resurrecting the Russian Service State," *Europe-Asia Studies,* 58, 5 (July 2006), 775–801; Richard Pipes, *Russia under the Old Regime* (Penguin, 1974).
13. Patrushev quoted in: Andrei Soldatov and Irina Borogan, *The New Nobility: The Restoration of Russia's Security State and the Enduring Legacy of the KGB* (Public Affairs, 2010), 5; Viktor Cherkesov, "Moda na KGB?," *Komsomol'skaya Pravda,* December 29,

2004; Viktor Cherkesov, "Nel'zya dopustit', chtoby voiny prevratilis' v torgovtsev," *Kommersant*", October 9, 2007.

14. Vladimir Putin, "Obrashcheniye Prezidenta Rossii Vladimira Putina," *Kremlin.ru*, September 4, 2004; "Stalin on the Ends and Means of Industrialization," in Robert V. Daniels, ed., *A Documentary History of Communism in Russia: From Lenin to Gorbachev* (University Press of New England, 1993), 180–183. On states as Janus-faced, see: Theda Skocpol, *States and Social Revolutions: A Comparative Analysis of France, Russia, and China* (Cambridge University Press, 1979), 32.

15. Vladimir Putin, "Poslaniye Prezidenta Rossiyskoy Federatsii Federal'nomu Sobraniyu Rossiyskoy Federatsii," *Kremlin.ru*, May 16, 2003; Vladimir Putin, "Vystupleniye na rasshirennom zasedanii Gosudarstvennogo soveta 'o strategii razvitiya Rossia do 2020 goda'," *Kremlin.ru*, February 8, 2008.

16. Vladimir Putin, "Vystupleniye i diskussiya na Myunkhenskoy konferentsii po voprosam politiki bezopasnosti," *Kremlin.ru*, February 10, 2007; Vladimir Putin, "Zasedaniye Mezhdunardonogo diskussionnogo kluba 'Valday'," *Kremlin.ru*, October 24, 2014.

17. Vladislav Surkov, "Russkaya politicheskaya kul'tura. Vzglyad iz utopii," in Konstantin Remchukov, ed., *Russkaya politicheskaya kul'tura. Vzglyad iz utopii. Lektsiya Vladislava Surkova* (Nezavisimaya Gazeta, 2007), 15.

18. Vladimir Putin, "Interv'yu britanskoy teleradiokorporatsii 'Bi-Bi-Si'," *Kremlin.ru*, June 22, 2003.

19. Author's interview with Valeriy Lavskiy, editor of *Kommersant"-Sibir'*, June 2015.

20. Andrey Rezchikov, "Putin utverdil osnovy kul'turnoy politiki Rossii," *Vzglyad*, December 24, 2014; David Remnick, "Watching the Eclipse," *New Yorker*, August 11, 2014.

21. I return to the issue of habits and emotions that feed into this anti-Westernism later.

22. Putin, "Obrashcheniye Prezidenta Rossii Vladimira Putina."

23. Vladimir Putin, "Poslaniye Federal'nomu Sobraniyu Rossiyskoy Federatsii," *Kremlin.ru*, May 10, 2006; Andrew Kramer, "Putin Is Said to Compare US Policies to Third Reich," *New York Times*, May 10, 2007; Nataliya Vasilyeva, "Putin Accuses US of Supporting Separatists in Russia," *AP*, April 26, 2015.

24. Sergei Medvedev, "'Juicy Morsels': Putin's Beslan Address and the Construction of the New Russian Identity," *PONARS Policy Memo*, 334 (November 2004); Author's interview with Sergey Medvedev, June 2015. On the incident in which Putin called Medvedev a moron, see: Viktoriya Vladimirova, "Vladimir Putin: professor VShYe—pridurok," *Slon*, October 3, 2013.

25. I am not suggesting that all of Putin's complaints about American foreign policy are wrong-headed. His objections to the 2003 Iraq war, or the expansion of NATO, make perfect sense from the point of view of Russian national interests. This reasonable critique of US foreign policy, which would be shared by many people around the world, including in the United States itself, is not surprising. But the belief that the United States has a strategy of supporting "colored revolutions" around the world, and in the former Soviet space in particular, all with a goal of overthrowing Putin, weakening Russia, and dividing up the country, goes much further, up to and including claims that the United States works with Islamic terrorists to achieve these goals. I see no serious evidence for these more extreme assertions. I return to this issue in chapter 6.

26. Dmitry Gorenburg, "Countering Color Revolutions: Russia's New Security Strategy and Its Implications for US Policy," *PONARS Eurasia Policy Memo*, 342 (September 2014); Brian Whitmore, "Paronia as Policy," *RFE/RL*, June 19, 2015; Brian Whitmore, "Putin Wants to Party Like It's 1815," *RFE/RL*, June 24, 2015.

27. Vladimir Putin, "Vystupleniye na forume storonnikov Prezidenta Rossii," *Kremlin.ru*, November 21, 2007; "Putin otvetil na predlozheniye vesti propagandu v svyazi s mitingami," *Lenta.ru*, December 8, 2011; "Vladimir Putin: Podderzhka Gosdepom SshA rossiyskoy oppozitsii—eto nepravil'no," *Russian.rt.com*, June 11, 2013.

28. Interview with Nikolay Patrushev, "Kto upravlyayet khaosom," *Rossiyskaya Gazeta*, February 10, 2015; Interview with Nikolay Patrushev, "'Za destabilizatsiyey Ukrainy skryvayetsya popytka radikal'nogo oslableniya Rossii,'" *Kommersant*, June 22, 2015; Anna Smolchenko, "Putting Words in Albright's Mouth," *Moscow Times*, November 7, 2007; Brian Whitmore, "Russia's Ministry of Mind Reading," *RFE/RL*, June 23, 2015.

29. Vladimir Putin, "Poslaniye Prezidenta Federal'nomu Sobraniyu," *Kremlin.ru*, December 12, 2013; Putin, "Rossiya na rubezhe tysyacheletiy."

30. Author's interview with Aleksey Makarkin, December 2014. For more on the Putinist claim that Russia embodies true conservative European values that have been left behind by Europe's liberal elites, see: Marlene Laruelle, "Beyond Anti-Westernism: The Kremlin's Narrative about Russia's European Identity and Mission," *PONARS Eurasia Policy Memo*, 326 (August 2014).

31. Brian D Taylor, "Putin's Crackdown: Sources, Instruments, and Challenges," *PONARS Eurasia Policy Memo*, 277, September 2013; Viatcheslav Morozov, *Russia's Postcolonial Identity: A Subaltern Empire in a Eurocentric World* (Palgrave Macmillan, 2015), esp. 103–134.

32. Elizaveta Surnacheva, "V poiskakh mudrosti," *Kommersant*, January 20, 2014; Alexander Sergunin, "Has Putin the Pragmatist Turned into Putin the Ideologue?," *Russia Direct*, April 14, 2014; Author's interview with Mikhail Remizov, July 2014.

33. Walter Laqueur, *Putinism: Russia and Its Future with the West* (St. Martin's Press, 2015), 120; Astrid S. Tuminez, *Russian Nationalism since 1856: Ideology and the Making of Foreign Policy* (Rowman & Littlefield, 2000), 2.

34. Vladimir Putin, "Rossiya: natsional'nyy vopros," *Nezavisimaya Gazeta*, January 23, 2012. On the more general point, see Tuminez, *Russian Nationalism since 1856.*

35. More precisely, we might say that Putin might be a "civic" or "statist" nationalist, but he is not an "ethnic" nationalist. See: Marlene Laruelle, "Misinterpreting Nationalism: Why *Russkii* Is Not a Sign of Ethnonationalism," *PONARS Eurasia Policy Memo*, 416, January 2016; Pål Kolstø and Helge Blakkisrud, eds., *The New Russian Nationalism: Imperialism, Ethnicity and Authoritarianism 2000–2015* (Edinburgh University Press, 2015).

36. Laqueur, *Putinism*, 69–108, 160–184; Vladimir Putin, "Razgovor s Vladimirom Putinym. Prodolzheniye," http://2010.moskva-putinu.ru/, December 16, 2010; Aleksandr Zadorozhnyy interview with Aleksey Venediktov, "Po prikazu Putina, Obamy, ili Poroshenko na yugo-vostoke Ukrainy nichego ne ostanovitsya," *Znak*, June 9, 2014.

37. Author's interview with Ol'ga Kryshtanovskaya, June 2015; Author's interview with Maria Lipman, May 2013. See also: Maria Lipman, "The Kremlin Turns Ideological: Where This New Direction Could Lead," in Maria Lipman and Nikolay Petrov, *Russia 2025: Scenarios for the Russian Future* (Palgrave Macmillan, 2013), 220–239.

38. Weber, *Economy and Society*, 25; Ted Hopf, "The Logic of Habit in International Relations," *European Journal of International Relations*, 16, 4 (2010), 544, 549.

39. An example of this type of analysis of Russian politics, by an excellent scholar who has written a large number of important books and articles, is: Daniel Treisman, "After Yeltsin Comes ... Yeltsin," *Foreign Policy*, No. 117 (Winter 1999–2000), 74–86. Writing at the end of the Yeltsin presidency, Treisman suggested that Yeltsin's successor would rule much like Yeltsin due to the constraints any new leader would face, the same constraints that hampered Yeltsin.

40. Hopf, "The Logic of Habit," 548.

41. Nils van der Vegte, "Kratkoye posobiye po lenivoy zhurnalistike, osveshchayushchey Rossiyu," in Jon Hellevig and Aleksandr Latsa, eds., *Putinskaya Rossiya Kak Ona Est'* (Kontinent SshA, 2013), 237; *Ot pervogo litsa*, 24–25.

42. *Ot pervogo litsa*, 21; http://putin.kremlin.ru/interests; Steven Lee Myers, *The New Tsar: The Rise and Reign of Vladimir Putin* (Knopf, 2015), 21.

43. Author's interview with Georgiy Satarov, December 2013; Yevgenia Albats, "In Putin's Kremlin, It's All about Control," *Washington Post*, December 12, 2004; Author's interview

with Dmitriy Trenin, July 2014; Michael Urban, *Cultures of Power in Post-Communist Russia: An Analysis of Elite Political Discourse* (Cambridge University Press, 2010), 17, 79.

44. Viktor Khamrayev, interview with Ol'ga Kryshtanovskaya, "'Polozheniye chekistov segodnya fantastitecheski ustoychivo,'" *Kommersant"-Vlast'*, March 19, 2007; Vladimir Putin, "Otvety na voprosy zhurnalistov posle pryamogo tele- i radioefira ("Pryamaya liniya s Prezidentom Rossii")," *Kremlin.ru*, October 18, 2007; Author's interview with Aleksandr Tsipko, December 2013.

45. Author's interview with Aleksandr Golts, May 2013; Soldatov and Borogan, *The New Nobility*, 4. I discuss the *siloviki* in: Brian D. Taylor, *State Building in Putin's Russia: Coercion and Policing after Communism* (Cambridge University Press, 2011), esp. 36–70.

46. Stanislav Belkovskiy and Sergey Korzun, "Bez durakov," *Ekho Moskvy*, May 17, 2014; Stanislav Belkovskiy, interviewed by Lola Tagayeva, "Lichnaya bezopasnost' Putina voobshche mozhet skoro prevratit'sya v natsional'nuyu ideyu Rossii," *Slon*, July 2, 2014; Author's interview with anonymous journalist, July 2014.

47. Ol'ga Malinova, "Tema proshlogo v ritorike prezidentov Rossii," *Pro et Contra*, 15, 3–4 (May–August 2011), 112; Putin, "Vladimir Putin otvetil na voprosy zhurnalistov o situatsii na Ukraine."

48. "Stenogramma zasedaniya 16 avgusta 1999 g.," State Duma of the Federal Assembly of the Russian Federation, http://transcript.duma.gov.ru/, August 16, 1999; Putin, "Poslaniye Prezidenta Rossiyskoy Federatsii," May 16, 2003; Putin, "Obrashcheniye Prezidenta Rossii Vladimira Putina," September 4, 2004; Dmitriy Medvedev, interviewed by Valeriy Fadeyev, "Chto kasayetsya bor'by gruppirovok v administratsii,- . . . my ne TsK KPSS," *Polit.ru*, April 5, 2005.

49. The term "fifth column" comes from the Spanish Civil War in the 1930s and refers to groups supporting an enemy from within a particular territory, usually a country. Quotes from: Vladimir Putin, "Obrashcheniye Prezidenta Rossiyskoy Federatsii," March 18, 2014; Vladimir Putin, "Vystupleniye na prazdnovanii Dnya znaniy s vospitannikami i pedagogami obrazovatel'nogo tsentra dlya odarennykh detey 'Sirius,'" *Kremlin.ru*, September 1, 2015.

50. Malinova, "Tema proshlogo v ritorike prezidentov Rossii," 114–115; Viatcheslav Morozov, "No Enemy at the Gate: An Unusual Election Cycle in Russia," *PONARS Eurasia Policy Memo*, 173, September 2011.

51. Author's interview with anonymous journalist, July 2014; Author's interview with Lipman; Author's interview with Kryshtanovskaya; Allen C. Lynch, *Vladimir Putin and Russian Statecraft* (Potomac Books, 2011), xiv.

52. Peter Baker and Susan Glasser, *Kremlin Rising*, updated ed. (Potomac Books, 2007), 47–53 (quote 47); Myers, *The New Tsar*, 97, 116–118, 136–142.

53. Aleksandr Panov and Andrey Degtyarev, "Venediktov: 'Yest' vragi i est' predateli,'" *Nastoyashcheye Vremya*, July 2, 2015; Putin, "Vystupleniye na prazdnovanii Dnya znaniy."

54. Alena V. Ledeneva, *Can Russia Modernise? Sistema, Power Networks and Informal Governance* (Cambridge University Press, 2013), 52; Urban, *Cultures of Power in Post-Communist Russia*, 111–112, 116, 182; Author's interview with Aleksey Mazur, June 2015.

55. See chapter 3 for further discussion.

56. Author's interview with Vladislav Bachurov, July 2014; Yelena Masyuk, "Gleb Pavlovskiy: 'Bol'she vsego Putin, po-moyemu, opasayetsya stat' lishnim,'" *Novaya Gazeta*, October 23, 2012; *Ot pervogo litsa*, 19–20.

57. Both of these episodes are discussed in Valerie Sperling, *Sex, Politics, and Putin: Political Legitimacy in Russia* (Oxford University Press, 2014), 30, 188–189. On Putin's use of criminal slang, see, for example: Michael S. Gorman, "Putin's Language," in Helena Goscilo, ed., *Putin as Celebrity and Cultural Icon* (Routledge, 2013), 82–103.

58. Sperling, *Sex, Politics, and Putin*, 4, 75–79.

59. Mikhail Zygar', *Vsya kremlevskaya rat': Kratkaya istoriya sovremennoy Rossii* (Intellektual'naya literatura, 2015), 215.

60. Weber, *Economy and Society*, 25; Jonathan Mercer, "Human Nature and the First Image: Emotion in International Politics," *Journal of International Relations and Development*, 9, 3 (September 2006), 288–303; Jonathan Mercer, "Feeling Like a State: Social Emotion and Identity," *International Theory*, 6, 3 (November 2014), 515–535. See also: Rose McDermott, "The Feeling of Rationality: The Meaning of Neuroscientific Advances for Political Science," *Perspectives on Politics*, 2, 4 (December 2004), 691–706.

61. Putin, "Zasedaniye Mezhdunardonogo diskussionnogo kluba 'Valday'"; Author's interview with Nikolay Troitskiy, December 2014; Nikolay Troitskiy, "Putin na Valdae. Pravota obizhennogo," *Ekho Moskvy*, October 27, 2014; Igor' Yurgens, interviewed by Andrey Lipskiy, "Razvernut' stranu nazad nevozmozhno," *Novaya Gazeta*, November 14, 2014.

62. Timothy Garton Ash, "Putin's Deadly Doctrine," *New York Times*, July 18, 2014; "Analiticheskaya programma 'Odnako', interv'yu V.V. Putina," *Pervyy kanal*, February 7, 2000; Author's interview with anonymous St. Petersburg journalist, July 2014; Author's interview with Leonid Smirnyagin, June 2015; Baker and Glasser, *Kremlin Rising*, p. 93.

63. Sergey Karaganov, "Izbezhat' Afganistana-2," *Vedomosti*, July 28, 2014; Author's interview with Medvedev.

64. Roger D. Petersen, *Understanding Ethnic Violence: Fear, Hatred, and Resentment in Twentieth-Century Eastern Europe* (Cambridge University Press, 2002), 40–41; Myers, *The New Tsar*, 52; Vladimir Isachenkov, "Book: Putin Had Taxi Backup Plan," *Moscow Times*, September 2, 2002.

65. E. D. Ponarin and B. O. Sokolov, "Global'naya politika glazami rossiyskoy elity," *Rossiya v global'noy politike*, November 11, 2014.

66. Ponarin and Sokolov, "Global'naya politika glazami rossiyskoy elity"; Olga Malinova, "Obsession with Status and *Ressentiment*: Historical Backgrounds of the Russian Discursive Identity Construction," *Communist and Post-Communist Studies*, 47, 3–4 (September–December 2014), 303. This Malinova article is part of a special issue on "Status and Emotions in Russian Foreign Policy." See also: Sergey Medvedev, "Russkiy resentiment," *Otechestvennye zapiski*, December 2014.

67. See chapter 6 on the importance of respect and resentment in the foreign policy realm.

68. Gleb Pavlovsky, interviewed by Tom Parfitt, "Putin's World Outlook," *New Left Review*, 88 (July–August 2014); Author's interview with Aleksandr Lukin, June 2014; Belkovskiy, "Lichnaya bezopasnost' Putina"; Author's interview with Dmitriy Babich, December 2013.

69. Pavlovsky, "Putin's World Outlook."

70. Lynch, *Vladimir Putin and Russian Statecraft*, xiv; Belkovskiy, "Lichnaya bezopasnost' Putina."

71. Pavlovsky, "Putin's World Outlook." See also: Zhurzhenko and Krastev, "Gleb Pavlovsky: The Final Act"; Ivan Krastev, Gleb Pavlovsky, and Tatiana Zhurzhenko, "The Politics of No Alternatives, or How Power Works in Russia," *Eurozine.com*, June 9, 2011; Masyuk, "Gleb Pavlovskiy."

72. Pavlovsky, "Putin's World Outlook."

73. Irving L. Janis, *Groupthink: Psychological Studies of Policy Decisions and Fiascoes*, 2nd ed. (Houghton Mifflin, 1982).

74. Rachel Donadio, "The Laureate of Russian Misery," *New York Times*, May 21, 2016.

75. Timothy J. Colton and Michael McFaul, "Are Russians Undemocratic?," *Post-Soviet Affairs*, 18, 2 (2002), 91–121; Henry E. Hale, "The Myth of Mass Russian Support for Autocracy: The Public Opinion Foundations of a Hybrid Regime," *Europe-Asia Studies* 63, 8 (2011), 1357–1375.

76. In other places Arutunyan goes much further, portraying Putin as a mystical, tsar-like figure who fulfilled Russians' desire to return to centuries-old "habits of subservience." Anna Arutunyan, *The Putin Mystique: Inside Russia's Power Cult* (Olive Branch Press, 2015), 4, 41.

77. Putin vowed to "snuff them out in the outhouse" at a press conference on September 24, 1999. The phrase became so famous that it even has its own page in Russian Wikipedia. For Lebed's memoir and his quip "like a goat after a carrot," see: Aleksandr Lebed', *Za derzhavu obidno . . .* (Moskovskaya Pravda, 1995), 453.

78. Boris Yel'tsin, *Prezidentskiy marafon: Razmyshleniya, vospominaniya, vpetchatleniya . . .* (AST, 2000), 254, 363, 368.

79. On elite versus mass opinion, see: Ponarin and Sokolov, "Global'naya politika glazami rossiyskoy elity."

80. Lynch, *Vladimir Putin and Russian Statecraft*, xvi.

81. Dmitry Babich, "No Unity in a Besieged Fortress," *Russia beyond the Headlines*, November 4, 2012.

Chapter 2

1. John Gooding, "Gorbachev and Democracy," *Soviet Studies*, 42, 2 (April 1990), 210; Boris Yeltsin, *Zapiski Prezidenta* (Ogonek, 1994), 16. On the changes in Russia as revolutionary, see, for example: Michael McFaul, *Russia's Unfinished Revolution: Political Change from Gorbachev to Putin* (Cornell University Press, 2001).

2. The best overview of electoral or competitive authoritarianism around the world is: Steven Levitsky and Lucan Way, *Competitive Authoritarianism: Hybrid Regimes after the Cold War* (Cambridge University Press, 2010). A brief introduction is: Andreas Schedler, "Electoral Authoritarianism," *The SAGE Handbook of Comparative Politics* (SAGE, 2009), 381–394.

3. Author's interview with Lipman, May 2013; Putin quoted in Peter Baker and Susan Glasser, *Kremlin Rising*, updated ed. (Potomac Books, 2007), 91. On the "menu of manipulation," see: Andreas Schedler, "The Menu of Manipulation," *Journal of Democracy*, 13, 2 (2002), 36–50.

4. Overviews of the September–October 1993 events include: Timothy J. Colton, *Yeltsin: A Life* (Basic Books, 2008), 272–280; McFaul, *Russia's Unfinished Revolution*, 161–204; Joel M. Ostrow, Georgiy A. Satarov, and Irina M. Khakamada, *The Consolidation of Dictatorship in Russia: An Inside View of the Demise of Democracy* (Praeger Security International, 2007), 15–35.

5. There were eighty-nine "subjects of the federation" in 1993, a number later reduced to eighty-three under Putin by combining some regions, and currently eighty-five with the addition of Crimea and the Crimean city of Sevastopol as new territories, although these are not recognized as part of Russia by most countries.

6. The 1993 Constitution can be found in Russian, English, French, and German at: http://www.constitution.ru/. On federalism as the best system of government for large multinational democracies, see: Alfred Stepan, "Russian Federalism in Comparative Perspective," *Post-Soviet Affairs*, 16, 2 (April–June 2000), 133–176.

7. Accounts of this period and elections under Yeltsin include: McFaul, *Russia's Unfinished Revolution*, 207–371; Stephen White, Richard Rose, and Ian McAllister, *How Russia Votes* (Chatham House Publishers, 1997).

8. Matthew Evangelista, *The Chechen Wars* (Brookings Institution Press, 2002); Gulnaz Sharafutdinova, *Political Consequences of Crony Capitalism inside Russia* (University of Notre Dame Press, 2010); Colton, *Yeltsin*, 425–435.

9. 2015 was the most recent year available when the book went to press. http://info.worldbank.org/governance/wgi/index.aspx#home.

10. https://freedomhouse.org/; Freedom House, *Freedom in the World: The Annual Survey of Political Rights & Civil Liberties, 2000–2001* (Freedom House, 2001), 447–448;

Mikhail Myagkov, Peter C. Ordeshook, and Dimitri Shakin, *The Forensics of Election Fraud: Russia and Ukraine* (Cambridge University Press, 2009), 135–137, 272; McFaul, *Russia's Unfinished Revolution*, 309–371.

11. Moshe Lewin, *The Gorbachev Revolution: A Historical Interpretation* (University of California Press, 1988); Stephen Kotkin, *Armageddon Averted: Soviet Collapse, 1970–2000*, rev. ed. (Oxford University Press, 2008).

12. Samuel P. Huntington, *The Third Wave: Democratization in the Late Twentieth Century* (University of Oklahoma Press, 1991); Levitsky and Way, *Competitive Authoritarianism*, 16–20; Francis Fukuyama, "The End of History?", *The National Interest* (Summer 1989), 3–18.

13. Vladimir Putin, "Poslaniye Prezidenta Federal'nomu Sobraniyu," *Kremlin.ru*, December 12, 2012; Vladislav Surkov, "Russkaya politicheskaya kul'tura. Vzglyad iz utopii," in Konstantin Remchukov, ed., *Russkaya politicheskaya kul'tura. Vzglyad iz utopii. Lektsiya Vladislava Surkova* (Nezavisimaya Gazeta, 2007), 16–21; Author's interview with Aleksandr Lukin, June 2015; Azar Gat, "The Return of Authoritarian Great Powers," *Foreign Affairs*, 86, 4 (2007), 59–69.

14. On a "Muscovite" political culture, see: Steven Rosefielde and Stefan Hedlund, *Russia since 1980* (Cambridge University Press, 2009), 9–19. Arguments suggesting the importance of climate and territory on Russian political development include: Marshall Poe, *The Russian Moment in World History* (Princeton University Press. 2003); Allen C. Lynch, *How Russia Is Not Ruled: Reflections on Russian Political Development* (Cambridge University Press, 2005). On Orthodoxy and democracy, see: M. Steven Fish, *Democracy Derailed in Russia: The Failure of Open Politics* (Cambridge University Press, 2005), 95–97.

15. Henry E. Hale, "The Myth of Mass Russian Support for Autocracy: The Public Opinion Foundations of a Hybrid Regime," *Europe-Asia Studies* 63, 8 (2011), 1357–1375.

16. Carles Boix and Susan Carol Stokes, "Endogenous Democratization," *World Politics*, 55, 4 (2003), 517–549; Adam Przeworski and Fernando Limongi, "Modernization: Theories and Facts," *World Politics*, 49, 2 (1997), 155–183; Fish, *Democracy Derailed in Russia*, 98–105; William Zimmerman, "'Normal Democracies' and Improving How They Are Measured: The Case of Russia," *Post-Soviet Affairs*, 23, 1 (Summer 2007), 1–17. World Bank income data available from: http://data.worldbank.org/country.

17. On the resource curse, see, for example: Michael L. Ross, "Does Oil Hinder Democracy?" *World Politics*, 53, 3 (2001), 325–361; Michael L. Ross, "Will Oil Drown the Arab Spring?" *Foreign Affairs*, 90, 5 (2011), 2–7. Applications to Russia include: Fish, *Democracy Derailed in Russia*, 114–138; Daniel Treisman, "Is Russia Cursed by Oil?", *Journal of International Affairs*, 63, 2 (Spring 2010), 85–102.

18. Henry E. Hale, *Patronal Politics: Eurasian Regime Dynamics in Comparative Perspective* (Cambridge University Press, 2014).

19. Comparisons based on Worldwide Governance Indicators 2014 Voice and Accountability ratings and 2014 Freedom House ratings.

20. In general, arguments about leadership beliefs are a relatively small part of the democratization literature, primarily because of the difficulty of coding this variable for statistical studies. A recent exception is a study by Scott Mainwaring and Anibal Perez-Linan, who analyzed regime patterns in Latin America over sixty years. They found that "a normative preference for democracy" (or its absence) among political elites played a key role in regime trajectories, along with policy moderation and the regional status of democracy. These variables were much more important than structural variables such as economic development. My interpretation of the Russian case is generally consistent with their argument about leadership preferences. Scott Mainwaring and Aníbal Pérez-Liñán, "Democratic Breakdown and Survival," *Journal of Democracy*, 24, 2 (2013): 123–137.

21. Experts suggesting a deliberate plan to build authoritarianism under Putin include: Michael McFaul, "Vladimir Putin's Grand Strategy . . . for Anti-Democratic

Regime Change in Russia," *Weekly Standard*, November 17, 2003; Karen Dawisha, *Putin's Kleptocracy: Who Owns Russia?* (Simon and Schuster, 2014).

22. *Ot pervogo litsa: Razgovory s Vladimirom Putinym* (Vagrius, 2000), 104–107, 119; Boris Yel'tsin, *Prezidentskiy marafon: Razmyshleniya, vospominaniya, vpetchatleniya* . . . (AST, 2000), 356; Michael R. Gordon, "Putin Running 'Uncampaign' on the Way to Election," *New York Times*, March 8, 2000.

23. Author's interview with Dmitriy Babich, December 2013.

24. See, for example: Schedler, "Electoral Authoritarianism"; Levitsky and Way, *Competitive Authoritarianism*; Hale, *Patronal Politics*, 66–71.

25. Eugene Huskey, "Overcoming the Yeltsin Legacy: Vladimir Putin and Russian Political Reform," in Archie Brown, ed., *Contemporary Russian Politics: A Reader* (Oxford University Press, 2001), 87.

26. Thomas F. Remington, "Parliamentary Politics in Russia," in Stephen White, Richard Sakwa, and Henry E. Hale, eds., *Developments in Russian Politics 8* (Duke University Press, 2014), 52–53; Matthew Hyde, "Putin's Federal Reforms and Their Implications for Presidential Power in Russia," *Europe-Asia Studies*, 53, no. 5 (July 2001), 719–743.

27. On electoral fraud in 2011, see: Ruben Enikolopov et al., "Field Experiment Estimate of Electoral Fraud in Russian Parliamentary Elections," *Proceedings of the National Academy of Sciences* 110, 2 (2013): 448–452. On electoral fraud in 2016, see: "Vizhu mnogo grafikov o fal'sifikatsii na vyborakh. Chto oni znachat?", *Meduza*, September 19, 2016. On earlier electoral fraud, see: Myagkov, Ordeshook, and Shakin, *The Forensics of Election Fraud*.

28. Discussions of these changes in electoral rules can be found in: Stephen White, "The Electoral Process," in White, Sakwa, and Hale, *Developments in Russian Politics 8*, 60–76; Henry E. Hale, "Russia's Political Parties and Their Substitutes," in White, Sakwa, and Hale, *Developments in Russian Politics 8*, 77–96.

29. Paul Chaisty, "The Legislative Effects of Presidential Partisan Powers in Post-Communist Russia," *Government and Opposition*, 43, 3 (2008), 424–453; Brian D. Taylor, "Police Reform in Russia: The Policy Process in a Hybrid Regime," *Post-Soviet Affairs*, 30, 2–3 (2014), 226–255; Thomas F. Remington, *Presidential Decrees in Russia: A Comparative Perspective* (Cambridge University Press, 2014), 105.

30. Yekaterina Shul'man, "Verkhovenstvo prava: Putevoditel' po zakonodatelyu," *Vedomosti*, January 22, 2014; Natalia Antonova, "Russian State Duma: 'Possessed Printer' or Executor of the People's Will?," *Moscow News*, January 29, 2014; Remington, *Presidential Decrees in Russia*, 106–107.

31. The origins of the Constitutional Court are actually in 1991, the last year of the Soviet Union, when it was written into the previous, Soviet-era constitution.

32. William E. Pomeranz, "President Medvedev and the Contested Constitutional Underpinnings of Russia's Power Vertical," *Demokratizatsiya*, 17, 2 (2009), 179–192; Alexei Trochev, *Judging Russia: The Role of the Constitutional Court in Russian Politics 1990–2006* (Cambridge University Press, 2008), esp. 139–157, 301–302; Kathryn Hendley, "Assessing the Rule of Law in Russia," in White, Sakwa, and Hale, *Developments in Russian Politics 8*, 149–150.

33. Ekaterina Mishina, "Tamara Morschakova: Recent Changes in Russian Legislation Resulted in a Considerable Decrease of the Legal Status of the Constitutional Court," *Institute of Modern Russia*, November 16, 2011; Peter H. Solomon Jr., "Law Courts and Human Rights," in Graeme Gill and James Young, eds, *Routledge Handbook of Russian Politics and Society* (Routledge, 2012), 189; Anna Pushkarskaya, "Konstitutsionnyy sud teryayet osobye mneniya," *Kommersant"*, December 2, 2009; Author's interview with Valeriy Lavskiy, June 2015. The dissents were described as "blistering" in Pomeranz, "President Medvedev and the Contested Constitutional Underpinnings . . . ," 184.

34. William Pomeranz, "Twenty Years of Russian Legal Reform," *Demokratizatsiya*, 20, 2 (2012), 141–147; Alexei Trochev, "All Appeals Lead to Strasbourg? Unpacking the

Impact of the European Court of Human Rights on Russia," *Demokratizatsiya*, 17, 2 (2009), 145–178; Ekaterina Mishina, "The Kremlin's Scorn for Strasbourg," *Institute of Modern Russia*, August 24, 2015; "Ekspert KGI Andrey Maksimov o novom zaslone ot resheniy ESPCh," *Komitet grazhdanskikh initsiativ*, December 15, 2015.

35. Grigorii V. Golosov, "The regional roots of electoral authoritarianism in Russia," *Europe-Asia Studies* 63, 4 (2011), 623–639; Stepan, "Russian Federalism," 170.

36. *Ot pervogo litsa*, 123. A comprehensive overview of Putin's early federal reforms is in: Peter Reddaway and Robert W. Orttung, eds., *The Dynamics of Russian Politics*, Volumes I and II (Rowman & Littlefield, 2004 and 2005).

37. Author's interviews with Smirnyagin, May 2001 and June 2015.

38. Cameron Ross, "Federalism and Electoral Authoritarianism under Putin," *Demokratizatsiya*, 13, 3 (Summer 2005), 363–365; J. Paul Goode, "The Revival of Russia's Gubernatorial Elections: Liberalization or Potemkin Reform?" *Russian Analytical Digest*, 139, November 18, 2013.

39. Author's interview with Dmitriy Oreshkin, November 2014.

40. On Russian political parties in the 1990s, see: Henry Hale, *Why Not Parties in Russia? Democracy, Federalism, and the State* (Cambridge University Press, 2006).

41. Author's interview with Lipman, May 2013. For a profile of Surkov, see: Peter Pomerantsev, "The Hidden Author of Putinism," *The Atlantic*, November 7, 2014.

42. Ellen Barry and Andrew E. Kramer, "Billionaire Condemns Party He Led as a Kremlin 'Puppet'," *New York Times*, September 15, 2011. For details, see: Anna Arutunyan, *The Putin Mystique: Inside Russia's Power Cult* (Olive Branch Press, 2015), 181–201.

43. Author's interview with political editor for Moscow newspaper, June 2015.

44. Author's interview with political editor for Moscow newspaper, June 2015; Aleksandr Kynev, "Perenosimye stradaniya: zachem nuzhny dosrochnye vybory," *RBK*, July 2, 2015; Mariya Rybakova, "Pravila s"ema s vyborov: oppozitsiyu upotreblyayut cherez fil'tr," *Moskovskiy Komsomolets*, July 28, 2015; "Kremlin Confirms Vyacheslav Volodin as New Duma Speaker," *Moscow Times*, September 23, 2016. The current deputy head of the Presidential Administration overseeing domestic politics is Sergey Kiriyenko, a previous prime minister under Yeltsin who has served in multiple positions under Putin.

45. Author's interview with Georgiy Satarov, December 2013; Yelena Tregubova, *Bayki kremlevskogo diggera* (Ad Marginem, 2003), 243–251, 274–282.

46. Good journalistic accounts include: Andrew Jack, *Inside Putin's Russia* (Oxford University Press, 2004), 131–173; Peter Baker and Susan Glasser, *Kremlin Rising*, updated ed. (Potomac Books, 2007), 78–98; Tregubova, *Bayki kremlevskogo digger*, 318–365 (esp. 323, 350–358); Mikhail Zygar', *Vsya kremlevskaya rat': Kratkaya istoriya sovremennoy Rossii* (Intellektual'naya literatura, 2015), 34–41.

47. The quote is from: Fish, *Democracy Derailed in Russia*, 30; Author's interview with Smirnyagin, June 2015.

48. Baker and Glasser 2007, 294; "A stat'ya naydetsya . . . Kak Administratsiya prezidenta fabrikuyet ugolovnye dela i publikatsii v presse," *The Insider*, January 29, 2015; "Kto vladeyet Natsional'noy Media Gruppoy," *RBK*, November 17, 2014.

49. Robert W. Orttung and Christopher Walker, "Putin and Russia's Crippled Media," *Russian Analytical Digest*, 123, February 21, 2013; Author's interview with Andrey Soldatov, December 2013; Andrey Soldatov and Irina Borogan, *The Red Web: The Struggle between Russia's Digital Dictators and the New Online Revolutionaries* (Public Affairs, 2015); Author's interview with media manager, July 2014; Irina Reznik, Ilya Khrennikov, and Henry Meyer, "Putin Allies Said Angling to Wrest Paper from WSJ, FT," *Bloomberg*, October 15, 2014; Masha Lipman, "The Demise of RBC and Investigative Reporting in Russia," *New Yorker*, May 18, 2016.

50. Sarah Henderson, *Building Democracy in Contemporary Russia: Western Support for Grassroots Organizations* (Cornell University Press, 2003).

51. Author's interviews with NGO representatives over the last 15 years in multiple Russian cities. See also: Alfred B. Evans Jr., "Vladimir Putin's Design for Civil Society," in Alfred B. Evans Jr., Laura A. Henry, and Lisa McIntosh Sundstrom, eds., *Russian Civil Society: A Critical Assessment* (M.E. Sharpe, 2006), 147–158.

52. Brian D. Taylor, *State Building in Putin's Russia: Policing and Coercion after Communism* (Cambridge University Press, 2011), 220–224, 236–238.

53. Vladimir Putin, interview with Aleksandr Gamov, "Gosudarstvennyy perevorot Rossii ne grozit," *Komsomol'skaya pravda*, August 7, 1999. See also: James Richter, "Civil Society and the Second Putinshchina," *PONARS Policy Memo*, 276, September 2013.

54. Author's interviews, June 2015; "Orthodox Church Receives Majority of Russian Government Grants," *Moscow Times*, December 21, 2015.

55. Mark R. Beissinger, *Nationalist Mobilization and the Collapse of the Soviet State* (Cambridge University Press, 2002), 334; Anatoliy Kulikov, *Tyazhelye zvezdy* (Voyna i Mir, 2002), 390–403; Yel'tsin, *Prezidentskiy marafon*, 31–33.

56. Vladimir Putin, "Nachalo vstrechi s zhitelyami Beslana, postradavshimi v rezul'tate terakta 1–3 sentyabrya 2004 goda," *Kremlin.ru*, September 2, 2005; Taylor, *State Building in Putin's Russia*.

57. Levitsky and Way, *Competitive Authoritarianism*.

58. Author's interview with Tatyana Dorutina, July 2014; Author's interview with Grigoriy Belonuchkin, July 2014.

59. Taylor, *State Building in Putin's Russia*, 95–97; Anastasiya Kornya, "Segodnya zavershayetsya registratsiya kandidatov v Mosgordumu—Bez Oppozitsii," *Vedomosti*, July 21, 2014.

60. Taylor, *State Building in Putin's Russia*, 98–99; Andrey Kolesnikov, "Vladimir Putin: dayu vam chestnoye partiynoye slovo," *Kommersant"*, August 30, 2010.

61. Graeme Robertson, *The Politics of Protest in Hybrid Regimes: Managing Dissent in Post-Communist Russia* (Cambridge University Press, 2011); Graeme Robertson, "Protesting Putinism," *Problems of Post-Communism*, 60, 2 (2013), 11–23; Leon Aron, "Russia's Protesters: The People, Ideals and Prospects," *American Enterprise Institute*, August 9, 2012.

62. Fred Weir, "How One Russian Became an Object Lesson for All Would-Be Protesters," *Christian Science Monitor*, December 31, 2015. For information on the so-called Bolotnoye Affair, named after the location of the rally, see: http://bolotnoedelo.info/.

63. Vladimir Putin, "Zasedaniye kollegii Federal'noy sluzhby bezopasnosti," *Kremlin.ru*, February 14, 2013; Vyacheslav Kozlov, "Will the Patriotic Stop List Kill Russia's NGOs?", *openDemocracy*, July 22, 2015; Fred Weir, "Can Russia's Only Independent Election Monitor Survive Kremlin Pressure?", *Christian Science Monitor*, August 27, 2015.

64. Irina Borogan, "Kak i dlya chego sostavlyayut 'chernye' spiski," *Yezhednevnyy zhurnal*, June 2, 2009; Valerie Sperling, *Sex, Politics, and Putin: Political Legitimacy in Russia* (Oxford University Press, 2014), 278–293.

65. Vadim Volkov, "Delo protiv pravosudiya," Vedomosti, December 26, 2014; Agence France-Presse, "Russia's conviction of opposition leader Alexei Navalny 'arbitrary', European court says," *The Guardian*, February 23, 2016; Ivan Nechepurenko, "Russia Bars Kremlin Critic From Running for President," *New York Times*, December 25, 2017. See also: Arutunyan, *The Putin Mystique*, 235–250.

66. Author's interview with Okhotin, November 2014. See also the reports at http://reports.ovdinfo.org.

67. Author's interview with Vladislav Bachurov, July 2014. On the "gray zone" between democracy and authoritarianism, see the classic article: Thomas Carothers, "The End of the Transition Paradigm," *Journal of Democracy*, 13, 1 (2002), 5–21.

68. On managed democracy, see, for example: Timothy J. Colton and Michael McFaul, "Russian Democracy under Putin," *Problems of Post Communism* 50, 4 (2003), 12–21.

69. Viktor Khamrayev, interview with Ol'ga Kryshtanovskaya, "'Polozheniye chekistov segodnya fantastitecheski ustoychivo'," *Kommersant"-Vlast'*, March 19, 2007.
70. Yelena Shishkunova, interview with Vladislav Surkov, "Sistema uzhe izmenilas'," *Izvestiya*, December 22, 2011.
71. Tat'yana Stanovaya, "Gvardiya prezidenta: kak novoye supervedomstvo menyayet konfiguratsiyu silovikov?" *Politkom.ru*, April 11, 2016; Yuriy Baluyevskiy, "Voyna ne konchayetsya, ona—zamirayet," *Nezavisimoye voyennoye obozreniye*, May 26, 2017.
72. Levada Center, "Vladimir Putin: udachi i neudachi, sila," *Levada.ru*, September 9, 2014; Author's interview with Dmitriy Oreshkin, November 2014; Author's interview with Nikolay Troitskiy, December 2014.
73. Vladimir Putin, "Otvety na voprosy zhurnalistov posle pryamogo tele- i radioefira ("Pryamaya liniya s Prezidentom Rossii")," *Kremlin.ru*, October 18, 2007; Author's interview with Dmitriy Trenin, July 2014; Author's interview with Aleksey Makarkin, December 2014.
74. Hale, "The Myth of Mass Russian support for autocracy"; Ol'ga Churakova, "Rossiyane ne veryat v vybory, khot' i otnosyatsya k demokratii khorosho," *Vedomosti*, August 11, 2015.

Chapter 3

1. On "parchment institutions," see, for example: John M. Carey, "Parchment, Equilibria, and Institutions." *Comparative Political Studies* 33, 6–7 (2000), 735–761. The conception of Putin as both president and boss comes from: Gleb Pavlovskiy, *Sistema RF v voyne 2014 goda: De Principatu Debili* (Yevropa, 2014), 28.
2. More generally, see Alena V. Ledeneva, *How Russia Really Works: The Informal Practices That Shaped Post-Soviet Politics and Business* (Cornell University Press, 2006).
3. Author's interview with Ol'ga Kryshtanovskaya, June 2015; personal correspondence with Kryshtanovskaya, August 2017.
4. On Putin as a deal-maker or fixer, see: Fiona Hill and Clifford G. Gaddy, *Mr. Putin: Operative in the Kremlin* (Brookings Institution Press, 2013), 144; Alena V. Ledeneva, *Can Russia Modernise? Sistema, Power Networks and Informal Governance* (Cambridge University Press, 2013), 13.
5. Richard Sakwa, *The Crisis of Russian Democracy: The Dual State, Factionalism, and the Medvedev Succession* (Cambridge University Press, 2011); Hill and Gaddy, *Mr. Putin*, 236; Vadim Kononenko and Arkady Moshes, eds., *Russia as a Network State: What Works in Russia When State Institutions Do Not* (Palgrave Macmillan, 2011); Henry E. Hale, *Patronal Politics: Eurasian Regime Dynamics in Comparative Perspective* (Cambridge University Press, 2014); Ledeneva, *Can Russia Modernise?*; Pavlovskiy, *Sistema RF v voyne 2014 goda*.
6. Author's interviews: Dmitriy Trenin, July 2014; Masha Lipman, May 2013; Aleksey Mazur, June 2015.
7. Ledeneva, *Can Russia Modernise?*; Kononenko and Moshes, *Russia as a Network State*; Gulnaz Sharafutdinova, *Political Consequences of Crony Capitalism inside Russia* (University of Notre Dame Press, 2010).
8. Hale, *Patronal Politics*, 21.
9. Hale, *Patronal Politics*; Allen C. Lynch, *How Russia Is Not Ruled: Reflections on Russian Political Development* (Cambridge University Press, 2005).
10. Thomas Graham, "Noviy rossiyskiy rezhim," *Nezavisimaya Gazeta*, November 23, 1995; Donald N. Jensen, "The Boss: How Yuri Luzhkov Runs Moscow," *Demokratizatsiya*, 8, 1 (2000), 83–122.
11. Key works include: Hale, *Patronal Politics*; Ledeneva, *Can Russia Modernise?*; Kononenko and Moshes, *Russia as a Network State*; Sharafutdinova, *Political Consequences of Crony Capitalism inside Russia*.

12. Anonymous interview by author, June 2008.

13. The officials in question were Vladimir Ustinov and Igor Sechin; their children have since divorced. For this and other examples, see: "Eti braki zaklyuchayutsya na politicheskikh nebesakh," *Trud*, September 20, 2007.

14. Sharafutdinova, *Political Consequences of Crony Capitalism inside Russia*, 2–3, 84–90.

15. On the gendered nature of informal clans in Russia, see: Janet E. Johnson and Alexandra Novitskaya, "Gender and Politics," in Stephen K. Wegren, ed., *Putin's Russia: Past Imperfect, Future Uncertain*, 6th ed. (Rowman & Littlefield, 2016), 219.

16. Author's interview with Valeriy Lavskiy, June 2015.

17. Hale, *Patronal Politics*.

18. *Ot pervogo litsa: Razgovory s Vladimirom Putinym* (Vagrius, 2000), 71–72.

19. Author's interview with anonymous St. Petersburg journalist, July 2014; *Ot pervogo litsa*, 77–80; Masha Gessen, *The Man without a Face: The Unlikely Rise of Vladimir Putin* (Penguin, 2012), 93–99.

20. Author's interview with Tatyana Dorutina, League of Women Voters, St. Petersburg, July 2014; Author's interview with Yuriy Nesterov, former city councilor, July 2014; Author's interview with an anonymous journalist; Author's interview with journalist Vladislav Bachurov, July 2014.

21. Hill and Gaddy, *Mr. Putin*, 162–164; Vadim Volkov, *Violent Entrepreneurs: The Use of Force in the Making of Russian Capitalism* (Cornell University Press, 2002). Volkov, it should be said, himself took the term from writings on the Italian mafia.

22. Karen Dawisha, *Putin's Kleptocracy: Who Owns Russia?* (Simon & Schuster, 2014).

23. Dawisha, *Putin's Kleptocracy*, 63–70; Dar'ya Petrova and Timofey Shirokov, "15 let samomu mutnomu 'Ozeru' v mire!," *Novaya Gazeta*, November 11, 2011.

24. Brian D. Taylor, *State Building in Putin's Russia: Coercion and Policing after Communism* (Cambridge University Press, 2011), 36–70; Jonathan Littell, *The Security Organs of the Russian Federation: A Brief History 1991–2004* (PSAN Publishing House, 2006), appendix; Dawisha, *Putin's Kleptocracy*, 51–56, 71–74, 85.

25. *Ot pervogo litsa*, 104–108; Author's interview with Yuriy Nesterov, July 2014; Vladimir Kovalev, "Yakovlev Appointed as New Deputy PM," *St. Petersburg Times*, June 17, 2003; Hill and Gaddy, *Mr. Putin*, 176–179.

26. Peter Baker and Susan Glasser, *Kremlin Rising*, updated ed. (Potomac Books, 2007), 47; Hill and Gaddy, *Mr. Putin*, 177. Putin himself describes St. Petersburg as "provincial" in his memoirs, echoing the older brother in *Brat*: *Ot pervogo litsa*, 122.

27. *Ot pervogo litsa*, 119–122; Author's interview with Nikonov, July 2014. The academic research is: Vladimir Gilpen'son and Vladimir Magun, "Na sluzhbe Gosudarstva Rossiyskogo: perspektivy i ogranicheniya kar'ery molodykh chinovnikov," *Vestnik obshchestvennogo mneniya*, 5 (September–October), 2004, 25–26.

28. *Ot pervogo litsa*, 181–183; Dawisha, *Putin's Kleptocracy*, 183–184; Author's interview with Bachurov, July 2014.

29. Varying accounts include: Dawisha, *Putin's Kleptocracy*, 184–190; Baker and Glasser, *Kremlin Rising*, 50–53; Gessen, *The Man without a Face*, 18–22.

30. Makarkin, *Politiko-ekonomicheskiye klany*, 15–58; Author's interview with Makarkin, December 2014; Mikhail Zygar', *Vsya kremlevskaya rat': Kratkaya istoriya sovremennoy Rossii* (Intellektual'naya literatura, 2015), 95. For an academic demonstration of Putin's solidifying control at the top around 2004, see: Alexander Baturo and Johan Elkink, "Dynamics of Regime Personalization and Patron–Client Networks in Russia, 1999–2014," *Post-Soviet Affairs*, 32, 1 (2016), 75–98.

31. Author's interview with Nikonov, July 2014.

32. Taylor, *State Building in Putin's Russia*, 63, 65–66; Zygar', *Vsya kremlevskaya rat'*, 222.

33. A. Makarkin, *Politiko-ekonomicheskiye klany sovremennoy Rossii* (Tsentr politicheskikh tekhnologiy, 2003); Author's interview with Aleskey Makarkin, December 2014. Other

Putin outsiders who have seemingly gained Putin's trust since 2000 include Moscow mayor Sergey Sobyanin and Duma Speaker Vyacheslav Volodin.

34. Author's interview with Aleskey Makarkin, December 2014; https://en.wikipedia.org/wiki/Konni_(dog); Zygar', *Vsya kremlevskaya rat'*, 332–335; Aleksey Venediktov, "Resheniye po Krymu real'no prinyal odin chelovek," *Noviy Kaliningrad*, August 20, 2015.

35. Viktor Dyatlikovich and Filipp Chapkovskiy, "Kto est' kto i pochemu v rossiyskoy elite" and "Klanovost': pol'za i preodoleniye," *Russkiy Reporter*, September 7, 2011. The authors break the data down by "Federal Districts," so the data for the areas around Moscow and St. Petersburg are for the Central and North-West Federal Districts. Data for the rest of the country includes all of the other Federal Districts (there were eight in 2011).

36. In fact, Putin did move part of the capital to St. Petersburg, relocating the Constitutional Court and naval headquarters from Moscow to St. Petersburg.

37. Dyatlikovich and Chapkovskiy, "Kto est' kto i pochemu v rossiyskoy elite" and "Klanovost'."

38. Author's interviews with Kirill Rogov, December 2013; Aleksey Makarkin, December 2014; Dmitriy Oreshkin, November 2014. A brief description in English of the origins of the Ozero collective is: Dawisha, *Putin's Kleptocracy*, 94–99. On the marriage of Putin's daughter Ekaterina, see: Jack Stubbs, Andrey Kuzmin, Stephen Grey, and Roman Anin, "The Man Who Married Putin's Daughter and Then Made a Fortune," *Reuters*, December 17, 2015. According to 2018 rumors, they later divorced.

39. Author's interview with Ol'ga Kryshtanovskaya, June 2015. See also: Olga Kryshtanovskaya, "The Tandem and the Crisis," *Journal of Communist Studies and Transition Politics*, 27, 3–4 (2011), 407–419; Olga Kryshtanovskaya, interview by Ilja Viktorov, "The Legacy of Tandemocracy: Russia's Political Elite during Putin's Third Presidency," *Baltic Worlds*, 7, 2–3 (2014), 14–21.

40. Nikolay Petrov, "Rossiya v 2014-m: skatyvaniye v voronku," *Pro et Contra*, 18, 3–4 (May–August 2014). Examples of other prominent expert schemes include: Minchenko Consulting, "'Politbyuro 2.0' i postkrymskaya Rossiya," October 22, 2014; V. Pribylovksiy, "Pyat' Bashen. Politicheskaya Topografiya Kremlya," 2007, at http://www.anticompromat.org/putin/5bashen.html.

41. The five models were from Kryshtanovskaya, Petrov, Minchenko, Pribylovskiy, and the newspaper *Nezavisimaya Gazeta*'s annual list of most influential politicians. For the latter, someone had to appear in the top 20 twice from the following three years: 2004, 2009, and 2014.

42. Luke Harding, "WikiLeaks Cables: Dmitry Medvedev 'Plays Robin to Putin's Batman,'" *The Guardian*, December 1, 2010; Author's interview with Kryshtanovskaya. The editor of *Ekho Moskvy*, Aleksey Venediktov, later claimed that he was the source of the Batman and Robin quip: "Putin—eto Batman, a Medvedev—eto Robin," *Diplomatrutube*, September 28, 2015, https://www.youtube.com/watch?v=e-D3o6OkpZ0.

43. Zygar', *Vsya kremlevskaya rat'*, 219.

44. These ten individuals are: Sergey Chemezov, Sergey Ivanov, Aleksey Kudrin, Sergey Lavrov, Elvira Nabiullina, Nikolay Patrushev, Arkady Rotenberg, Sergey Sobyanin, Gennadiy Timchenko, and Vladimir Yakunin.

45. Andrew Jack, *Inside Putin's Russia* (Oxford University Press, 2004), 317.

46. This paragraph is based on insights from multiple interviews.

47. Yekaterina Shul'man, quoted in Joshua Yaffa, "Oligarchy 2.0," *New Yorker*, May 29, 2017, 52.

48. Discussions include: Tat'yana Stanovaya, "Kak rabotayet novaya kadrovaya politika Putina," *Carnegie Moscow Center*, August 2, 2016; Aleksey Nikol'skiy and Elena Mukhametshina, "Prezident sozdayet novyy kadrovyy rezerv iz svoikh byvshikh okrannikov," *Vedomosti*, August 1, 2016; Oleg Kashin, "How Do You Get to Be a Governor in Vladimir Putin's Russia?", *New York Times*, September 8, 2016; Ilya Arkhipov, Henry

Meyer, and Gregory White, "Putin Grooms a New Generation of Leaders," *Bloomberg*, September 8, 2016. On Viktor Ivanov's role in recruiting Putin, see: Sergey Mikhalych and Aleksey Polukhin, "2008? Net problemy," *Novaya Gazeta*, December 8, 2005; Pavel Fel'gengauer, "Stolonachal'niki derzhat oboronu," *Novaya Gazeta*, February 2, 2007.

49. Stanovaya, "Kak rabotayet novaya kadrovaya politika Putina"; Vladimir Pastukhov, "Otstavka Ivanova kak Osusheniye 'Ozera'," *BBC Russian Service*, August 13, 2016. See also: Brian Whitmore, "Russia's Solitary Man," *RFE/RL*, August 15, 2016.

50. Interview respondents who made this analogy include: Ol'ga Kryshtanovskaya, June 2015; Nikolay Petrov, May 2013, and Kirill Rogov, December 2013. See also: Ol'ga Kryshtanovskaya, "Rossiyskaya elita na perekhode," *Polit.ru*, July 31, 2008. Western journalists sometimes use the "mafia state" label in a more literal way. See, for example: Luke Harding, *Expelled: A Journalist's Descent into the Russian Mafia State* (St. Martin's Press, 2012); Brian Whitmore, "The Putin Syndicate," *RFE/RL*, June 9, 2015.

51. Author's interview with Georgiy Satarov, December 2013; Author's interview with Makarkin, December 2014; Zygar', *Vsya kremlevskaya rat'*, 370.

52. Sharafutdinova, *Political Consequences of Crony Capitalism inside Russia*. This view is different from that of Henry Hale, who sees both the Yeltsin and Putin systems as being "single pyramid," a consequence of the superpresidential institutional design.

53. Vladimir Pribylovsky, "Power Struggles inside the Kremlin," *openDemocracy*, December 31, 2014; Stanislav Belkovskiy, "Bor'ba za vlast' v Rossii: vesenneye obostreniye— 2015," *Slon*, May 27, 2015; "Patrioty Rossii i ee vragy," *Novaya Gazeta*, March 10, 2015; David Herszenhorn, "Chechen's Ties to Putin Are Questioned amid Nemtsov Murder Case," *New York Times*, March 19, 2015.

Chapter 4

1. Warren Zevon is probably best known to older readers for "Werewolves of London," whereas he is probably best known to younger readers for absolutely nothing.

2. Anna Arutunyan, *The Putin Mystique: Inside Russia's Power Cult* (Olive Branch Press, 2015), 101.

3. Gerald M. Easter, "Revenue Imperatives: State over Market in Postcommunist Russia," in Neil Robinson, ed., *The Political Economy of Russia* (Rowman & Littlefield, 2013), 62.

4. Gulnaz Sharafutdinova, *Political Consequences of Crony Capitalism inside Russia* (University of Notre Dame Press, 2010).

5. I use the term "communism" as shorthand for the type of economic system that existed in the Soviet Union from roughly the 1930s to 1991, and have no stake and little interest in debates about what "socialism" or "communism" really are, and whether these labels are appropriate for the Soviet economic system.

6. Stephen E. Hanson, "Analyzing Post-Communist Economic Change: A Review Essay," *East European Politics and Societies*, 12, 1 (1997), 145–170; Jeffrey S. Kopstein and David A. Reilly, "Geographic Diffusion and the Transformation of the Postcommunist World," *World Politics*, 53, 1 (2000), 1–37; Vladimir Popov, "Shock Therapy versus Gradualism: The End of the Debate," *Comparative Economic Studies*, 42, 1 (2000), 1–57; Mitchell A. Orenstein, "What Happened in Eastern European (Political) Economies?", *East European Politics and Societies*, 23, 4 (2009), 479–490; Timothy Frye, *Building States and Markets after Communism: The Perils of Polarized Democracy* (Cambridge University Press, 2010); Andrew Barnes, "From the Politics of Economic Reform to the Functioning of Political Economies," *Demokratizatsiya*, 20, 2 (2012), 79–86; Clifford G. Gaddy and Barry Ickes, *Bear Traps on Russia's Path to Modernization* (Routledge, 2013).

7. Data from: Yoshiko M. Herrera, "Russian Economic Reform, 1991–1999," in Zoltan Barany and Robert G. Moser, eds., *Russian Politics: Challenges of Democratization* (Cambridge University Press, 2001), 145.

8. Andrew Barnes, *Owning Russia* (Cornell University Press, 2006), 110–115; Daniel Treisman, "'Loans for Shares' Revisited," *NBER Working Paper No. 15819*, March 2010; J. David Brown, John S. Earle, and Scott Gehlbach, "Privatization," in Michael Alexeev and Shlomo Weber, eds., *The Oxford Handbook of the Russian Economy* (Oxford University Press, 2013), 161–185.

9. Stephen Kotkin, *Armaggedon Averted: The Soviet Collapse 1970–2000*, updated ed. (Oxford University Press, 2008), 122.

10. Stephen F. Cohen, *Bukharin and the Bolshevik Revolution* (Oxford University Press, 1971), 89; Gerard Roland, *Transition and Economics: Politics, Markets and Firms* (MIT Press, 2000), 153–170.

11. Source for the figure: World Bank, *World Development Indicators*. See also: Andrei Shleifer and Daniel Treisman, "A Normal Country: Russia after Communism," *Journal of Economic Perspectives*, 19, 1 (2005), 151–174.

12. Kotkin *Armaggedon Averted*, 178; Allen C. Lynch, *How Russia Is Not Ruled: Reflections on Russian Political Development* (Cambridge University Press, 2005), 41–46; Gaddy and Ickes, *Bear Traps*, 33; Fiona Hill and Clifford G. Gaddy, *The Siberian Curse: How Communist Planners Left Russia Out in the Cold* (Brookings Institution Press, 2003); Natalia Zubarevich, "Four Russias: Human Potential and Social Differentiation of Russian Regions and Cities," in Maria Lipman and Nikolay Petrov, eds., *Russia 2025: Scenarios for the Russian Future* (Palgrave Macmillan, 2013), 75–78; Richard E. Ericson, "Command Economy and Its Legacy," in Alexeev and Weber, *The Oxford Handbook of the Russian Economy*, 70–71.

13. Elena Shomina and Frances Heywood, "Transformation in Russian Housing: The New Key Roles of Local Authorities," *International Journal of Housing Policy*, 13, 3 (2013), 312–324; Sergey Aleksashenko, "Russia's Economic Agenda to 2020," *International Affairs* 88, 1 (2012), 35; Joel S. Hellman, "Winners Take All: The Politics of Partial Reform in Postcommunist Transitions," *World Politics*, 50, 2 (1998), 203–234.

14. Andrew Kuchins, "Vladimir the Lucky," *Carnegie Russia and Eurasia Program*, July 25, 2006; Clifford Gaddy and Barry Ickes, "Russia after the Global Financial Crisis," *Eurasian Geography and Economics*, 51, 3 (2010), 282–287.

15. Aleksashenko, "Russia's Economic Agenda to 2020," 34–35; Daniel Treisman, *The Return: Russia's Journey from Gorbachev to Medvedev* (Free Press, 2011), 232–236.

16. Gleb Pavlovsky, interviewed by Tom Parfitt, "Putin's World Outlook," *New Left Review*, 88 (July–August 2014).

17. Richard E. Ericson, "The Russian Economy in 2008: Testing the 'Market Economy'," *Post-Soviet Affairs*, 25, 3 (2009), 213–214; Easter, "Revenue Imperatives"; Gaddy and Ickes, "Russia after the Global Financial Crisis." See also Fiona Hill and Clifford G. Gaddy, *Mr. Putin: Operative in the Kremlin* (Brookings, 2013), 206–249.

18. Daniel Treisman, "Presidential Popularity in a Hybrid Regime: Russia under Yeltsin and Putin," *American Journal of Political Science*, 55, 3 (2011), 590–609.

19. On Putin's thesis, see: Hill and Gaddy, *Mr. Putin*, 222–223; Harley Balzer, "The Putin Thesis and Russian Energy Policy," *Post-Soviet Affairs* 21, 3 (2005), 210–225.

20. For a well-supported argument that leaving oil wealth in private hands would actually have helped avoid many of the common political and economic "curses" of oil, see: Pauline Jones Luong and Erika Weinthal, *Oil Is Not a Curse: Ownership Structure and Institutions in Soviet Successor States* (Cambridge University Press, 2010).

21. Peter Rutland, "The Oligarchs and Economic Development," in Stephen K. Wegren and Dale R. Herspring, *After Putin's Russia*, 4th ed. (Rowman & Littlefield, 2010), 174–175; Vladimir Soldatkin and Andrew Callus, "Russia's Rosneft Pays Out $40-Billion in Historic TNK-BP Deal Completion," *Reuters*, March 21, 2013; "In Russia, Privatisation Can Mean Selling One State-Owned Company to Another," *The Economist*, October 22, 2016.

22. Aleksey Navalny, "i snova zdravstvuyite," http://navalny.livejournal.com/823877. html?page=41, July 19, 2013. Data on exports from the state statistical service Rosstat. For representative examples of statements by Putin and Medvedev, see, for example: Vladimir Putin, "Poslaniye Federal'nomu Sobraniyu Rossiyskoy Federatsii," *Kremlin.ru*, April 3, 2001; Dmitriy Medvedev, "Rossiya, vpered!," *Gazeta.ru*, September 10, 2009; Vladimir Putin, "Nam nuzhna novaya ekonomika," *Vedomosti*, January 30, 2012. On resources as a disincentive for reform, see also: Sergei Guriev and Ekaterina Zhuravskaya, "Why Russia Is Not South Korea," *Journal of International Affairs*, 63, 2 (2010), 125–139.

23. Rutland, "The Oligarchs and Economic Development," esp. 168. See also Peter Rutland, "The Political Economy of Putin 3.0," *Russian Analytical Digest*, 133, July 18, 2013, 2–5.

24. For accounts, see: Ol'ga Kryshtanovskaya, *Anatomiya Rossiyskoy elity* (Zakharov, 2005), 359–362; Peter Baker and Susan Glasser, *Kremlin Rising*, updated edition (Potomac Books, 2007), 84–87; Roman Kutuzov, "Oligarkhy," *Forbes (Russia)*, October 20, 2010; Hill and Gaddy, *Mr. Putin*, 208–210.

25. Vadim Volkov, *Violent Entrepreneurs: The Use of Force in the Making of Russian Capitalism* (Cornell University Press, 2002), 181–186.

26. William Tompson, "Putting Yukos in Perspective," *Post-Soviet Affairs*, 21, 2 (2005), 168–171; Lilia Shevtsova, *Putin's Russia* (Carnegie Endowment for International Peace, 2003), 16; Hill and Gaddy, *Mr. Putin*, 163, 166. The Nobel prize–winning economist Douglass North observed, "If the state has coercive force, then those who run the state will use that force in their own interest at the expense of the rest of society." Douglass C. North, *Institutions, Institutional Change and Economic Performance* (Cambridge University Press, 1990), 59–60.

27. The references are to Norilsk Nickel's Vladimir Potanin, Lukoil's Vagit Alekperov, and TNK's (Tyumen Oil Company) Mikhail Fridman. See: Kryshtanovskaya, *Anatomiya Rossiyskoy elity*, 360–361; Barnes, *Owning Russia*, 175.

28. Richard Sakwa, "Systematic Stalemate: *Reiderstvo* and the Dual State," in Robinson, *The Political Economy of Russia*, 78. A brief overview is in Baker and Glasser, *Kremlin Rising*, 272–292. Useful analyses include Barnes, *Owning Russia*, 209–226; Tompson, "Putting Yukos in Perspective,"; Vadim Volkov, "'Delo Standard Oil' i 'delo Yukosa'," *Pro et Contra*, 9, 2 (September–October 2005), 66–91.

29. Mikhail Zygar', *Vsya kremlevskaya rat': Kratkaya istoriya sovremennoy Rossii* (Intellektual'naya literatura, 2015), 220–221.

30. Easter, "Revenue Imperatives"; Gerald M. Easter, "The Russian State in the Time of Putin," *Post-Soviet Affairs*, 24, 3 (2008), 199–230; Philip Hanson, "Networks, Cronies, and Business Plans: Business-State Relations in Russia," in Vadim Kononenko and Arkady Moshes, eds., *Russia as a Network State: What Works in Russia When State Institutions Do Not?* (Palgrave Macmillan, 2011), 113; Andrei Vandenko, interview with Gennadiy Timchenko, "Timchenko: Everything Has to Be Paid For, and Acquaintance with Top Officials as Well," *TASS*, August 4, 2014.

31. Author's interview with St. Petersburg journalist, July 2014. A detailed report on multiple examples of this practice in Russian is: "Izobrazhaya zhervovatelya. Kto dayet den'gi na proyekty, svyazannye s Putinym," *Slon*, August 9, 2016.

32. Ellen Barry, "Putin Plays Sheriff for Cowboy Capitalists," *New York Times*, June 4, 2009; Vera Kholmogorova, Mariya Buravtseva, and Bela Lyauv, "Poshel i podpisal," *Vedomosti*, June 5, 2009. For a detailed discussion of how profitable oil, gas, and metal companies are expected to support the rest of the economy, see Gaddy and Ickes, *Bear Traps*.

33. Charles Clover, "Russian Puzzle Proves Hard to Crack," *Financial Times*, October 24, 2013.

34. Sharafutdinova, *Political Consequences of Crony Capitalism inside Russia*.

35. "Ikh dom Rossiya," *New Times*, November 2, 2011; author's research. On Surgutneftegaz, see: Mariya Ignatova, "Surgutskiy Pas'yans," *Russkiy Forbes*, April 2004.

36. Hill and Gaddy, *Mr. Putin*, 224–228; Ben Aris, "Meeting the Stoligarchs, Putin's Pals Who Control a Fifth of the Russian Economy," *Intellinews.com*, July 11, 2016; Hanson, "Networks, Cronies, and Business Plans," 122–126.

37. In addition to the sources in chapter 3, see, for example: Vladimir Pribylovskiy, *Pereklichka Vladimira Putina: Kto vybyvayet, a kto ostayetsya?* (Algorithm, 2013), 78–164; V. Milov, B. Nemtsov, V. Ryzhkov, and O. Shorina, *Putin. Korruptsiya. Nezavisimyy ekspertnyy doklad* (Partiya narodnoy svobody, 2011), 10–24; Andrew E. Kramer and David M. Herszenhorn, "Midas Touch in St. Petersburg: Friends of Putin Glow Brightly," *New York Times*, March 1, 2012.

38. "Koroli goszakaza—2016," *Forbes*, February 25, 2016; Joshua Yaffa, "Oligarchy 2.0," *New Yorker*, May 29, 2017, 45–55.

39. Yaffa, "Oligarchy 2.0," 50–51. For a comparison to Chinese-style crony capitalism, see: David Barboza and Sharon LaFraniere, "'Princelings' in China Use Family Ties to Gain Riches," *New York Times*, May 17, 2012; David Barboza "Billions in Hidden Riches for Family of Chinese Leader," *New York Times*, October 25, 2012.

40. Gaddy and Ickes, "Russia after the Global Financial Crisis." See also Hill and Gaddy, *Mr. Putin*, 206–249.

41. Hanson, "Networks, Cronies, and Business Plans," 119–120; Tat'yana Stanovaya, "Vosstavshiy iz gaza: 'Gazprom' prizvali na voynu," *Slon*, October 29, 2013.

42. Nadezhda Krasnushkina, "FAS vzyalas' za tarify," *Kommersant*", June 5, 2017;Vladimir Putin, "Interv'yu radiostantsii 'Mayak'," *Kremlin.ru*, March 18, 2000.

43. Lukas Alpert, "Who Wants to Be a Russian Billionaire," *Wall Street Journal*, October 9, 2013; Credit Suisse, *Global Wealth Report 2013*, 53. A critique of the report's methodology that claims it overstates the degree of inequality by miscounting the household wealth of average Russians, is: Leonid Bershidsky, "Just How Rich Are Russia's Billionaires?," *Bloomberg*, October 10, 2013.

44. Julia Kollewe, "Russia Leads Shopping Mall Building Resurgence across Europe," *The Guardian*, April 2, 2014; Andrew E. Kramer, "Malls Blossom in Russia, with a Middle Class," *New York Times*, January 1, 2013.

45. The Russian scholar Nataliya Zubarevich conceives of "four Russias": one-third live in cities of over 250,000 people; one-quarter live in industrial towns between 25,000-250,000; one-third live in rural or "semiurban" areas on the edge of cities; and the remaining 5 to 10 percent live in "underdeveloped Russia," such as the North Caucasus or the Altai in southern Siberia. Zubarevich, "Four Russias."

46. OECD, *Russia: Modernising the Economy*, April 2013, 20. The China figure is from Kotkin, *Armageddon Averted*, 197.

47. Two recent sweeping and forceful statements of this view are: Daron Acemoglu and James Robinson, *Why Nations Fail: The Origins of Power, Prosperity, and Poverty* (Crown, 2012); Douglass C. North, John Joseph Wallis, and Barry R. Weingast, *Violence and Social Orders: A Conceptual Framework for Interpreting Recorded Human History* (Cambridge University Press, 2012).

48. Arto Ojala and Hannakaisa Isomaki, "Entrepreneurship and Small Businesses in Russia: A Review of Empirical Research," *Journal of Small Business and Enterprise Development*, 18, 1 (2011), 112, 114.

49. For a detailed overview, see the report: "Pytki i ubiystvo Sergeya Magnitskogo. Sokrytiye pravdy gosudarstvennymi organami" at the website: http://russian-untouchables.com/rus/docs/P01RUS.pdf. An account in English is: Arutunyan, *The Putin Mystique*, 155–168.

50. Vladimir Putin, "Poslaniye Prezidenta Federal'nomu Sobraniyu," *Kremlin.ru*, December 3, 2015; V. V. Volkov, E. L. Paneyakh, and K. D. Titayev, *Proizvol'naya aktivnost' pravookhranitel'nykh organov v sfere bor'by s ekonomicheskoy prestupnost'yu. Analiz statistiki* (IPP EUSPB, 2010); Vadim Volkov, "Socioeconomic Status and Sentencing Disparities: Evidence from Russia's Criminal Courts," Working Paper IRL-01/2014

(IPP EUSPB, 2014); Jordan Gans-Morse, "Threats to Property Rights in Russia: From Private Coercion to State Aggression," *Post-Soviet Affairs*, 28, 3 (2012), esp. 278–287; Author's interview with Vladislav Bachurov, July 2014. See also: Sakwa, "Systematic Stalemate"; Thomas Firestone, "Criminal Corporate Raiding in Russia," *International Lawyer*, 42 (2008), 1207–1229; Michael Rochlitz, "Corporate Raiding and the Role of the State in Russia," *Post-Soviet Affairs*, 30, 2–3 (2014), 89–114.

51. Gans-Morse, "Threats to Property Rights in Russia"; Kathryn Hendley, "Suing the State in Russia," *Post-Soviet Affairs*, 18, 2 (2002), 148–181.

52. Vladimir Putin, "Poslaniye Prezidenta Rossiyskoy Federatsii V.V. Putina Federal'nomu Sobraniyu Rossiyskoy Federatsii," *kremlin.ru*, April 18, 2002; Dmitriy Medvedev, "Poslaniye Federal'nomu Sobraniyu Rossiyskoy Federatsii," *kremlin.ru*, November 5, 2008; Igor' Nikolayev, "Zaplati nalogi i ne spi," *gazeta.ru*, October 29, 2013; "Putin uprsotil vozbuzhdeniye ugolovnykh del po nalogovym prestupleniyam," *Forbes.ru*, October 22, 2014; "Medvedev o prave SK vozbuzhdat' nalogovye dela: 'Eta model' mozhet rabotat'," *RBK Daily*, January 15, 2014.

53. Sergei Guriev and Oleg Tsyvinsky, "Clock Is Ticking on Putin's Economic Pledges," *Moscow Times*, February 21, 2013; Shawn Donnan, "Russia Rises in World Bank's 'Doing Business' Rankings," *Financial Times*, October 27, 2015; The World Bank, "Doing Business," http://www.doingbusiness.org/rankings.

54. In the next chapter we consider other cross-national measures of the quality of the Russian state.

55. Byung-Yeon Kim, "The Unofficial Economy in Russia," in Alexeev and Weber, *The Oxford Handbook of the Russian Economy*, 265–285; Evgenia Pismennaya and Ilya Arkhipov, "Putin Peers into Shadows Where 30 Million Toil on Fringes," *Bloomberg*, July 13, 2016.

56. Anna Andrianova and Andre Tartar, "Oil Must Go to $40 and Stay There to Buy Russia Some Reforms," *Bloomberg*, July 17, 2016; "Deneg net, no vy derzhites'," *Meduza*, May 24, 2016; "World Bank Says Russian Economy to Grow 1.3 Percent in 2017, 1.4 Percent in 2018," *RFE/RL*, June 5, 2017. On the difference between oil dependence and addiction, see: Gaddy and Ickes, "Russia after the Global Financial Crisis."

57. "Across the World, Politically Connected Tycoons Are Feeling the Squeeze," *Economist*, May 7, 2016; Sergei Guriev, "Political Origins and Implications of the Economic Crisis in Russia," in Leon Aron, ed., *Putin's Russia: How It Rose, How It Is Maintained, and How It Might End* (American Enterprise Institute, 2015), 8–21; Kramer, "A Russian Oil Company Is for Sale—Again"; " 'Downshifter' Russia Is Losing Global Competition, Warns State Bank Chief," *Moscow Times*, January 15, 2016.

58. Dmitriy Medvedev, "Vystupleniye Dmitriya Medvedeva," V Gaidar Forum, Moscow, January 15, 2014 (http://government.ru/news/9741); Anton Feynberg, Anna Mogilevskaya, and Vladimir Dergachev, " 'Vsye ochevidno: nuzhny strukturnye reformy . . . ,'" *RBK*, June 2, 2017.

59. Gaddy and Ickes, *Bear Traps*.

60. Peter B. Evans, "Predatory, Developmental, and Other Apparatuses: A Comparative Political Economy Perspective on the Third World State," *Sociological Forum*, 4, 4 (1989), 561–587; Atul Kohli, *State-Directed Development: Political Power and Industrialization in the Global Periphery* (Cambridge University Press, 2004); Guriev and Zhuravskaya, "Why Russia Is Not South Korea," 130. For a good short statement of how Russian capitalism is more predatory than developmental, see Neil Robinson's introductory and concluding chapters in: Robinson, *The Political Economy of Russia*, esp. 1–6, 191–197.

Chapter 5

1. Merle Fainsod, *How Russia Is Ruled* (Harvard University Press, 1953); Robert Levgold, "Significant Books: How Russia Is Ruled," *Foreign Affairs*, 76, 5 (September–October 1997): 229–230; Jerry F. Hough and Merle Fainsod, *How the Soviet Union Is governed*

(Harvard University Press, 1979); Allen C. Lynch, *How Russia Is Not Ruled: Reflections on Russian Political Development* (Cambridge University Press, 2005).

2. I developed these arguments about the relatively low quality of the Russian state under Putin in: Brian D. Taylor, *State Building in Putin's Russia: Policing and Coercion after Communism* (Cambridge University Press, 2011).

3. National Research Council and Institute of Medicine, *U.S. Health in International Perspective: Shorter Lives, Poorer Health* (National Academies Press, 2013); Kirill Rogov, " 'Krymskiy sindrom': mekhanizmy avtoritarnoy mobilizatsii," *Kontrapunkt*, 1 (2015), 3; Kirill Rogov, "Resursnyy natsionalizm—ot Yukosa do Kryma," *Vedomosti*, October 15, 2014.

4. For a study of the Russian policy process, see: Brian D. Taylor, "Police Reform in Russia: The Policy Process in a Hybrid Regime," *Post-Soviet Affairs*, 30, 2–3 (2014), 226–255.

5. Author's interview with Ol'ga Kryshtanovskaya, June 2015; Aleksandr Zadorozhnyy, interview with Aleksey Venediktov, "Po' prikazu Putina, Obamy ili Poroshenko na yugo-vostoke Ukrainy nichego ne ostanovitsya," *Znak*, June 9, 2014; Author's interview with Nikolay Troitsky, December 2014; Author's interview with Aleksandr Sergunin, June 2017.

6. Author's interview with Nikolay Petrov, May 2013; Author's interview with Ivan Rodin, June 2015; Author's interview with Georgiy Satarov, December 2013.

7. Andrey Sukhotin and Ruslan Dubov, "Prezidenta ostavlyayem na brustvere . . . ," *Novaya Gazeta*, August 11, 2014. A discussion in English is: Patrick Reevell, "Geopolitical Football Engulfs Top Teams in Russia," *New York Times*, August 12, 2014.

8. Author's interview with Leonid Smirnyagin, May 2001; Author's interview with Leonid Smirnyagin, June 2015; Author's interview with Natal'ya Zubarevich, July 2014; Zubarevich lecture at Tartu University, Estonia, November 2014, attended by author; Author's interview with Mikhail Remizov, July 2014.

9. Author's interview with Maria Lipman, May 2013; "Vse vzyatki Moskvy," *Bol'shoy Gorod*, February 21, 2011; Anatoliy Temkin, "Putin otchital Dvorkovicha i Yakunina za elektrihcki i inostrannye poyezda," *RBK*, February 19, 2015.

10. Open Society Institute, *Corruption and Its Consequences in Equatorial Guinea: A Briefing Paper*, March 2010.

11. Interview with Lipman; Alexander Kliment, "Putin's Fairy Tale: Why Russia Will Try—and Fail—to Build a New Empire," *Council on Foreign Relations*, March 31, 2014.

12. See, for example: Evgeniy Gontmakher, "Kholodil'nik pobedit televizor," *Ekho Moskvy*, May 12, 2015.

13. Francis Fukuyama, "What Is Governance?," *Governance*, 26, 3 (2013): 347–368.

14. Russia has a type of bureaucracy closer to what Max Weber called "patrimonial," rather than a modern "rational-legal" system based on merit and rules. Vladimir Gilpen'son and Vladimir Magun, "Na sluzhbe Gosudarstva Rossiyskogo: perspektivy i ogranicheniya kar'ery molodykh chinovnikov," *Vestnik obshchestvennogo mneniya*, 5 (September–October), 2004, 25–26; Karl W. Ryavec, *Russian Bureaucracy: Power and Pathology* (Rowman & Littlefield, 2003); Max Weber, *Economy and Society*, edited by Guenther Roth and Claus Wittich (University of California Press, 1978), 956–1110.

15. Author's interview with Ol'ga Vlasova, June 2015.

16. Levada Center data, multiple years, collected from http://www.levada.ru/.

17. Levada Center data, multiple years, collected from http://www.levada.ru/.

18. "Rossiya—velikaya nashi derzhava," *VTsIOM*, June 10, 2016.

19. Levada Center, "Vospriyatiye deyatel'nosti Vladimira Putina," September 10, 2015.

20. Stephen Whitefield, "Russian Citizens and Russian Democracy: Perceptions of State Governance and Democratic Practice, 1993–2007," *Post-Soviet Affairs*, 25, 2 (2009), 99–100; Paul Chaisty and Stephen Whitefield, "The Effects of the Global Financial Crisis

on Russian Political Attitudes," *Post-Soviet Affairs*, 28, 2 (2012), 190; Levada Center, "Vospriyatiye deyatel'nosti Vladimira Putina."

21. Budget data from Russian Ministry of Finance. These are obviously not the only categories, or even the biggest, but they do give a good idea of state priorities.

22. Taylor, *State Building in Putin's Russia*, 52–55; Brian D. Taylor, "Kudrin's Complaint: Does Russia Face a Guns vs. Butter Dilemma?" *PONARS Eurasia Policy Memo*, 254, June 2013; Julian Cooper, "The Funding of the Power Agencies of the Russian State: An Update, 2005 to 2014 and Beyond," *Journal of Power Institutions in Post-Soviet Societies*, 16, 2014; Anastasiya Manuilova, "Na lyudey vse sredsvta khoroshi," *Kommersant*", June 5, 2017.

23. Taylor, "Kudrin's Complaint"; Thomas Remington, "10 explanations for Russia's Coming Fiscal Squeeze," *Washington Post*, February 13, 2014; Ezekiel Pfeifer, "Russia's $100 Billion Pension System Is a Dangerous Zombie," *Institute of Modern Russia*, September 2 and 3, 2015.

24. Peter Spinella, "Moscow and St. Petersburg Lead Europe in Traffic Jams," *Moscow Times*, April 1, 2015; Ellen Barry, "The Russia Left Behind," *New York Times*, October 13, 2013; Yulia Ponomareva, "Snowfall Blocks Miles of the Moscow-St. Petersburg Highway for Days," *Russia beyond the Headlines*, December 6, 2012.

25. Anna Arutunyan, "Road Rage: Reality in Russia," *Moscow News*, November 2013; Rick Archer, "The Russian Highway from Hell," January 2007, http://www.ssqq.com/archive/vinlin27c.htm.

26. Data from multiple sources, including: World Health Organization, *Global Status Report on Road Safety 2013: Supporting a Decade of Action* (WHO, 2013); "List of Countries by Traffic-Related Death Rate," *Wikipedia*; data collected from national statistical services by research assistant.

27. Alina Raspopova, "Putin ustroil dorozhnuyu razborku," *gazeta.ru*, October 8, 2014; Boris Nemtsov and Vladimir Milov, *Putin. Itogi. 10 let* (Solidarnost', 2010); Ivan Buranov, "Dorozhnye plany zakatayut v asfal't," *Kommersant*", March 19, 2015; Barry, "The Russia Left Behind"; Mariya Zholobova, "Pochemu v Rossii malo mostov," *RBK*, May 24, 2016.

28. "Stoimost' stroitel'stva rossiyskikh dorog," *RIA Novosti*, August 31, 2010; Dmitriy Ponomarev, "Skol'ko stoyat avtomobil'nye dorogi v Rossii," *Rosavtodor*, August 7, 2010; Anastasiya Bashkatova, "Tak skol'ko zhe stoyat dorogi Rossii," *Nezavisimaya Gazeta*, December 7, 2011. See also: Peter Podkopaev and Natalie Duffy, "Russia's Pothole Predicament: Beneath the Pavement, Corruption," *Foreign Affairs*, August 10, 2017.

29. Elena Polyakovskaya, "Doroga cherez Khimkinskiy Les," *Radio Svoboda*, December 26, 2014; Rinat Sagdiyev, "Predstavitel' Rotenberga v sovete direktorov kompanii, kotoraya rubit Khimkinskiy les," *Vedomosti*, August 26, 2010; "Koroli goszakaza-2014: reyting Forbes," *Forbes.ru*, March 13, 2014; Aleksandra Galaktionova and Anatoliy Temkin, "Rotenberg naznachil otvetsvennogo za stroyku Kerchenskogo mosta," *RBK*, March 26, 2015; Zholobova, "Pochemu v Rossii malo mostov"; Sergey Stel'makh, "Kerchenskiy most ostanovil stroitel'stvo dorog v Rossii?", *Krym.Realii*, February 17, 2017; Joshua Yaffa, "Oligarchy 2.0," *New Yorker*, May 29, 2017.

30. World Economic Forum, *Global Competitiveness Index 2014–2015*, Russian Federation Profile.

31. Masha Gessen, "The Dying Russians," *New York Review of Books*, September 2, 2014.

32. Nicholas Eberstadt and Hans Groth, "Russia's Human Resources Crisis in Numbers," in Nicholas Eberstadt, Hans Groth, and Judy Twigg, *Addressing Russia's Mounting Human Resources Crisis* (American Enterprise Institute, 2013), 19–24, 44–50.

33. World Health Organization, "Global Health Observatory Data Repository: Life Expectancy—Data by Country," 2016 (data for 2015); "Life Expectancy Grows in Russia," *Opec.ru*, January 22, 2015; Social Progress Index, "Russia," 2015, http://www.socialprogressimperative.org.

34. Eberstadt and Groth, "Russia's Human Resources Crisis in Numbers," 26–33; Mark Adomanis, "8 Things Masha Gessen Got Wrong about Russian Demography," *Forbes*, September 3, 2014; "Life Expectancy Grows in Russia," 2015.
35. "Life Expectancy Grows in Russia," 2015.
36. OECD, *OECD Reviews of Health Systems: Russian Federation*, 2012, 33–36; Sergey Shishkin, "Russia's Health Care System: Difficult Path of Reform," in Michael Alexeev and Shlomo Weber, eds., *The Oxford Handbook of the Russian Economy* (Oxford University Press, 2013), 753–755; Evsei Gurvich, "A New Step in Russia's Budget Policy," *Russian Analytical Digest*, 121, December 21, 2012, 7.
37. *OECD Reviews of Health Systems: Russian Federation*, 100–101.
38. Judy Twigg, "Russia's Human Capital Challenges and Potential for International Collaboration," in Eberstadt, Groth, and Twigg, *Addressing Russia's Mounting Human Resources Crisis*, 3; *OECD Reviews of Health Systems: Russian Federation*, 12.
39. See, for example: *OECD Reviews of Health Systems: Russian Federation*, 77–84.
40. Diana Quirmbach, "Smoking in Russia: Kicking the Habit," *openDemocracy*, June 3, 2014; Peter Orszag, "Putin's Other War? Russians' Binge Drinking," *Bloomberg*, August 11, 2015; "Skvortsova: Grazhdane Rossii stali men'she pit' i kurit'," *Regnum*, June 8, 2017; Emily Jane Fox, "Putin Works Out in a $3,220 Sweat Suit as Only Putin Would," *Vanity Fair*, September 2, 2015.
41. Taylor, *State Building in Putin's Russia*, 319.
42. Vladimir Putin, "Poslaniye Federal'nomu Sobraniyu Rossiyskoy Federatsii," *Kremlin.ru*, April 25, 2005; Leonid Nikitinskiy, "Vladimir Vasil'ev: V militsiyu popadayut lyudi, kotoriye mogli by sidet' v tyur'me," *Novaya Gazeta*, July 10, 2009; Taylor, "Police Reform in Russia."
43. The evidence for this paragraph can be found in: Taylor, *State Building in Putin's Russia*. The Stepashin and Latynina quotes appear on p. 176.
44. Russian Federal State Statistics Service; United Nations Office on Drugs and Crime; Alexandra Lysova and Nikolay Shchitov, "What Is Russia's Real Homicide Rate? Statistical Reconstruction and the 'Decivilizing Process'," *Theoretical Criminology*, 19 (May 2015): 257–277; Evgeny Andreev, Vladimir M. Shkolnikov, William Alex Pridemore, and Svetlana Yu. Nikitina, "A Method for Reclassifying Cause of Death in Cases Categorized as 'Event of Undetermined Intent'," *Population Health Metrics*, 13 (2015).
45. Social Progress Index, "Russia," 2015; World Justice Project, *Rule of Law Index*, 2016.
46. "One of the World's Richest Men Went to Solitary Because of This Interview," www.esquire.com, October 10, 2008; Vadim Volkov, "Delo Naval'nogo: predely proizvola razdvigayutsya," April 27, 2013; Aleksandr Sokolov and Igor' Terent'ev, "Issledovaniye RBK: skol'ko v Rossii chinovnikov i mnogo li one zarabatyvayut," *RBK*, October 15, 2014.
47. Taylor, *State Building in Putin's Russia*, 172–175; Alena V. Ledeneva, *Can Russia Modernise? Sistema, Power Networks and Informal Governance* (Cambridge University Press, 2013), 182–188; Leonid Nikitinskiy, "Who Is Mister Dvoskin?," *Novaya Gazeta*, July 21, 2011.
48. C. J. Chivers, "Power. The Vladimir Putin Story," *Esquire*, October 1, 2008.
49. Sources for this section include: Martin Muller, "Higher, Larger, Costlier: Sochi and the 2014 Winter Olympics," *Russian Analytical Digest*, 143, February 9, 2014; Robert W. Orttung, "Olimpstroy: Building the Sochi Olympics from Scratch," *Russian Analytical Digest*, 143, February 9, 2014; Joshua Yaffa, "The Waste and Corruption of Vladimir Putin's 2014 Winter Olympics," *Bloomberg/Business Week*, January 2, 2014; Boris Nemtsov and Leonid Martynyuk, *Zimnyaya olimpiada v subtropikakh* (Solidarnost', 2013); Brett Forrest, "Putin's Run for Gold," *Vanity Fair*, February 2014. For a complete account, see: Robert W. Orttung and Sufian N. Zhemukhov, *Putin's Olympics: The Sochi Games and the Evolution of Twenty-First Century Russia* (Routledge, 2017).

50. Quotes are from: Yaffa, "The Waste and Corruption of Vladimir Putin's 2014 Winter Olympics," citing Russian *Esquire*; Muller, "Higher, Larger, Costlier."

51. Andrew Kramer, "Russian Environmentalist, and Critic of Olympics, Gets 3-Year Prison Sentence," *New York Times*, February 12, 2014.

52. Dmitri Trenin, "Sochi: Olympics and Politics," Carnegie Moscow Center, July 15, 2013; Yaffa, "The Waste and Corruption of Vladimir Putin's 2014 Winter Olympics."

53. "McLaren Independent Investigations Report into Sochi Allegations," World Anti-Doping Agency, July 18, 2016; Vladimir Putin, "Zayavleniye v svyazi s dokladom Komissii Vsemirnogo antidopingovogo agenstva," *Kremlin.ru*, July 18, 2016; Neil MacFarquhar, "Putin Cites Politics in Answer to Report," *New York Times*, July 19, 2016.

54. For an overview of the academic debate about whether Putin has been a successful state-builder, see: Brian D. Taylor, "The Transformation of the Russian State," in Stephan Leibfried, Evelyne Huber, Matthew Lange, Jonah D. Levy, Frank Nullmeier, and John D. Stephens, eds., *The Oxford Handbook of Transformations of the State* (Oxford University Press, 2015), 637–653.

55. Data and further information at: www.govindicators.org. At the time of writing, the most recent ratings were for 2015.

56. Note that the income category groups were created based on where that country was placed by the World Bank in 2016. So, for example, the upper-middle income line shows the overall WGI score for every country given that designation by the World Bank in 2016.

57. World Economic Forum, *The Global Competitiveness Report 2015–2016*, available at: http://reports.weforum.org/global-competitiveness-report-2015-2016/.

58. 2017 Social Progress Index, available at: http://www.socialprogressindex.com/.

59. Author's interview with Georgiy Satarov, December 2013; Sarah Lindemann-Komarova, "The Flood: A Tree Is Best Measured When It Is Down . . . ," *Medium.com*, March 31, 2015; Sarah Lindemann-Komarova, "Running for Office in Siberia," multipart series, *Medium.com*, August 3, 14, 21, 27, September 5, 11, 17, 2015; Author's discussions with Sarah Lindemann-Komarova; Author's interview with St. Petersburg journalist, July 2014.

60. Yuliya Latynina, "Kod dostupa," *Ekho Moskvy*, October 24, 2015.

61. Insiders will recognize a subtle reference here to Vitaliy Shlykov, a former military colonel who influenced the defense reforms undertaken by Anatoliy Serdyukov after 2008. On the relative success of military reform, often against the expectations of experts, see: Pavel Baev, "Ukraine: A Test for Russian Military Reform," *Russie.Nei.Reports*, 19, May 2015; Marysya Zlobek, "Kak baby podveli rossiyskuyu armiyu" (based on a speech by Aleksandr Gol'ts), *Slon.ru*, October 28, 2014.

Chapter 6

1. Maxim Trudolyubov, "The Year Putin Won," *The Russia File*, December 20, 2016; Julia Ioffe, "The End of the End of the Cold War," *Foreign Policy*, December 21, 2016; Sergey Karaganov, "2016—A Victory of Conservative Realism," *Russia in Global Affairs*, February 13, 2017.

2. Author's interview with Dmitriy Trenin (July 2014).

3. Inevitably, many nuances will be overlooked in order to keep the narrative compact, hopefully without distorting too much the central issues.

4. As Viatcheslav Morozov puts it, "The only subject on the horizon of Russian politics is the West." Viatcheslav Morozov, *Russia's Postcolonial Identity: A Subaltern Empire in a Eurocentric World* (Palgrave Macmillan, 2015), 6.

5. Vladimir Putin, "Poslaniye Federal'nomu Sobraniyu Rossiyskoy Federatsii," *Kremlin. ru*, April 25, 2005. Putin's exact meaning is a source of heated arguments among specialists—did he say "the greatest" or simply "one of the greatest" or even "major?"

My understanding of the original Russian suggests that "one of the greatest" is the most accurate translation.

6. The idea for the graph came from a similar figure prepared in 2011 by Kingsmill Bond of Citigroup and featured in a blogpost in the *Financial Times*; see Jonathan Wheatley, "Russian Imperialism: Should We Worry?", *beyondbrics*, October 24, 2011: http://blogs. ft.com/beyond-brics/2011/10/24/russian-imperialism-should-we-worry/. The data through 2008 come from the work of the economic historian Angus Maddison. Census data after 2008 are from the UN 2015 census projection, and economic data are from the IMF. Thus, some of the jumps in the GDP line after 2008 in particular are probably more dramatic than they should be. But the overall trend over the last several centuries is clear. The point about losing more territory than the EU comes from: Stephen Kotkin, "Russia's Perpetual Geopolitics," *Foreign Affairs*, 95, 3 (2016), 3.

7. For example, the British historian Dominic Lieven, quoted in: "Take care of Russia," *The Economist*, October 22, 2016.

8. Dmitri Trenin, "Russia's Great Power Problem," *The National Interest*, October 28, 2014.

9. Denis Volkov, "Russian Elite Opinion after Crimea," *Carnegie Moscow Center*, March 23, 2016. For excellent scholarly explorations of the role of emotion in Russian foreign policy, see "Special Issue: Status and Emotions in Russian Foreign Policy," *Communist and Post-Communist Studies* 47, 3 (2014).

10. Steve Heisler, "Interview: Nathan Fillion," *A.V. Club*, March 9, 2009.

11. See the discussion in chapter 1.

12. Vladimir Putin, "Bol'shaya press-konferentsiya Vladimira Putina," *Kremlin.ru*, December 18, 2014.

13. Max Fisher, "Putin's Insane-Sounding Quote about Bears Is Essential for Understanding Russia Today," *Vox*, December 18, 2014.

14. Robert Legvold, *Return to Cold War* (Polity, 2016).

15. *Ot pervogo litsa: Razgovory s Vladimirom Putinym* (Vagrius, 2000), 156, 159; Angela E. Stent, *The Limits of Partnership: US-Russian Relations in the Twenty-First Century* (Princeton University Press, 2015), 75–76; Mikhail Zygar', *Vsya kremlevskaya rat': Kratkaya istoriya sovremennoy Rossii* (Intellektual'naya literatura, 2015), 137; Stephen Sestanovich, "Could It Have Been Otherwise?", *The American Interest*, 10, 5 (2015).

16. "Stenogramma vstrechi prezidenta Rossii V. Putina s rodstvennikami ekipazha podvodnoy lodki Kursk 22 avgusta," available at: https://www.gazeta.ru/stenogram. shtml; Zoltan Barany, *Democratic Breakdown and the Decline of the Russian Military* (Princeton University Press, 2007), 19–43.

17. Vladimir Putin, "Nachalo vstrechi s zhitelyami Beslana, postradavshimi v rezul'tate terakta 1–3 sentyabrya 2004 goda," *Kremlin.ru*, September 2, 2005; Clifford G. Gaddy and Barry W. Ickes, "Russia after the Global Financial Crisis," *Eurasian Geography and Economics*, 51, 3 (2010), 288–289.

18. Stent, *The Limits of Partnership*, 62–72; Jeffrey Mankoff, *Russian Foreign Policy: The Return of Great Power Politics*, 2nd ed. (Rowman & Littlefield, 2012), 102–106.

19. Stent, *The Limits of Partnership*, 78, 81–84; Fiona Hill and Clifford G. Gaddy, *Mr. Putin: Operative in the Kremlin*, new and expanded ed. (Brookings Institution Press, 2015), 304–305; Zygar', *Vsya kremlevskaya rat'*, 49–51.

20. Vladimir Putin, "Obrashcheniye Prezidenta Rossii Vladimira Putina," *Kremlin. ru*, September 4, 2004; Interfaks, "Putin rasskazal o kontaktakh severokavkazskikh boyevikov so spetssluzhbami SShA," *Meduza*, April 26, 2015.

21. On the Kremlin reaction, see: Zygar', *Vsya kremlevskaya rat'*, 118–120. Brief analyses include: Henry Hale, *Patronal Politics: Eurasian Regime Dynamics in Comparative Perspective* (Cambridge University Press, 2014), 182–190; Lucan Way, *Pluralism by Default: Weak Autocrats and the Rise of Competitive Politics* (Johns Hopkins University Press, 2015), 65–72. On the role of civil society and foreign support, see: Valerie J. Bunce and Sharon

L. Wolchik, *Defeating Authoritarian Leaders in Postcommunist Countries* (Cambridge University Press, 2011), 114–147.

22. Zygar', *Vsya kremlevskaya rat'*, 120; see also 127, 132.
23. Vladimir Putin, "Vystupleniye i diskussiya na Myunkhenskoy konferentsii po voprosam politiki bezopasnosti," *Kremlin.ru*, February 10, 2007; Vladimir Putin, "Interv'yu zhurnalu 'Taym'," *Kremlin.ru*, December 19, 2007.
24. NATO, "Bucharest Summit Declaration," April 3, 2008; Ol'ga Allenova, Yelena Geda, and Vladimir Novikov, "Blok NATO razoshelsya na blokpakety," *Kommersant*, April 7, 2008. See: Hill and Gaddy, *Mr. Putin* (2015), 307–308; Stent, *The Limits of Partnership*, 159–168.
25. Samuel P. Huntington, "The Lonely Superpower," *Foreign Affairs*, 78, 2 (1999), 42; Richard Haass, quoted in Stent, *The Limits of Partnership*, 75.
26. Sestanovich, "Could It Have Been Otherwise?"; U.S. European Command, "U.S. Military Presence in Europe (1945–2016)," May 26, 2016. Note that in response to the annexation of Crimea and the Russian-backed war in Ukraine, discussed below, the United States and NATO have taken steps to deploy additional combat battalions to Poland and the Baltic states on a rotational basis.
27. Ellen Barry, "Georgia Challenges Report That Says It Fired First Shot," *New York Times*, September 30, 2009.
28. Stephen Kotkin, *Armaggedon Averted: The Soviet Collapse 1970–2000*, updated ed. (Oxford University Press, 2008), 218.
29. "Interv'yu Dmitriya Medvedeva rossiyskim telekanalam," *Kremlin.ru*, August 31, 2008; "The Draft of the European Security Treaty," *En.Kremlin.ru*, November 29, 2009; Author's interview with Alexander Sergunin, June 2017. For analysis, see: Irina Kobrinskaya, "Russia and the Eastern Partnership States in a New European Security Architecture," *PONARS Eurasia Policy Memo*, 128 (October 2010); Richard Weitz, "The Rise and Fall of Medvedev's European Security Treaty," *On Wider Europe* (German Marshall Fund, May 2012).
30. Zygar', *Vsya kremlevskaya rat'*, 240–243, 249–250; Stent, *The Limits of Partnership*, 247–250; Hill and Gaddy, *Mr. Putin*, new and expanded ed., 310; "Razgovor s Vladimirom Putinym. Prodolzheniye," http://2011.moskva-putinu.ru/, December 15, 2011; "Peskov: destabilizatsiya v Sirii nachalas' analogichno stsenariyu tsvetnoy revolyutsii na Ukraine," *Tass*, December 20, 2015.
31. Brian D. Taylor, "Putin's Crackdown: Sources, Instruments, and Challenges," *PONARS Eurasia Policy Memo*, 277, September 2013; Brian Whitmore, "The Kremlin's New Deal," *RFE/RL*, March 11, 2013; Paul J. Saunders, "U.S. Ambassador's Rough Welcome in Moscow: Is the Reset Failing?", *The Atlantic*, January 23, 2012; Vladimir Putin, "Press-konferentsiya Vladimira Putina," *Kremlin.ru*, December 20, 2012.
32. Zygar', *Vsya kremlevskaya rat'*, 107, 317–320.
33. Steven Lee Myers, *The New Tsar: The Rise and Reign of Vladimir Putin* (Knopf, 2015), 451–452.
34. Far-right Ukrainian nationalists were responsible for some of the violence, although it appears that the regime initiated the major moments of escalation during the multimonth crisis. For a brief summary of the 2014 Euromaidan revolution in Ukraine, see: Way, *Pluralism by Default*, 81–88. For a longer, even-handed account of the origins and course of the Ukraine crisis, although one which in my view underplays the importance of Putin's mentality, see: Samuel Charap and Timothy J. Colton, *Everyone Loses: The Ukraine Crisis and the Ruinous Contest for Post-Soviet Eurasia* (IISS/Routledge, 2017).
35. "Krym: Put' na rodinu," documentary film, https://www.youtube.com/watch?v=t42-71RpRgI; Zygar', *Vsya kremlevskaya rat'*, 336. Other people mentioned as possible participants include Putin's foreign policy adviser Yuriy Ushakov and the chief of the General Staff: Ivan Davydov, "My ne banda, my—khunta," *The New Times*, June 30, 2015; Tat'yana Melikyan, "Krym. Put' na ekran," *Lenta.ru*, March 11, 2015. Not mentioned

in any accounts I have read are Prime Minister Dmitriy Medvedev or Foreign Minister Sergey Lavrov.

36. The closest analogy is probably Turkey's occupation of about 40 percent of Cyprus since 1974, but Turkey never went so far as to formally annex the territory.

37. Vladimir Putin, "Vladimir Putin otvetil na voprosy zhurnalistov o situatsii na Ukraine," *Kremlin.ru*, March 4, 2014.

38. Vladimir Putin, "Obrashcheniye Prezidenta Rossiyskoy Federatsii," *Kremlin.ru*, March 18, 2014; Zygar', *Vsya kremlevskaya rat'*, 337, 346. See also: Daniel Treisman, "Why Putin Took Crimea," *Foreign Affairs*, 95, 3 (2016), 47–54.

39. Yuliya Taratuta and Maksim Tovkaylo, "'Minfin ne sprashivali, vo skol'ko oboydetsya resheniye po Krymu,'" *Forbes Woman*, March 5, 2015; Author's interview with Sergunin; Stanislav Belkovskiy, interviewed by Igor' Poroshin, "'Ya uberu vsekh, kto posmeyet posyagnut' na russkiy yazyk': Belkovskiy o slovesnosti," *Vozdukh*, April 23, 2015. For a debate about who is to blame for the Ukraine crisis, the United States or Russia, see the exchange between John Mearsheimer, Michael McFaul, and Stephen Sestanovich in the November 2014 issue of *Foreign Affairs*. I find McFaul's and Sestanovich's arguments more persuasive.

40. Vladimir Putin, "Pryamaya liniya s Vladimirom Putinym," *Kremlin.ru*, April 17, 2014. On Russian military involvement in Ukraine, see: Michael Kofman et al., *Lessons from Russia's Operations in Crimea and Eastern Ukraine* (RAND Corporation, 2017); Nikolay Mitrokhin, "Infiltration, Instruction, Invasion: Russia's War in the Donbass," *Journal of Soviet and Post-Soviet Politics and Society*, 1 (2015), 219–250.

41. Zygar', *Vsya kremlevskaya rat'*, 357; Andrey Vandenko interview with Gennadiy Timchenko, "Za vse v zhizni nado platit'. I za znakomstvo s rukovodstvom strany tozhe," *ITAR-TASS*, August 4, 2014; Stanislav Belkovskiy, *Biznes Vladimira Putina* (Algoritm, 2002), 229–230; Viktoriya Sunkina, Aleksey Pastushin, and Elena Myazina, "Rassledovaniye RBK: v kakikh stranakh u rossiyskikh chinovnikov est' nedvizhimost'," *RBK*, July 21, 2014.

42. Lucian Kim, "Putin the Pariah," *Slate*, November 18, 2014; "Battle for Ukraine: How the West Lost Putin," *Financial Times*, February 3, 2015; Author's interview with Vladislav Bachurov, June 2017. On the clear evidence of responsibility for the shooting down of flight MH-17, see especially the September 2016 presentation of the Joint Investigation Team, available at: https://www.om.nl/onderwerpen/mh17-vliegramp/presentaties/presentation-joint/.

43. Joshua Yaffa, "Putin, Syria, and Why Moscow Has Gone War-Crazy," *New Yorker*, October 14, 2016; Scott Wilson, "Obama Dismisses Russia as 'Regional Power' Acting out of Weakness," *Washington Post*, March 25, 2014; Fedor Luk'yanov, "Neobkhodimo, no nedostatochno," *Rossiyskaya gazeta*, March 8, 2016. See also: Fyodor Lukyanov, "Putin's Foreign Policy: The Quest to Restore Russia's Rightful Place," *Foreign Affairs*, 95, 3 (2016), 30–37.

44. Andrew Higgins, "Maybe Private Russian Hackers Meddled in Election, Putin Says," *New York Times*, June 2, 2017.

45. Office of the Director of National Intelligence, "Assessing Russian Activities and Intentions in Recent US Elections," January 6, 2017; Philip Bump, "Here's the Public Evidence That Supports the Idea That Russia Interfered in the 2016 Election," *Washington Post*, July 6, 2017; Thomas Rid, "How Russia Pulled Off the Biggest Election Hack in U.S. History," *Esquire*, October 20, 2016; Eric Lipton, David E. Sanger, and Scott Shane, "The Perfect Weapon: How Russian Cyberpower Invaded the U.S.," *New York Times*, December 13, 2016; Laura Hautala, "How US Cybersleuths Decided Russia Hacked the DNC," *CNET*, May 2, 2017; Evan Osnos, David Remnick, and Joshua Yaffa, "Active Measures," *New Yorker*, March 6, 2017; Matthew Cole et al., "Top-Secret NSA Report Details Russian Hacking Effort Days before 2016 Election," *The Intercept*, June 5, 2017; Massimo Calabresi, "Inside Russia's Social Media War on America," *Time*, May 18, 2017;

Ned Parker, Jonathan Landay, and John Walcott, "Putin-Linked Think Tank Drew Up Plan to Sway 2016 U.S. Election—Documents," *Reuters*, April 20, 2017.

46. Office of the Director of National Intelligence, "Assessing Russian Activities . . . ," ii; "Lavrov o rusofobii v SShA," *RIA Novosti*, July 24, 2017; Dmitriy Medvedev, *Facebook*, August 2, 2017, https://www.facebook.com/Dmitry.Medvedev/posts/10154587161801851.

47. Dov H. Levin, "Partisan Electoral Interventions by the Great Powers: Introducing the PEIG Dataset," *Conflict Management and Peace Science*, Online First (2016); Mark Kramer, "The Soviet Roots of Meddling in US Politics," *PONARS Eurasia Policy Memo*, 452, 2017; Strobe Talbott, *The Russia Hand: A Memoir of Presidential Diplomacy* (Random House, 2002), 189–213; Tom Malinowski, "Did the United States Interfere in Russian Elections?," *Washington Post*, July 21, 2017; Dmitry Gorenburg, "Russia's Strategic Calculus: Threat Perceptions and Military Doctrine," *PONARS Eurasia Policy Memo*, 448, 2016; Dmitry Gorenburg, "Countering Color Revolutions: Russia's New Security Strategy and Its Implications for U.S. Policy," *PONARS Eurasia Policy Memo*, 342, 2014. Mikhail Zygar claims that among Putin's close associates, only the former finance minister Aleksey Kudrin doesn't believe that the United States is waging war against Russia and Putin: Zygar', *Vsya kremlevskaya rat'*, 360.

48. Office of the Director of National Intelligence, "Assessing Russian Activities . . . ," 1; Scott Shane, "Russian Intervention in American Election Was No One-Off," *New York Times*, January 6, 2017.

49. I make no judgment here on perhaps the two biggest issues about Russian interference in the election—whether members of the Trump campaign colluded with Russia, and whether this interference influenced the results of the election. I think we don't know enough yet about either question to say definitively, and both are matters of American politics, not Russian politics.

50. On democracy promotion, see: Josh Rogin, "State Department Considers Scrubbing Democracy Promotion from Its Mission," *Washington Post*, August 1, 2017. On sanctions: Olga Oliker, "Punishing Russia with Sanctions Will Not Stop the Kremlin," *The Hill*, July 29, 2017; Paul Pillar, "Sanctions as Feckless Disapproval," *The National Interest*, July 30, 2017.

51. The quote by a Putin ally is from: Sergey Naryshkin, "Vossoyedineniye Kryma s Rossiyey—krupneysheye sobytiye sovremennoy istorii," *Izvestiya*, March 17, 2016. For similar statements by Putin and his top associates just from the first half of 2016, see, for example: Nikolay Patrushev, interviewed by Mikhail Rostovskiy, "Mirovoye soobshchestvo dolzhno skazat' nam spasibo za Krym," *Moskovskiy Komsomolets*, January 26, 2016; Vladimir Putin, "Mediaforum regional'nykh i mestnykh SMI 'Pravda i spravedlivost'," *Kremlin.ru*, April 7, 2016; Vladimir Putin, "Plenarnoye zasedaniye Peterburgskogo mezhdunarodnogo ekonomicheskogo foruma," *Kremlin.ru*, June 17, 2016. The ex-diplomat quoted is: Kirk Bennett, "Condemned to Frustration," *The American Interest*, April 1, 2016. ·

52. Andrey Soldatov, quoted in Andrew Roth and Dana Priest, "Russian Hacking a Question of Revenge and Respect," *Washington Post*, September 16, 2016.

53. As the American expert Angela Stent put it, "The United States and its allies have repeatedly underestimated Russia's determination to revise the global order that Moscow feels the West has imposed on Russia since the fall of the Soviet Union." Angela Stent, "Putin's Power Play in Syria," *Foreign Affairs*, 95, 1 (2016), 106–113.

54. Vladimir Putin, "70th session of the UN General Assembly," *En.kremlin.ru*, September 28, 2015; Karaganov, "2016—A Victory of Conservative Realism."

55. Neil MacFarquhar, "In Talks with Merkel, Putin Calls for Improving Relations with Europe," *New York Times*, May 10, 2015; Andrew Rettman, "Merkel: Russia Cannot Veto EU Expansion," *euobserver*, November 17, 2014.

56. Bennett, "Condemned to Frustration." See also: Jeffrey Mankoff, "Russia's Latest Land Grab: How Putin Won Crimea and Lost Ukraine," *Foreign Affairs*, 93, 3 (2014); Igor Zevelev, "The Russian World in Moscow's Strategy," *Center for Strategic and International Studies*, August 22, 2016.

57. Charap and Colton, *Everyone Loses*, esp. 40–54. See also: Kotkin, "Russia's Perpetual Geopolitics"; James Goldgeier, "Promises, Made, Promises Broken? What Yeltsin Was Told about NATO in 1993 and Why It Matters," *War on the Rocks*, July 12, 2016; Kimberly Marten et al., "Roundtable on Robert Legvold, *Return to Cold War*," *H-Diplo/ISSF Roundtable*, 9, 12 (2017). The point about colored revolutions was made by former secretary of state Condoleezza Rice.

58. Mikhail Zygar, "Why Putin Prefers Trump," *Politico*, July 27, 2016.

59. Paul T. Christensen, "Russia as Semiperiphery," in Neil Robinson, ed., *The Political Economy of Russia* (Rowman & Littlefield, 2012), 171. For an excellent summary by a Russian author of why Russian great power aspirations are unrealistic, see: Anton Barbashin, "Dorogiye mechty o velikoderzhavii," *Intersection*, June 1, 2016. Military spending data are from SIPRI, economic data from the World Bank, and population data from Wikipedia.

60. Thomas E. Graham, "America Needs to Break Its Old Habits on Russia," *The National Interest*, June 6, 2016; Max Fisher (quoting Mark Galeotti), "In Syrian War, Russia Has Yet to Fulfill Superpower Ambitions," *New York Times*, September 24, 2016.

Chapter 7

1. Musa Muradov, " 'Putin—dar bozhiy'," *Kommersant"-Vlast'*, June 18, 2007.

2. Aleksandr Yunashev, "Volodin: U tekh, kto khochet mirnoy Rossii, kandidat v prezidenty tol'ko odin," *Life.ru*, June 13, 2017.

3. Mikhail Zygar', *Vsya kremlevskaya rat': Kratkaya istoriya sovremennoy Rossii* (Intellektual'naya literatura, 2015), 264, 307.

4. Jason Brownlee, "The Limited Reach of Authoritarian Powers," *Democratization*, Online First (2017), 6–9; Burgess Everett, "McCain: Russia Is a 'Gas Station'," *Politico*, March 26, 2014; Timothy J. Colton, "Paradoxes of Putinism," *Daedalus* 146, 2 (2017), 16–17.

5. Alexey Makarkin, "The Test for Russia Is Not the 2018 Election but What Follows," *Carnegie Moscow Center*, May 25, 2017.

6. Vladimir Gel'man, "The Unrule of Law in the Making: The Politics of Informal Institution Building in Russia," *Europe-Asia Studies* 56, 7 (2004), 1021–1040.

7. As Max Weber observed, "It would be very unusual to find concrete cases of action . . . which were oriented *only* in one or another of these ways." Weber's four ways in which action could be oriented were instrumentally rational, value rational (ideas), affectual (emotions), and traditional (habits): Max Weber, *Economy and Society* (University of California Press, 1978), 24–26. Further, one can almost always find a post hoc rationalist explanation that seems to "fit" the circumstances, making it difficult to convince skeptics that factors like ideas and emotions also played a role.

8. Pauline Jones Luong and Erika Weinthal, *Oil Is Not a Curse: Ownership Structure and Institutions in Soviet Successor States* (Cambridge University Press, 2010).

9. Olexiy Haran and Mariia Zolkina, "The Demise of Ukraine's 'Eurasian Vector' and the Rise of Pro-NATO Sentiment," *PONARS Eurasia Policy Memo*, 458, February 2017; Sergey Shelin, "Vezeniye konchilos', pravleniye—net," *Rosbalt*, August 8, 2017. See also: Brian D. Taylor, "Putin's Own Goal," *Foreign Affairs* online, March 6, 2014.

10. Vladimir Putin, "Stenograficheskiy otchet o vstreche s uchastnikami tret'ego zasedaniya Mezhdunarodnogo diskussionnogo kluba 'Valday'," *Kremlin.ru*, September 9, 2006; Vladimir Putin, "Intervyu zhurnalistam pechatnykh sredstv massovoy informatsii iz stran—chlenov 'Gruppy vos'mi'," *Kremlin.ru*, June 4, 2007; Vladimir Putin, "Bol'shaya press-konferentsiya Vladimira Putina," *Kremlin.ru*, December 18, 2014.

11. Vladimir Putin, "Rossiya na rubezhe tysyacheletiy," *Nezavisimaya Gazeta*, December 30, 1999.

12. Vladimir Putin, "Otvety na voprosy zhurnalistov posle pryamogo tele- i radioefira ("Pryamaya liniya s Prezidentom Rossii")", *Kremlin.ru*, October 18, 2007.

13. Vladimir Putin, "Interv'yu Predsedatelya Pravitel'stva Rossiyskoy Federatsii V.V. Putina," http://archive.premier.gov.ru, October 17, 2011; Vladimir Putin, "Predsetatel' Pravitel'stva Rossiyskoy Federatsii V.V. Putin vstretilsya v Sochi s uchastnikami VII zasedaniya mezhdunarodnogo diskussionnogo kluba 'Valday'," http://archive.government.ru, September 6, 2010.

14. Putin, "Rossiya na rubezhe tysyacheletiy"; Shelin, "Vezeniye konchilos', pravleniye—net." Economic data are from World Bank World Development Indicators. On the economic diversity of Russia's regions, see: Natalia Zubarevich, "Four Russias: Human Potential and Social Differentiation of Russian Regions and Cities," in Maria Lipman and Nikolay Petrov, eds., *Russia 2025: Scenarios for the Russian Future* (Palgrave Macmillan, 2013), 70–80.

15. Author's interview with Dmitriy Trenin, July 2014; Dmitri Trenin, "Russia's Great Power Problem," *The National Interest*, October 28, 2014.

16. Jack Snyder, "The Modernization Trap," *Journal of Democracy*, 28, 2 (2017), 78. See also: Andrei Kolesnikov, "The Burden of Predictability: Russia's 2018 Presidential Election," *Carnegie Moscow Center*, May 18, 2017.

17. For some examples of the positioning of the children of close Putin associates in important state or private companies see: Roman Rozhkov, "Zolotye deti Rossii," *Kommersant'-Den'gi*, March 7, 2011; Aleksey Navalny, "Neofeodal'naya sistema uzhe zdes'. I eto ne preuvelicheniye," https://navalny.com/p/4084/, January 22, 2015; Aleksandr Birman, "Lyubov' k otechestkim delam," *Forbes.ru*, April 8, 2015; Stephen Grey and Elizabeth Piper, "Rising Stars among Children of Russia's Elite," *Reuters*, November 10, 2015.

18. Karen Dawisha, *Putin's Kleptocracy: Who Owns Russia?* (Simon & Schuster, 2014), 294–304; Jack Stubbs, Andrey Kuzmin, Stephen Grey, and Roman Anin, "The Man Who Married Putin's Daughter and Then Made a Fortune," *Reuters*, December 17, 2015; Irina Reznik, Ilya Arkhipov, and Alexander Sazonov, "Putin Family Split Offers Peek at Secret Dealings of Russia Inc.," *Bloomberg*, January 25, 2018.

19. Irina Reznik, "A Fallen Russia Oligarch Sends Warning to Rest of Putin Insiders," *Bloomberg*, January 12, 2016.

20. Gleb Pavlovskiy, interviewed by Tom Parfitt, "Putin's World Outlook," *New Left Review*, 88 (July–August 2014). On muddling through leading to muddling down, see: Pavel Baev, "It Is Indecision Time for Putin, as Russia Muddles Down Ungoverned," *Eurasian Daily Monitor*, January 25, 2016.

21. Ilya Arkhipov, Henry Meyer, and Gregory White, "Putin Grooms a New Generation of Leaders," *Bloomberg*, September 8, 2016; "Government Hasn't Adjusted to Economic Reality," *Moscow Times*, October 31, 2016; "Economy Ministry: No Change in Russian Living Standards before 2035," *Moscow Times*, October 20, 2016; "Russians' Political Engagement Shrinking, Poll Shows," *Levada.ru*, August 24, 2016; Kolesnikov, "The Burden of Predictability."

22. Those suggesting Russia under Putin was heading toward a dead end included Aleksey Makarkin (December 2014), Dmitriy Oreshkin (November 2014), and Nikolay Troitskiy (December 2014).

23. Author's interview with Dmitriy Oreshkin, November 2014. For a comprehensive discussion of what comes after Putin, see the contributions to the following special issue: "Russia Beyond Putin," *Daedalus*, 146, 2 (2017).

24. Henry E. Hale, "The Myth of Mass Russian Support for Autocracy: The Public Opinion Foundations of a Hybrid Regime," *Europe-Asia Studies* 63, 8 (2011), 1357–1375.

25. Author's interview with Russian political scientist, December 2014. For similar lines of argument, see the comments in the panel discussion with Fred Hiatt, Leon Aron,

Vladimir Kara-Murza, and Stephen Sestanovich, "Russia: Politics, Protests, and the Presidential Election," *Council on Foreign Relations*, February 29, 2012.

26. Henry E. Hale, *Patronal Politics: Eurasian Regime Dynamics in Comparative Perspective* (Cambridge University Press, 2014); "Irina Nagornykh, 'Neryadovye zapasa,' *Kommersant*", August 21, 2017.

27. Tat'yana Stanovaya, "Rossiya posle Putina: pyat' krugov ada dlya preyemnika," *Slon*, September 10, 2014.

28. For this debate, see, for example: Roberto Stefan Foa and Yascha Mounk, "The Signs of Deconsolidation," *Journal of Democracy*, 28, 1 (2017), 5–15; Ronald F. Inglehart, "How Much Should We Worry?," *Journal of Democracy* 27, 3 (2016), 18–23. A highly stimulating essay on the topic is: Pankaj Mishra, "Welcome to the Age of Anger," *The Guardian*, December 8, 2016.

29. Vladimir Putin, "Priyem po sluchayu Dnya Rossii," *Kremlin.ru*, June 12, 2017.

30. Journalists remarking in interviews on Putin's concern with his legacy include: Vladislav Bachurov, July 2014; Ivan Rodin, June 2015. More generally, see the account of Putin "the history man" in Fiona Hill and Clifford G. Gaddy, *Mr. Putin: Operative in the Kremlin* (Brookings Institution Press, 2013), 63–77. The quote is from: Sergey Markov, "Interv'yu," *Ekho Moskvy*, October 23, 2014. Andrei Kolesnikov remarked, similarly, "Putin himself remains the only effective institution in Russia": Kolesnikov, "The Burden of Predictability."

INDEX